The Complete Book of Running

The Complete Book of Running

James F. Fixx

1979
CHATTO & WINDUS
LONDON

Published by
Chatto & Windus Ltd
40 William IV Street
London, WC2N 4DF

British Library Cataloguing in Publication
Data
Fixx, James F.
    The complete book of running
    1. Running
    I. Title
    796.4'26   GV1061

ISBN 7011 2392 3

Printed in Great Britain by
Cox & Wyman Ltd,
London, Fakenham and Reading

This one,
at last,
is for my mother

Acknowledgments

I am particularly grateful for the long-suffering aid and counsel of Bob Anderson, Thomas Bassler, M.D., Hal Bowser, Ted Corbitt, David Costill, Ph.D., Leroy Getchell, Ph.D., Bob Glover, Joe Henderson, Martin Hyman, Nina Kuscsik, R.N., Kathryn Lance, John Moe, George Sheehan, M.D., Roger Smith, Charles Steinmetz, M.D., Peter Travers, M.B., B.S., M.R.C.S., L.R.C.P., D.Phys. Med., and John Williams, M.Sc., F.R.C.S., running aficionados all; for permission to quote a number of passages from *Runner's World, The Jogger,* and *The Physician and Sportsmedicine*; for the incalculable help of my wife, Alice; and above all, for the indispensable assistance of all those running companions and competitors on both sides of the Atlantic who, usually without knowing it, offered ideas and inspiration when I could not have taken another step without them.

J.F.F.

Contents

Foreword

On the subversive nature of this book

The purposes of this book are, first, to introduce you to the extra-ordinary world of running, and second, to change your life.

Until recently those goals, particularly the second, would have seemed laughably grandiose. Today, however, we are in the midst of a worldwide running revolution, a revolution that is beyond question changing—and saving—lives. This book was first published, in a different form, in the United States. When I began writing it surveys showed that there were some six million runners there. Within a few months the figure had increased to twenty-five million. I quickly saw convincing evidence of the boom: almost upon publication, *The Complete Book of Running* rose to the top of all the nation's best-seller lists and simply perched there, as tirelessly as any long-distance runner, for months on end. In the United Kingdom, as I write, similar surveys have indicated that two million Britons pull on their running shoes at least once a week.*

The current running phenomenon is largely a reflection, I think, of the peculiar attractiveness of the sport. It can be done almost anywhere by almost anybody, requires a minimum of equipment, and is among the most beneficial and inexpensive of sports. The preparations are no more time-consuming than those required for taking a walk, and the pleasures are far greater. Furthermore, running has an appealing and often amusing body of lore that tends to bind all runners together, no matter where they live. In visiting Britain to prepare this edition I had some vivid, and occasionally curious, glimpses of that lore. In the United States, for example, it is well known that the proper treatment for an inflamed Achilles tendon is

* Research conducted for Robbie Brightwell, former captain of the British Olympic team and now managing director of Le Coq Sportif, revealed that in a sample of 5000, chosen from the ITV regions, 4% of those interviewed described themselves as runners. Running was defined as one two-mile run per week. The male/female ratio among runners was 78:22. By age-group runners divided thus: 23% (15–18 years); 21% (19–24 years); 23% (25–34 years); 21% (35–44 years); 12% (over 45 years).

to run only on hard surfaces, avoiding grass and springy tracks as if they were Scylla and Charybdis. In Britain, on the other hand, it is beyond dispute that soft surfaces are the only sure cure.

Running in Britain, I have learned, has its own special character. Whereas in the United States the typical runner, man or woman, is a free spirit who belongs to no club and only infrequently seeks out the hurly-burly of competition, in Britain, a sizeable proportion of runners are team members who regularly race. As the running movement sweeps Britain this difference is becoming less pronounced.

There is at least one other way in which running in Britain is different from running elsewhere, and it is simply that no more pleasing place for the sport exists anywhere. Even in the hearts of cities, a park is seldom far away. In densely populated Surrey, for example, there is more common land than in any other county. But you don't need a park or forest to run. Even in the middle of London you will no longer attract the slightest notice if you simply pop out of your door and start running.

If you are not yet a runner, this book will show you how to become healthier and happier than you have ever imagined you could be. It will do so no matter how out of shape or fat or old or ungraceful you are, and no matter how many times you have tried and failed with other exercise programmes. With proper preparation and a few elementary precautions, practically anyone who can walk can run.

If, as I hope, you are already a runner, and even if you are already a very good one, this book will help make you fitter, faster, more knowledgeable, and better able to enjoy your sport's special pleasures and avoid its occasional hazards.

Whatever your skill, or lack of it, this book will acquaint you with the many benefits of running and show you how to share them. In these pages you will learn, among other phenomena, about:

The remarkable adaptations the human body makes to training, even in old age.
Running as a natural tranquillizer.
Running as an enhancer of sexual pleasure.
The nutritional secret that lets runners eat foods absolutely forbidden to most dieters, and lets them lose weight while doing it.

Runners who, without strain, cover as many as 200 miles at a time.

Heart-attack victims who, with their doctors' blessing, not only compete in twenty-six-mile races but feel better than they did before their attacks.

You will, in short, discover that running has a vast number of beneficial effects, some of which are only beginning to be understood.

It will not be surprising if the foregoing claims strike you as extravagant, and you have every right to ask who is making them and on what authority. The answers to those questions will emerge piece by piece throughout these pages, but a preliminary summary may be in order.

One day, almost a decade ago, I was playing tennis with a friend named Walter Guzzardi. He and I were evenly matched, and we always played hard. I was in my mid-thirties and worked on a big magazine in Manhattan. One of my more pleasant duties was to entertain authors at lunches and dinners, and what with too many martinis and too little exercise my weight had climbed, ounce by flabby ounce, from the 170 lbs it had been during my teens to a beefy 213¾ lbs. (This figure is absolutely precise. I still have in my files a sobering report, dated November 25, 1968, from a medical institution I visited for a physical.)

None the less, by virtue of ancient reflexes and guile I still played a respectable, if roly-poly, game of tennis. Moreover—I confess it—I prided myself on my game. That is why I was so irritated when, as Guzzardi and I played that day, I felt a ripping sensation in my right calf. I had been running towards the left side of the court and Guzzardi, in order to catch me off balance, had hit the ball to the right. His strategy worked. I tried to change direction too fast, and the effort pulled the muscle.

The injury was not serious, and even though I limped painfully for a week or two, the leg soon healed.

What lingered longer than the pain was the way I felt about the damage. My body had betrayed me, and I was angry. I still thought of myself, secretly at least, as an athlete. Someone who all his life had played tennis and Saturday-afternoon football shouldn't be laid low in this way.

So I was not prepared to accept my fate. As soon as the pain had

eased, I decided to do some running to strengthen my legs. Incidentally, we may as well dispose of a question of definition right away.
Although some would argue the point, there is no particular speed at
which jogging turns into running. If you feel that you're running, no
matter how slow you're going, no one can say you're not. For the
purposes of the present discussion, therefore, I'll always refer to
running, no matter what the speed.

As it happened, the only running I had ever done had been in
Army basic training, and I had hated it. I can still hear the voice of the
tall, dyspeptic sergeant as he shuffled alongside us puffing 'Hut-
two-three-four', just as I can still feel the summer sun tormenting me
and my fellow recruits as we tried to keep up. But because Army
running was all I knew, I laced on a pair of heavy boots, went
outdoors, and started shuffling slowly along the pavement.

I saw no sign that in doing so I had begun to change my life, yet
this is exactly what was happening. Although my thighs ached and
my lungs burned—it didn't help that I smoked two packets of
cigarettes a day—I kept at my running. I very much wanted to avoid
another pulled muscle. Three or four times a week I would shuffle
half-a-mile or so, seldom more. When the pressures of work became
too great I would stop altogether, but sooner or later I always drifted
back to it.

Eventually I moved from New York to suburban Connecticut,
where running was more pleasant. There were country roads,
streams and rivers, grassy parks and woods. I stopped smoking and
began to run more. Sometimes I ran with a young neighbour, Ned
Tuthill, who had just been discharged from the Marines and was
very fit. He ran faster than I really wanted to, but his ebullient spirit
cheered me on, and if he didn't press too hard I could usually stay
with him.

One day I read in our local newspaper that in two or three weeks
there was to be a five-mile race right in the town where I lived.
Anyone could enter, even thirty-five-year-old overweight geriatric
cases like myself.

Next day, in my naïve enthusiasm, I tried running five miles,
much farther than any reasonably prudent person would have
attempted. My pace was snail-like, especially toward the end, but
somehow I managed to finish. I posted in an entry form for the race
and trained hard, running every morning before work.

The night before the race I slept badly, just as I had years earlier whenever I faced an important tennis match. At the starting line I looked around. There must have been two hundred runners, most of them young and lean. Their ribs showed; their cheeks were hollow. But there were also a good many men in their forties, fifties and even sixties, and a scattering of women and children. With luck, I might not do badly. The town mayor was introduced, wished us well, and then fired the starting gun.

I couldn't believe the pace. The front runners had turned the first corner almost before I had taken a dozen steps. But at least I was not in last place. I kept moving—under a bridge and some railway lines, over another bridge that spanned a stream, and into a park. Although my legs were getting heavy I pushed on. I looped through the park and started uphill, but now I was slowing down badly. Women and children had begun to pass me. Soon I was last. Ahead of me the women and children moved steadily away.

I was discouraged and mystified. Just why had I done so badly? I had tortured myself with all that training, and I was plainly not the fattest, oldest, or clumsiest runner in the race.

I went to the local library and hunted down some books on running. A friend lent me some copies of a magazine. I began to learn what training was. I also learned why, if you did it right, you would not only get faster and healthier, but, in both the psychological and physiological senses, younger. I found myself thinking more and more about running. Not everyone likes it, but I did. I forced myself to lose weight in order to do better at it, and I began to run every day. Friends started to tell me I looked wonderful. No one had said *that* for a long time. Finally, two years after I had taken my first running steps, I even managed to win a minor championship, the Connecticut 10 000-metre title, in my age category.

But what I found even more interesting were the changes that had begun to take place in my mind. I was calmer and less anxious. I could concentrate more easily and for longer periods. I felt more in control of my life. I was less easily rattled by unexpected frustrations. I had a sense of quiet power, and if at any time I felt this power slipping away I could call it back by going out and running.

Every runner is familiar with these changes. Though they have been compared with those that occur in transcendental meditation, they are something more than that, perhaps because they are magnified by an unusual degree of physical fitness.

I am steadfastly suspicious when it comes to out-of-the-ordinary psychological states. But even my most hard-headed, sceptical self admits that running has produced some remarkable psychological benefits. One might even say they have been spiritual. The wife of a running friend of mine, asked how her husband reconciled his Methodist convictions with the fact that in the United States nearly all races are held on Sundays, replied 'Tom *used* to be a Methodist. Now he's a runner.' The distinguished historian Johan Huizinga, author of *Homo Ludens: A Study of the Play Element in Culture*, has probably given as much thought to the meaning of recreation as anyone. Citing the fact that Plato equated play with ritual, Huizinga wrote: 'The Platonic identification of play and holiness does not defile the latter by calling it play; rather it exalts the concept of play to the highest regions of the spirit.'

When I first began to suspect that there was considerably more to running than met the casual eye, I wondered whether mine was so private a view that it had little application to anyone else. So I asked other runners about their experiences. It turns out that a great many other runners have had experiences much like my own. There is, in fact, an almost invariable pattern of development. Typically, a person begins running in search of fitness, to lose weight and to look and feel better. After several months or years, he or she gradually begins to spend far more time running than the requirements of fitness alone would dictate. Finally, he or she realizes that something in running has a uniquely salutary effect on the mind.

This aspect of running is what makes this book such an incongruous combination of elements. Whoever heard of a book that dealt with both transcendental meditation and blisters? Yet running cannot be adequately or accurately described without giving equal attention to the physical and the psychological.

The physical benefits (and hazards) of running have long been under scientific scrutiny, while the psychological effects are only in the earliest stages of exploration. Still, it would be misleading to slight running's physical benefits, for there are many of them and they are closely related to the psychological.

The plan of this book, therefore, is this:

In Part One we will look at the ways in which running changes you, physically, mentally, socially and spiritually.

In Part Two, we will examine the various theories and techniques of running to find out how to search for, and find, the beneficial changes and the improvement that all runners experience.

In Part Three we will look into the world of running, its mystique and some of its odder aspects, to see what awaits you.

There is one final step, one necessarily beyond the compass of this book. That is the running itself. This is up to you. It is also up to you to decide, with the help, probably, of a coach and perhaps a doctor who specializes in athletics, how long and how far you will run. But remember, especially at first, that long-distance running requires training. Researchers who have studied running's physical effects agree that fifteen or twenty minutes as few as three days a week are enough to produce measurable benefits. (At first this may seem like a lot, but it doesn't take much training to be able to do that much.) On the other hand, many beginners find, as I did, that as they get stronger and fleeter they want to run more just because it's fun. Many cover eight to ten miles a day, and find the hour to hour-and-a-half a stimulating interlude. But each of us is different, and each of us responds differently to running. You may feel just as refreshed after a mile as I do after ten, so listen carefully to your body for its own special complaints and exultations. Run as much or as little as you want to. Whatever you decide, you should find yourself perfectly at home in this book; most of its principles are as applicable to a run around the block as to a marathon.

James F. Fixx

PART ONE
The Whys of Running

1 · Feeling better physically

Running as an antidote to what ails us

One grey November morning I was running near the edge of a lake. On the path ahead of me an old man shuffled along slowly, using a cane. As I ran by I called out, 'Good morning!' He returned my greeting and then called after me unexpectedly, 'What do you gain by running?' I shouted back: 'It makes you feel good!'

What I said was true enough, but it was hardly the whole answer. This chapter is an attempt to do belated justice to the old man's question.

For convenience, running's benefits can be divided into the physical and the psychological, even though the demarcation between them is not really clear. (The psychological lift of running, for example, goes hand in hand with exercising for a certain length of time, forty-five minutes or so.) In this chapter, we will look briefly into some of the physical benefits of running.

The people of most industrial nations are in terrible shape. They smoke and drink too much, weigh too much, exercise too little and eat too many of the wrong things. One pathologist, Thomas Bassler, says that on the basis of autopsies he has performed, two out of every three deaths in America are premature; they are related to what he calls loafer's heart, smoker's lung and drinker's liver. Thomas Cureton, a professor at the University of Illinois Physical Fitness Laboratory, has said, 'The average American young man has a middle-aged body. He can't run the length of a city block, he can't climb a flight of stairs without getting breathless. In his twenties, he has the capacity that a man is expected to have in his forties.'

What about people who aren't so young? Cureton goes on: 'The average middle-aged man in this country is close to death. He is only one emotional shock or one sudden exertion away from a serious heart attack.' If that strikes you as overdramatic, for the next few days notice the ages in the deaths columns and bear in mind that, among British men, a third of all deaths result from heart disease.

But isn't there a contradiction here? Participation in sports has doubled since World War II, and a glance at any tennis court or golf course is enough to suggest that the rate of growth is currently accelerating. Unfortunately, however, only a fraction of the population does most of the participating. The rest are spectators.

The experience of Neil Carver, a lawyer, is typical. Carver is tall, rangy and sturdily built, but at thirty-three he was out of shape. 'I was carrying my two children upstairs one night to put them to bed,' he told me. 'I got so winded I could hardly breathe. I said to myself, I've got to do something about this.' Carver started running. Today, seven or eight years later, he has not only competed in an eight-mile race but spends part of every summer climbing mountains with his wife and children.

Even young people are out of shape. In one American school only eight ten-year-olds out of a class of fifty-two were fit enough to earn physical fitness awards. Not long ago a study at Massachusetts General Hospital showed that fifteen percent of 1900 pre-teenagers had high cholesterol levels and eight percent had high blood pressure. (Both conditions are associated with an increased likelihood of heart attacks and strokes.) Nor, despite our growing interest in sport, is our children's physical fitness getting any better. When twelve million youngsters from ten to seventeen years old were tested for the U.S. Office of Education, strength, agility and speed showed no improvement over a ten year period. (There was one exception: girls had slightly more endurance.) Conditions are not significantly better in England.

Doctors, the very people we might reasonably look to for guidance, are in no better shape than the rest of us. In Southern California not long ago, 58 doctors were given physicals. Most were found to be in poor physical condition. One out of five smoked; two out of three were overweight; one in four had high blood pressure; one in five had an abnormal electro-cardiogram while exercising; more than half had high serum lipid levels, which are thought to be associated with heart disease. Their condition may reflect the attitude of a young doctor friend of mine who smokes heavily. 'I don't worry about lung cancer,' he told me. 'By the time I get it they'll have a cure for it.'

Not all doctors are so devil-may-care. Many, because they are so grievously overworked, give most of their time to emergencies or cases in which pain must be alleviated. Inevitably, giving advice on how to stay well falls to the bottom of their list of priorities. Dr John Williams, medical director of the Farnham Park Rehabilitation Centre and Secretary-General of the International Federation of Sports Medicine, told me, 'The doctor's biggest problem is the pressure of work.'

If our doctors can't be expected to bring us good health, to whom can we look? The answer is plain: to ourselves. This conclusion received support recently from Dr John Knowles, President of the Rockefeller Foundation. Noting that many people regard 'sloth, gluttony, alcoholic intemperance, reckless driving, sexual frenzy and smoking' as constitutional rights and expect the Government to pay for the consequences, Knowles argued that this attitude, and the kind of medical system it produces, will inevitably lead to higher costs. The next major breakthrough in medicine, he predicted, will come through changes in the way we live, not through anything doctors, hospitals or drugs can do to cure what Dr Williams has called 'the pathology of pleasure'.

An easy way to effect a favourable change in your way of living is by running. Running is one of the best exercises there is, and certainly the simplest. When workers in a Soviet factory took up running, they reduced the number of days lost annually through sickness from 436 to 42. Furthermore, studies have shown that practically everyone can benefit from the sport. The University of Michigan's Physical Performance Research Laboratory has demonstrated that even extremely overweight people can significantly improve their physical condition in as little as three weeks.

An important indicator of overall health is cardio-vascular endurance, which is what running, particularly when done at a pace fast enough to make you breathe hard, develops. Of course, there are other exercises that build such endurance, bicycling, swimming and rowing among them. But only running can be done anywhere, requires practically no equipment and costs almost nothing. You can go right out of your front door and get started. You don't need a bicycle, a swimming pool, a boat or a court. You don't need a track, either. I have run on paths, roads and highways, in parks and fields and on the main roads of London, New York, Florence, Vienna and Paris. You can run at dawn, at midnight or whenever it suits your schedule and your fancy. I have run—and enjoyed it—in snow, sleet, wind and hail, and on the most forbiddingly hot days of an Athens summer. As a runner named Stan Gerstein told me, 'There's nothing quite like the feeling you get from knowing you're in good physical condition. I wake up alert and singing in the morning, ready to go.'

Running's physiological values are attested to by the growing number of physicians who use running as a form of preventive medicine, in the belief that it's better to keep someone well than to cure him after he gets sick. Dr George Sheehan, an American cardiologist, says running 'is a physiologically perfect exercise. Running uses large thigh and leg muscles in rhythmic fashion at a personally controlled rate. This is the requirement for safely developing maximum cardiopulmonary function.' It is for this reason that Sheehan recently referred to 'a new trend in medicine: prescribing sport instead of drugs.' (It is not, of course, really new at all but merely a rediscovery of a truth that was well known in, among other periods of British history, the seventeenth century.) In our own time, the philosopher Paul Weiss, writing in *Sport: A Philosophic Inquiry*, has said: 'Athletics, because it enables one to move from a poor to a better state of being, can be viewed as a branch of medicine, but one which fortunately finds room for the expression of spontaneity, ingenuity and judgment.'

For the moment, let us consider only the way running combats the risk of developing heart trouble. Dr Robert Jones, a preventive-medicine specialist, cites fifteen factors that indicate the likelihood of having a heart attack:

Blood pressure
Activity
Weight
Mood and coping style
Fasting blood sugar
Triglycerides
Fibrinolysins
Cigarette smoking
Diet
Electro-cardiogram readings
Uric acid
Pulmonary function

Glucose tolerance
Heredity
Cholesterol*

Of the fifteen, exercise may improve all except heredity, and there is strong suspicion that it is not heredity itself but family living patterns that are most significant. Although smoking and dietary habits, for example, are not directly altered by running, anyone who becomes a regular runner will probably stop smoking, eat less and eat a more balanced diet. Running can therefore significantly reduce the risk of developing coronary heart disease. It can also, as will be discussed in Chapter 21, help to bring heart-attack victims back to full vigour, even allowing them to compete in gruelling marathons.

While not all the physical effects of running are so dramatic, most of them are equally welcome. A doctor named William Fortner told me that his chronic tension headaches go away when he runs. And Barbara Orr, a Californian doctor, said, 'I love running because you feel so good. It keeps my tennis game in shape. I can get to the ball better. And it makes my legs slim.'

Running does some other startling things. We live in an age when it is considered desirable to be young and unfortunate to be old, so if staying young is what you want, running can help. Dr Fred Kasch studied 43 middle-aged men for ten years, checking at intervals on their maximum heart rate, their oxygen-processing ability, the pumping power of their hearts and what doctors call peripheral vascular resistance, all of them commonly accepted indicators of ageing. Previous studies had shown what would happen to a group of sedentary middle-aged men during a similar period. Kasch was interested to find out what, if anything, would happen if the men exercised, so he put them on a programme of either running or swimming. At the end of the decade none of the four indicators showed any signs of increasing age, and two of them (the body's oxygen-processing capacity and the amount of blood pumped in a single heartbeat) suggested a decrease in age. As a side benefit, blood pressure stayed below average and in a number of cases even declined.

These scientific findings are borne out by common-sense

* Recent research suggests that cholesterol itself is probably not the chief culprit. Rather, the significant factor seems to be the ratio of high-density and low-density lipoproteins, the compounds that transport the cholesterol.

Stephen Richardson

observation. In their sixties and seventies, runners move with an easy grace not often found in people even two or three decades younger. I have often seen what I took to be a young man or woman running towards me, then been startled to discover that he or she was in fact middle-aged.

Stephen Richardson is such a person. In his late fifties, he is tall and lean. When training for marathons he runs as many as twenty miles a day, and he has run them fast enough to be the envy of many twenty-year-olds. Richardson is almost always taken for a man several years younger than he is. (For what it's worth, people usually think I am seven or eight years younger than I actually am. At any rate, they *say* that's what they think. It may just be that I look as if I could use a little flattery.) This sort of compliment can, however, have its grisly side effects. Richardson works at a medical college. Not long ago an anatomist colleague looked him up and down and remarked, 'You'll make a fine corpse—no fat to cut through.'

Another benefit of getting into shape through running is that the pleasure of sex, for both men and women, is invariably heightened. The reason is not at all mysterious. Being in good physical condition involves not just muscles, the heart and the lungs but all the senses. Runners are more aware of themselves and of others and are able to participate more fully in all aspects of life, including the sexual.

Despite this beneficial effect on physical vigour and the ageing process, however, running has not yet been shown to make people live longer, though in all likelihood, as Chapter 4 suggests, it will one day be demonstrated that this is so. Robert Glover, one-time physical fitness director at a large Y.M.C.A. in New York City and a tireless proselytizer of running, says: 'We don't guarantee to add years to your life, but we will add life to your years.'

Unlike many other physical activities, running qualifies as a 'lifetime sport', one that can be enjoyed long after contact sports have become too hazardous. This is why so many Government-sponsored fitness campaigns stress running over other sports. To launch a keep-fit programme in Scotland in 1978, for example, three Scottish MPs—Teddy Taylor, Harry Ewing and Hector Monro—went jogging in St James's Park (and, needless to say, made sure that news photographers were there to give the event its proper place in the annals of British history). The Health Council, for its part, launched its fitness programme with the catchy slogan 'Improve Your Sex Life with a Pair of Plimsolls'.

Running helps your entire body, not just your legs and lungs, feel better. When you run regularly you feel lithe, springy and energetic. You have a sense of power obtainable from few other sources. Furthermore, an easy run of a few miles can cure minor indispositions, such as headaches or upset stomachs. Once, when a friend told me he wasn't feeling well, I asked him whether he was going to see a doctor. 'Running is my doctor,' he replied.

This comment contains a profound truth. Dale Nelson, who teaches physical fitness, told me recently about a 45-year-old student of his named Quintin Snow. A former pilot, Snow had undergone surgical removal of one third of his stomach. He weighed 221 lbs, could barely climb out of a swimming pool, and suffered from a variety of medical problems. Snow joined Nelson's physical fitness class, started running, and within three and a half months had lost 40 pounds and had recovered from many of his ailments. At the last report he could run six miles without stopping.

The list of disorders that can be helped by running is a long one. Mike Levine has cerebral palsy. In spite of it, he not only completed a marathon, but also gained first place in the college and university division, and in the process gave his self-confidence an incomparable lift. His father, Jack, an orthopaedic surgeon, told me, 'Running has played a vital role in Mike's life. The change in his self-image permitted him to expand what had been an extremely circumscribed social life.'

Most important, though, running is fun. Many of us have been brought up to feel that any physical effort must be made out of a sense of duty, not for the joy in it. Most physical training programmes in schools certainly make us feel that way. But if you miss the pleasure in running you miss its essence. Imagine an autumn day. The air is crisp and filled with bright, swirling leaves. I head out of my door, down a hill, through a park, and along a road that leads to woodland paths and broad beaches. I am stiff and creaky as I start, but within a few minutes I begin to sweat lightly and my stride smoothes out. Pheasants, rabbits and squirrels scatter at the sound of my footsteps. I reach the halfway point, near a flower garden and an old brick wall. Running easily, I glide along the edge of the sea, through marsh grasses and then along a beach. Soon I am home again, breathing lightly and feeling both spent and exhilarated. Much the same thing happens, by the way, to runners who must do their running in competition with exhaust smoke, smog and eighteen-wheelers.

Any description of such an hour pales beside the experiencing of it. But the experience is—I guarantee it—very much there, waiting for you. This helps to account for the growing popularity of running. It is why, for example, there are today some two million runners in the United Kingdom and more than twenty-five million in the United States.

But the physical benefits of running, as we shall see in the next chapter, are only the beginning.

2 · What happens to your mind

The brain–body phenomenon

Few psychological frontiers are more fascinating than those that you cross in your mind as you run. Profound and far-reaching, such changes provide clues to the intricate relationship between our minds and our bodies. For several months, as I did research for this book, I travelled a great deal, talking with all sorts of runners who I hoped could supply me with information about various aspects of running. In almost every case I would start the discussion with a specific subject in mind—running following a heart attack, say, or racing tactics, or the types of muscle tissue involved in running—and for a while we would stick to that subject. But at some point the conversation would invariably slip off into a topic I had not brought up: the psychology of running. Everyone, it seemed, was secretly interested in, and in a surprising number of cases obsessed by, what goes on in runners' minds and how the sport changes people.

Western society today puts considerable emphasis on personal development and the maximizing of one's potential. Zen Buddhism, transcendental meditation, assertiveness training, and similar movements are all directed at making us fulfilled human beings. Sometimes, to judge by the testimony of their adherents, they work well. Sometimes, however, they do not, and I suspect the reason in many cases is that they fail to mesh with the inescapable peculiarities and idiosyncrasies of individual character. In contrast, while running often alters a person profoundly, the changes all come from within and are therefore tightly integrated with the total personality. To some extent, of course, this is true of all athletics, since they alter the mind by altering the body. Dr J. E. Kane of the University of London, who is well-known for his investigations of the psychology of sport, has written: 'The way an individual characteristically perceives his body has long been held as an important factor in forming his image of himself and his general integration.' This seems to be truer in running than in team sports and those individual sports that are of less sustained intensity.

In this chapter I plan to discuss the psychological changes that result from running. First, we will examine some of the emotions runners feel as a result of running. Then we will look at the ways in which the psychological phenomena of running work to change lives.

The majority of the people I have talked to about running have told me they felt they had benefited psychologically from it. This did not surprise me, for I myself have long known that I have. Some of the benefits, as already indicated, are easily described: a sense of enhanced mental energy and concentration, a feeling of heightened mental acuity. Other benefits are more difficult to put into words. To cite only one example, the qualities and capacities that are important in running—such factors as will-power, the ability to apply effort during extreme fatigue, and the acceptance of pain—have a radiating power that invariably influences one's life.

The people I spoke with described these phenomena in persuasive and even poetic terms. Nancy Gerstein, for example, is a young editor who runs six miles four or five times a week. She told me: 'Running gives me a sense of controlling my own life. I feel I'm doing something for myself, not depending on anyone else to do it for me. I like the finiteness of my runs, the fact that they have a clear beginning and end: I set a goal and I achieve it. I like the fact, too, that there's real difficulty in running; when you have to push yourself to finish a run, you feel wonderful afterwards. A good run makes you feel sort of holy.' Louise Foottit, a London girl who runs for half-an-hour every morning in Kensington Gardens, is equally insistent about the importance of running in her life. 'When you run, you're free,' she says. 'No boss bothers you. The falsity of so much of modern life becomes irrelevant. You're just completely yourself. It's possibly the only time you can say that.'

Allan Ripp is in his early twenties. For years he was bothered by asthma. ('Every gasp was terrible,' he told me. 'I couldn't think about anything else.') Then he took up running. Although he is careful not to claim that running cured his asthma, he does say that it has made it easier to tolerate the attacks when they come. Ripp said: 'Running is the greatest thing that ever happened to me. It's the focus of my daily routine, the source of everything. It gives my life a sense of rhythm. It's not just a game or a sport, something *outside* of life; it's *part* of life. It's an adjective, something that defines me.'

Ted Corbitt was a member of the 1952 U.S. Olympic marathon

team and two years later became America's marathon champion. He has competed in some 200 marathons, many longer races and innumerable shorter ones—enough, certainly, to have squashed any lingering romanticism about running. Yet when I talked with him he said in his soft-spoken, understated manner: 'People get a relief of tension from running. It's like having your own psychiatrist. You have various feelings. Sometimes it's joyous. Everyone benefits from running, both in ways they recognize and in ways they don't. One thing that almost always happens is that your sense of self-worth improves. You accept yourself a little better.'

Nina Kuscsik is another veteran runner who, in 1972, won the women's division of the world-renowned Boston Marathon. She told me: 'There isn't much freedom in our lives any more. Running gives you freedom. When you run, you can go at your own speed. You can go where you want to go and think your own thoughts. Nobody has any claim on you.' And Joe Henderson, a writer who has thought as deeply as anyone about running, said, 'Running is a childish and a primitive thing to do. That's its appeal, I think. You're moving like a child again. You strip away all the chains of civilization. While you're running, you go way back in history.'

No one, however, has put the matter as succinctly as a runner named Mark Hanson. 'To run is to live,' he told me. 'Everything else is just waiting.'

Hanson is not the only person who equates running with living fully. As I talked with people all over the world I discovered that many of them regarded their running hours as their happiest, partly because running is such a powerful antidote to anxiety and depression. A runner named Monte Davis told me: 'Running long and hard is an ideal anti-depressant, since it's hard to run and feel sorry for yourself at the same time. Also, there are those hours of clear-headedness that follow a long run.' Beth Richardson, a Boston runner, said, 'I feel less cranky and bitchy when I run.' Bill Copeland, a witty newspaper columnist, speaks evocatively about running on the beach: 'As you run, you sink your bare feet into the moistly yielding sand along the surf and invoke the known benefit of sole massage, the next best thing to soul massage for curing the blues.' Finally, a runner named Russel Gallop said, 'Several years after college I was struck with both a failing marriage and a leg injury. I had to face a psychologically debilitating divorce and the physical limitations that come with knee surgery. I was in a physical and psychological rut. Running seemed the logical way to get my knee back to its normal function. The unexpected dividend was that I got my head together, too.'

The feelings these runners describe have been documented. Richard Driscoll, a psychologist, found that running makes people less anxious, particularly if they think pleasant thoughts as they train. Dr Michael Mock of the U.S. National Heart, Lung and Blood Institute told me that 'in a society where for many reasons there is a tendency for a majority of people to have depression, exercise has been found to counter depressed feelings by increasing one's feeling of self-esteem and independence.' I even came across one psychiatrist, Dr John Greist, who, having assigned a group of abnormally depressed patients either to a ten-week running programme or to ten weeks of traditional psychotherapy, found the running programme more effective.

The sense of well-being that comes with running is corroborated by other observers. Dr Fredrick Harper reports on a research project designed to assess, among other things, the psychological changes that occurred when students worked their way up from a quarter of a mile to several miles of running. Among the results reported by the participants were decreased anxiety, greater sexual appreciation and a better feeling about themselves, including, in Dr Harper's words, 'positive feelings about their body'. He also reports on some side effects of the project: 'By jogging on the athletic track, the students were subject to spectators, including the football team, which practised around the same time. Some of the girls felt self-conscious in the beginning because of wisecracks from male bystanders. At the end of the jogging project, the girls had gained respect for their ability and perseverance in getting up to a distance of four and five miles. Some of the football players even commented that the joggers inspired them to practise harder.'

The same diminution of anxiety cited by Dr Harper and others has been reported in a study carried out by Dr Herbert deVries and Gene Adams in California. They asked for volunteers from a retirement community. These ranged in age from 52 to 70, and all suffered from such symptoms as nervous tension, sleeplessness, irritability, continual worry and feelings of panic in everyday situations. The researchers tested the volunteers after 400-milligram doses of meprobamate, a widely used tranquillizer; after taking an identical-looking placebo; and after exercising moderately for fifteen minutes. The exercise, it turned out, reduced the volunteers' tension more effectively than the tranquillizer.

Even without the benefit of a formal study, most runners come to value the tranquillizing effect of their sport. Robert Gene Fineberg reports: 'My vocation, market analysis, puts me under extreme pressure each day, but nothing seems too big when I know that these miles after work will be as smooth as silk. Running gives the mind a boost worth all the tranquillizers in the world.' Similarly, Dr Stephen Storey, an orthopaedic surgeon, said: 'I find that running allows me to escape from the numerous pressures of private practice. I usually do my running at lunchtime, and I feel much less hassled during the afternoon. I have been through a transcendental meditation programme and for a period of time meditated regularly. Running has much the same effect on me as transcendental meditation.' Dr Terence Kavanagh, medical director of the Toronto Rehabilitation Center, asserts that most heart patients in his running programme report 'a great improvement in mood and morale'. And Dr Alan Clark, who is frequently asked to prescribe tranquillizers, says, 'It is well known that exercise is the best tranquillizer. I refuse to medicate patients with simple neurotic anxiety until they give aerobic exercises an adequate trial.'

In a well-known study at Purdue University, 60 middle-aged faculty and staff members, all of them in sedentary jobs, participated in a four-month exercise programme consisting chiefly of running. Before and after the programme their personalities were evaluated by a standard test, the Cattell 16 Personality Factor Questionnaire. As they became fitter, the subjects were found to become more emotionally stable, self-sufficient, imaginative and confident.

While I was looking into the mental dimensions of running, I noticed that many writers have in fact been circling round the subject for some time. Sir Roger Bannister, the first person to run the four-minute mile, once wrote:

I can still remember quite vividly a time when as a child I ran barefoot along damp, firm sand by the seashore. The air there had a special quality, as if it had a life of its own. The sound of breakers on the shore shut out all others, and I was startled and almost frightened by the tremendous excitement a few steps could create. It was an intense moment of discovery, of a source of power and beauty that one previously hardly dreamed existed. ... The sense of exercise is an extra sense, or perhaps a subtle combination of all the others.

Another runner, Annette McDaniels, says: 'I experience a complete unification of body and mind.'

Finally, a runner and writer named David Bradley has described one of his runs in these words:

I am producing alpha brain waves. I am hurting far more than most people ever do unless they are sick or injured, yet feel relaxed, almost happy. I am deeply inside myself and yet totally aware of my surroundings. ... I no longer touch the ground: I am moving through the air, floating. The incline is not a hill, it is just air that is a little thicker, and I can breathe deeply and draw myself up without effort. My body is producing draughts of a hormone called epinephrine, which researchers have linked with feelings of euphoria. This, combined with the alpha waves and the repetitive motion of running which acts as a sort of mantra, makes me higher than is legally possible in any other way.

Many of the states these people describe are, of course, much like those that occur occasionally in the lives of all of us, whether we run or not. The important difference is that running makes them totally predictable; if you are a runner, you can summon them whenever you want to.

Some runners even argue that running brings about mental states so remote from those of everyday life as to be unimaginable to most of us. Michael Murphy, the founder of Esalen, says many athletes are 'closet mystics', people who have paranormal experiences during competition. A professional football player, for example, has described a game in which all the players were inexplicably surrounded by 'auras'. By looking at a player's aura, he reported, he could tell which way the man was planning to move. Another psychological researcher, Mike Spino, has written: 'Running ... can be a way of discovering our larger selves. I am finding that average people as well as superstars touch spiritual elements when they least expect it.'

John Walker of New Zealand, who as I write is history's fastest miler (3:49.4), has in these remarkable words described his victory in an Olympic 1500 metre race: 'When I hit the front I got a flash of compelling certainty. I didn't look over my shoulder, but I sensed someone coming up on me fast. And I knew it was Rick Wohlhuter of the United States, even though I couldn't see who it was. I just knew it. I was already at full stretch. But I went into a sort of mental overdrive, and my subconscious mind took over completely.

I've experienced it in races before, and I can't explain it. I burned Wohlhuter off.'

Re-reading William James's *Varieties of Religious Experience* not long ago, I was struck by how similar runners' language is to that of many of the mystics whose minds James explores. It is not difficult, in fact, to find explicit references to the religious qualities of running. A 30-year-old runner, Coreen Nasenbeny, told me of having become a 'true convert' to running in 1976. Then she added: 'And I don't think I'm far off in equating my experience with a conversion.'

No one has yet undertaken a comprehensive investigation of the mental changes that occur as a result of running. Although several writers—Sir Roger Bannister, Joe Henderson, George Sheehan and the psychiatrist Thaddeus Kostrubala prominent among them—have touched upon the subject, no one has yet attempted a full-scale description of the mental phenomena associated with running. In *The Madness in Sports*, Arnold Beisser suggests a reason for the neglect: 'The reluctance to penetrate into comprehending the meaning of sports is understandable. We prefer not to know too much about what we treasure. ... The lover of a beautiful woman protects his cherished concept of her from anything which may detract from her beauty.'

None the less, a few adventurous thinkers have tried to unravel what it is about sport in general that tugs at us so strongly. Let us see how much light their thoughts shed on the running experience.

Any thorough inquiry into the meaning of sport will eventually bring us to Johan Huizinga's *Homo Ludens: A Study of the Play Element in Culture*, mentioned earlier. Published in 1949, the book argues that man is not best defined as *Homo sapiens* (man the thinker) or *Homo faber* (man the maker) but as *Homo ludens* (man the game player). This is so, Huizinga says, because we have a propensity for turning all aspects of life, no matter how serious, into games. Beethoven, writing his Fifth Symphony, was playing a game. Faulkner, writing his complex Yoknapatawpha County novels, was playing a different game. Whether corporation president, general or surgeon, when we are at work we are playing games.

If we accept the idea that our lives are games, might it not also be true that what we call our games are in fact a deeper part of our lives than we may hitherto have suspected? This would help to explain the frenzied intensity of the football fan, the ascetic concentration of the chess player, the scholarly zeal with which some people devote themselves to Wisden.

None of this would explain why sport penetrates our lives so deeply. For that, we need to turn to another clue, this one in Paul Weiss's *Sport: A Philosophic Inquiry*. Weiss holds that champion athletes are more than merely themselves; they are excellence in human form. We like to watch a Rosewall backhand not just for what it is but for what it represents: pure, platonic perfection. So it is with running, both the running of champions and our own. The champion—Chris Stewart or Filbert Bayi, let us say—is excellence in human form, and we just as surely are our own excellence. When you next watch a race, notice the expressions of ecstasy on the faces of those who cross the finishing line many minutes or, in the case of long races like the marathon, even hours after the winner. These slower runners have pushed themselves quite as hard as the winner and, like him, have overcome fatigue and the agony of too much pain too long endured. In the context of the race, they have become as excellent as they are capable of being. That is the rare and wonderful feeling you are seeing.

Sport also does other things if we let it. It teaches us lessons in human limits. Because sport offers no hiding places, it also teaches honesty and authenticity. In short, it teaches us something about personal fulfilment and integrity. And if we give it the respect and attention it deserves, it teaches us something about joy.

These are not lessons in any formal schoolroom sense. Rather, they are scraps of knowledge received piecemeal through Bannister's 'extra sense'. Because they are won by so much effort, they are that much more impressive and memorable. In *Leisure: The Basis of Culture*, Josef Pieper remarks that people mistrust rewards that come with too little effort: '[Man] can only enjoy, with a good conscience, what he has acquired with toil and trouble.' There is enough toil and trouble in running to ease the conscience of the most puritanical of athletes, and this is one of running's clearest pleasures.

Perhaps the simplest way to understand this paradox is to consider the pain of running. It is possible to run without pain, but as soon as you start trying to improve, pain—or at least some mild distress—will be your companion. Let's assume you are accustomed to running a mile a day. You want to increase that distance, so one day you decide to try running two miles. No doubt you will be able to do it, but towards the end you will be tired and your legs will feel heavy.

Then, as you push on, you will feel worse. The pain is the result of a struggle between your mind ('Keep running' it tells your body) and your legs ('Stop!' they plead).

The severity of pain in running depends on the intensity of the mind–body struggle. If you just want to cover the two miles, you can slow down, ease the discomfort, and probably experience nothing more than a persistent ache. But if you try to run really hard despite the pain—the way you might if you were battling a rival in a race—it can be fairly intense. (One doctor has compared it with the pain of childbirth: not unbearable but not particularly pleasant either.)

Yet pain of that intensity or greater is something runners regularly experience. Rick Wohlhuter once declared, 'I'm willing to accept any kind of pain to win a race.' Still, to assert that discomfort is a reasonable price to pay for the fruits of victory doesn't get to the heart of the pain question. In most races, even important ones, the prizes are inconsequential—an inexpensive trophy or medal, a round of applause. And in a training run the prize is only what you make it—a rest, a long, cold drink, the satisfaction of finally being home.

Why, then, do runners so willingly accept and even embrace pain? I suspect that it is because there is a close kinship between pain and pleasure. Almost two thousand years ago, Seneca remarked that 'there is a certain pleasure which is akin to pain'. And Socrates said, 'How singular is the thing called pleasure, and how curiously related to pain, which might be thought to be the opposite of it ... yet he who pursues either is generally compelled to take the other; their bodies are two but they are joined by a single head.' In his book: *Pain: Why it Hurts, Where it Hurts, When it Hurts*, Richard Stiller sheds light on the pain-pleasure phenomenon: 'We think of [pain and pleasure] as opposites. Yet our language betrays the confusion that can exist between the two. We describe the pleasure as being so intense as to be "unendurable", something we "can't stand". We talk of "exquisite" pain. From the physiological point of view, agony and ecstasy seem remarkably similar.'

The pleasure that conceals itself in pain is familiar to most runners. At the finishing line of a recent Boston Marathon, a spectator, Kitty Davis, noticed a runner crying. His face was contorted like a child's, and tears were running down his weather-tanned cheeks.

'Why are you crying, sir?' Mrs Davis asked. 'Are you hurt?'

'No,' the runner replied, 'I'm crying because I'm so happy.'

Perhaps, then, there is in us a need to experience pain and, through it, pleasure. Aside from this, however, a number of other needs are fulfilled when we run, among them:

The need for movement.   Watch a child at play. It runs for a while, rests, then runs again. Now it runs quickly, now slowly, now briefly, now for a longer time. At school our running becomes more institutionalized. We run a few yards on a football field or twenty-two yards on a cricket pitch. Once out of school we hardly run at all. Our style of living slowly squeezes the running out of us. Yet the need to run never leaves us, and we are the poorer if we do not somehow find a way to keep at it.

The need for self-assertion.   In *Science and Sport*, Vaughan Thomas observes that we spend much of our lives dominated by others: sergeants, bosses, mothers-in-law. As a result, our need for self-assertion is constantly being pushed out of sight. Running gives us a socially acceptable way of asserting ourselves, of being as competitive, either with ourselves or with others, as we want to be. If at work you try too noticeably to claw your way upward at the expense of your fellow employees, people frown on your behaviour. But in a race, improving your position at the expense of others is considered admirable, so long as it is done with at least an outward show of humility.

The need for alternations of stress and relaxation. Dr Hans Selye has been studying stress for four decades. Each of us, he believes, possesses at birth a given amount of what he calls 'adaptational energy'. When that energy is used up, we experience a mental or physical breakdown. One way to avoid such a breakdown is by deliberately directing stress at varying body systems. 'Often,' Dr Selye writes in *Stress without Distress*, 'a voluntary change of activity is as good as or even better than rest. ... For example, when either fatigue or enforced interruption prevents us from finishing a mathematical problem, it is better to go for a swim than simply to sit around. Substituting demands on our muscles for those previously made on the intellect not only gives our brain a rest but helps us avoid worrying about the other.' Dr Clinton Weiman, medical director of one of the world's largest banks, found that employees had less disease—high blood pressure, overweight, and so forth—if they worked under an optimum amount of stress. Either too much or too little was associated with more disease.

Suppose you work in an office and you come home tired, washed out, your energy gone. You dread the thought of running. Yet as soon as you start you feel better, and by the end of half an hour you are restored. You may have felt tired, but you'll find to your surprise that you weren't tired at all. It's a pleasant discovery.

The need for mastery over ourselves. Too many of us live underdisciplined lives. By giving us something to struggle for and against, running provides an antidote to slackness. 'This urge to struggle lies latent in everyone,' Sir Roger Bannister has written, 'and the more restricted our lives become in other ways, the more necessary it will be to find some outlet for this craving for freedom. No one can say, "You must not run faster than this or jump higher than that." The sportsman is consciously or unconsciously seeking the deep satisfaction, the sense of personal dignity, which comes when body and mind are fully coordinated and they have achieved mastery over themselves.'

Mao Tse-tung was of the same mind. 'In general,' he wrote in 1918, 'any form of exercise, if pursued continuously, will help to train us in perseverance. Long-distance running is particularly good.'

The need to indulge ourselves.   When we run regularly we get into such good physical condition that we can afford occasional excesses. Five hundred calories of chocolate cake replace all the calories we burn up during a five-mile run, but at least the balance is zero, not an excess of five hundred. And the effects of an extra drink can be quickly burned off the next morning. Jack Gianino, a runner and actor, likes to eat chocolate-covered sweets while he watches television. 'They're not good for me,' he says, 'but I don't care. I run enough to get rid of the calories.' Gianino is right; despite his secret vice he is as thin as anyone could want to be.

The need to play.   Although many of us virtually stop playing at some point in our lives, we never outgrow our need for it. Play not only keeps us young but also maintains our sense of perspective about the relative seriousness of things. Running is play, for even if we try hard to do well at it, it is a relief from everyday cares. As a result, our worries and responsibilities seem less pressing. Look at a group of runners at a race. Among them may be a heart surgeon, a judge, an airline pilot, an investment banker. All of them have heavy responsibilities, yet they are as light-hearted as schoolchildren. When they return to their duties later, some of the light-heartedness will remain, for they know that tomorrow there will be another hour of running. Thorstein Veblen understood this phenomenon well when he referred to 'the peculiar boyishness of temperament in sporting men'. He attributed it to 'the large element of make-believe that is present in all sporting activity. . . .'

Many people ask nothing more from running than this sense of play. Dale Van Meter exults in the way the world looks when he runs. He described running early one spring morning while visiting New York: 'I had never seen the beauty of Fifth Avenue before. The streets, empty of people were filled with brilliant early-morning light. The New York Public Library appeared newly washed and clean. St Patrick's Cathedral seemed to stand straighter in the early dawn of that March morning. It was a great experience and one of the high points of my trip.' Van Meter's feeling for the scenic pleasure of running is echoed in the words of Janis Taketa, a 26-year-old runner from Arizona. She said: 'For me, running isn't drudgery but an effortless joy. My home town is on the Navajo Indian reservation, at an elevation of 7000 feet. We are in a canyon surrounded by mountains, trees and sagebrush. Running while it's snowing is breathtaking. There are many places to run here, the air is clean, and there is no traffic. You can't get bored running in a place like this. I prefer running while the sun is coming up. By the time it's light, you're warmed up, you've got your second wind and your whole body feels right. It's great!' I asked a runner who took up the sport nine years ago how he thought his life had changed. His reply was an eloquent summary of the pleasures many people find in running: 'My life has been much more exciting, much more *fun*, as a result of running. The first bird in the spring, robins singing in snow, the perfume of early morning—I would have missed those things and many others. Life is so much richer as a result of running. Running gives me more than I have ever given.'

The need to lose ourselves in something greater than ourselves. The appeal of religion and of many mass movements lies, as Eric Hoffer demonstrates in *The True Believer*, in their capacity for allowing us to forget ourselves, to submerge ourselves in a cause we regard as greater than ourselves. Something like this happens in running. Running is such an intense experience, both physically and psychologically, that we shed self-consciousness and live solely in the moment of running. A psychologist named Mihaly Csikszentmihalyi has done research on activities that are intrinsically rewarding. Whenever we are involved in such activities, he has found, we experience a feeling he calls 'flow'. In this state, according to a recent report in *Psychology Today*, 'we are completely immersed in what we are doing . . . the person loses a self-conscious sense of himself and of time. He gains a heightened awareness of his physical involvement with the activity. The person in flow finds, among other things, his concentration vastly increased and his feedback from the activity enormously enhanced.' What Dr Csikszentmihalyi calls 'flow' is a common experience among runners.

The need to meditate. Unless we make an effort to set aside specific periods of time, our lives seldom allow quiet intervals for thought. Even people employed for their thinking ability usually become so bogged down in daily minutiae that they don't have a chance to do much thinking at all. Running changes that. While we run, we have time to follow our thoughts. Phones don't ring; visitors don't intrude. Even if it is only twenty minutes, we can count on that time as our own. We can, if we wish, address ourselves to particular problems. While writing books on games, puzzles and human intelligence I often solved problems as I ran. It was hard work (I'm not much good at doing maths without pencil and paper), but if I concentrated, I could usually accomplish something. The kind of thinking I most like to do while I run, though, is just to let my thoughts wander. What is important is not *what* we think about, but the fact that we are free to think at all. Even many people who for one reason or another are not eager to face all their thoughts, find that thinking while running is a pleasant and restoring experience.

The need to live to our own rhythms. Large portions of our lives are governed by schedules imposed upon us by other people. Running offers an escape from that. We can run where we want to. We can go fast or slow, hard or easy. We can run by ourselves or with friends. We can get out seven days a week. We can think or let our minds go blank. All these choices are entirely ours; furthermore, we can change them according to the minute-by-minute requirements and fancies of our minds and bodies. 'Rhythm is as much a part of our structure as our flesh and bones,' says Bertram Brown, director of the U.S. National Institute of Mental Health. Running lets us adjust our lives to our rhythms. When our rhythms are at a low ebb, we can cosset ourselves by running slowly and for a short time. When we feel strong and purposeful we can test ourselves by running up steep hills, by finding trails that require us to wade streams and vault fallen trees, by sprinting until we gasp for air. Whatever our need of the moment, running offers an answer.

If what I have been describing as needs are, in fact, true human needs, and if they are met through running, it should follow that runners are somehow different from other people. Are they? Evidence might be mustered either by demonstrating that running has influenced specific people's behaviour in specific ways, or by showing that where objective evidence is absent, so many people report having the same feelings that it is justifiable to give them credence.

As I was working on this section I received a letter from Dr Shew Lee, an optometrist. Lee, who is in his early fifties, started running seven years ago for his health. He had become worried when at a convention he felt his heart beating too rapidly. He thought, *I'm not even fit enough to relax!* This is how Dr Lee feels now: 'Some days I feel so energetic that I can fly up to my second floor office, taking two steps at a time. My patients sense my new enthusiasm for life and work. They're glad to refer their families and friends to an optometrist with such eagerness and vitality.'

Like Dr Lee, most runners find they have more energy than non-runners, and this contributes to a feeling of greater control over their lives. Recently Les Anderson, the mayor of Eugene, Oregon, and a runner himself, said, 'I feel a lot better generally. I know that I can do more things physically and that I recover from them quickly. I also think my mental processes are better.'

Experiences like these have been corroborated by a study conducted at Exxon's physical fitness laboratory. Dr Albert Paolone, the laboratory supervisor, said that after six months on an exercise programme practically everyone reports an increased capacity for work, while a significant proportion say they feel less tired at the end of the day. This reflects my own experience. Before I became a runner I was often sleepy after lunch and had to force myself through a difficult hour or two until my brain crept back to life. Now I have high energy all day long, and at night I invariably sleep well.

Most people who take up running find that their morale and general outlook improve. In his book *Running Scarred*, Tex Maule tells how running helped him find his way back to normal living after a heart attack. Of the psychological effect of running, he writes: 'Although jogging is not an unalloyed pleasure, it *does* have a very pleasant side effect. I can't think of anything which relaxes you more mentally or eases tensions more completely than a leisurely run. While you are running, you do not worry about anything. It is an all-absorbing occupation. When you have finished, the pleasant fatigue combined with the sense of accomplishment keeps tension away for a long time.'

Similarly beneficial results have been reported by Thaddeus Kostrubala. In *The Joy of Running* he tells how, when he was in his early forties and weighed 230 lbs, he started running, lost 55 lbs, felt better, and eventually wondered what effect running might have on his patients. As it turned out, running accomplished what conventional treatment had not: 'To my own surprise and pleasure, the running therapy opened up a new therapeutic aspect. For as I ran along with my patients, my own unconscious was stimulated. And as we explored the meanings and stimuli for both the patient and therapist, it became quite evident that I could no longer adhere to any stereotyped rules.'

Kostrubala reports on the improvements not just in his patients but also in himself: 'We all changed our life habits.... Smoking decreased, then stopped. Drinking followed the same pattern. My obesity fell away. Depressions lifted. Excessively bizarre thought processes were eliminated without destroying the verve and spontaneity of that person. New friends appeared. In short, the group was successful, and the combination of running and therapy seemed to be the key.'

Diminished smoking and drinking are common by-products of running. A businessman named Frank Adams, who runs four to six miles a day in a park just down a hill from my home, told me, 'When I used to get tense at the office I'd stop off on the way home and have a couple of martinis. Now I take a run instead.' And Dr Ronald Lawrence, founder of the American Medical Joggers Association and a fellow of the American College of Sports Medicine, said not long ago: 'You stop smoking in order to run long distances. Your consumption of alcohol drops for the same reason. You simply have more fun if drinking and smoking don't slow you down. Eating habits change because good nutrition is an integral part of aerobic exercises. Your total well-being improves. You sleep better. Your sex life is enhanced. Anxieties decrease and you're better prepared to cope with stress. Work productivity improves. You get away from the television and begin seeing a new world around you.'

Another doctor, William Glasser, has written a book on what he calls 'positive addiction'—the abandonment of bad habits like drug-taking and excessive drinking through the substitution of good habits. 'A positive addiction,' Dr Glasser writes, 'increases your mental strength and is the opposite of a negative addiction, which seems to sap the strength from every part of your life except in the area of the addiction.... Negative addicts are totally involved with their addiction, having long since given up on finding love and worth. The positive addict enjoys his addiction, but it does not dominate his life.' Glasser thinks running is the surest route to positive addiction, an almost infallible way to shake yourself loose from habits that make life more difficult than you want it to be.

Glasser is not the only person to have noticed that running is a powerful enemy of bad habits. Some years ago Kurt Freeman, who runs a rehabilitation centre, noticed that alcoholics tend to lack any leisure activities. What would happen, he wondered, if alcoholics could be induced to develop an interest in something else? By chance, one of his patients was a former high school sprinter who was interested in getting back into shape. Freeman encouraged him to enter some local track meets. The sprinter's condition improved so rapidly that Freeman started urging other alcoholics to take up running. Today Freeman puts on an annual Alcoholics Olympics in California. Recently some 1500 athletes, both men and women, participated. One of Freeman's first alcoholic runners has said of his running: 'It has helped me more than anything to stay sober, to understand myself, to find out what my good points were.'

Other people have reported further benefits. The writer and researcher Robert Bahr takes issue with the argument that competitive sports like running encourage aggression. On the contrary, he says, what it teaches is how to *control* aggression. 'The next time you're running,' says Bahr, 'when your lungs are burning, your feet are blistered, and you think you can't go another step, look at it this way: every mile you cover may be putting more distance between you and your destructive tendencies.'

There seems little doubt that running does enhance mental health, but does anyone know why? The answer is, Not really, though there are some theories. One is that the brain, nourished by an unusually rich supply of oxygen, responds by calling into play its self-correcting mechanisms. Another is that the body and the mind are so closely linked that when you help the body you inescapably help the mind as well. You hear from your mind when you listen to your body.

Listening to your body is, in fact, something you hear a lot about when you are a runner. Let's say your foot hurts. Should you run that day? If you pay attention to your body, it will give a virtually infallible answer. Simply *try* running on it gently, enough to warm up. If your foot continues to hurt or feels worse, your body is telling you not to run. But if the pain diminishes, it's probably safe.

Listening to your body is not only a technique for monitoring your day-to-day condition, but also one of running's pleasures. Most members of our sedentary society feel remote from their bodies; knowing little about how they work or what they are capable of, people fear and mistrust them. Runners, on the other hand, like their bodies. It is those bodies, after all, that carry them across all those miles and bring them all the pleasant experiences discussed in these pages. Because runners do like their bodies and think about how they function, they learn more about them than most people. 'Do you realize how privileged runners are?' Nina Kuscsik asked me as we ran together one day. 'We discover things about our bodies that most people, even doctors, never learn. We're so much more in touch with ourselves.'

Consider, too, runners' attitudes towards bodily functions, both those freely talked about and those that are ordinarily left undiscussed. For example, most of us don't think a great deal about how much water we drink or when we drink it. Runners, especially when a run is long or the weather hot, must think about this. They know that physical efficiency drops sharply if they drink substantially less water than they lose. Instead of drinking merely because they feel thirsty (or not drinking because they don't feel thirsty), they drink consciously, deliberately, for the good of their bodies. They have learned how much their bodies need, and how often.

Under the stress of hard exercise the functions we don't customarily talk about—belching, spitting, breaking wind—inevitably occur. If they happen when you are in the company of other runners, no one takes any notice. Runners come to accept the way the body works.

In the 1972 Boston Marathon, for example, Nina Kuscsik was on her way to winning the women's division when, at thirteen miles, she had an attack of uncontrollable diarrhoea. 'I got a little self-conscious,' she told me at a party after the marathon. 'I thought maybe I should stop. But I wasn't feeling as bad as I looked, so I figured I'd just keep running if I could. After all, what was happening to me happens to everybody at one time or another; the only difference was that it was happening to me in public. I'd done a lot of training and I didn't want to stop if I didn't have to.' She kept running and beat her closest rival by a comfortable nine minutes.

A sign 'DEFEAT IS WORSE THAN DEATH. YOU HAVE TO LIVE WITH DEFEAT' was once posted in a football team's changing room. Although there are indications today of a shift in these attitudes, most of us still think it is good to win and bad to lose. We haven't learned how to handle not winning, and when it happens we don't know quite what to do about it.

Running changes one's attitude towards defeat. When you run, even in competition, you compete not only against others but also against yourself. 'You can succeed by finishing last,' Joe Henderson said as we talked about running one day. 'Maybe this is why so many people of small stature are runners. They've always done badly at athletics. Then they discover running. It's something small people can do. For the first time they succeed at a sport. So their attitude is "Even if I'm not winning the race, I'm winning *something*".'

To learn the meaning of not winning in running is to learn the meaning of not winning elsewhere in our lives. For what we learn through running has a value in the remotest corners of everything we do, making everyday failures seem less dispiriting. Perhaps some day the lessons of running will radiate into other sports as well. The time will come, Mike Spino predicts, when athletics will change markedly. 'They will remain serious but become joyful,' he writes. 'Old concepts of superiority and dominance will subside. Individuals who have prepared for an event will see it as their day to experience something special together. The training build-up will be seen as a preparation rite for a voyage into the physical/spiritual world.'

Spino may underestimate the mud-spattered joy of a hard-fought bone-wrenching football game. Still, his vision reflects an attitude that can be seen in an increasing number of runners, at least in Britain and the United States. I know of no closer feeling between two athletes than when they run stride for stride in the twenty-fifth mile of a gruelling marathon. Both know that one will cross the finishing line first, and will thus, for the record book, win, but each also knows that his own fatigue and pain are indistinguishable from the other's. This shared experience draws them together just as strongly as their competitiveness drives them apart.

Any account of running's psychological pleasures would be incomplete if it failed to mention the ways in which it enhances other activities. For example, my wife is fond of travelling: to her way of thinking no year is complete without a trip abroad. Running makes travel more interesting, for there is no better way to explore a new place. I have had some of my pleasantest runs in the grassy fields near the River Avon in Stratford, in the hills above Florence, along the mountain paths of Jamaica, along the Danube in Vienna, and through the sheep pastures of Wales. Not long ago, on a visit to

London, I arose at dawn and, in my running clothes, crept from our hotel room. For an hour I ran through the deserted streets, reconnoitering in preparation for our sightseeing later that day. By the time my wife was up I was able to tell her exactly where the sights we wanted to see were to be found.

An account of the psychological element in running would be incomplete without an acknowledgement of the problems running sometimes creates or exposes. At least one doctor has expressed the view that the stress of too much running may make mental problems more acute. Runners' spouses, especially during periods of intensive training such as occur before a marathon, sometimes feel neglected. ('It isn't easy being the wife of an athlete,' said the wife of record-breaking Olympian George Young. 'The season never seems to end.') Once addicted, runners sometimes put their running above all other activities, neglecting family, friends and jobs. A student named Daniel Glickenhaus told me: 'I sometimes wonder whether running ten to thirteen miles a day has affected my ambition. My mother worries when I tell her that all I want out of life is to be a track bum, with a job that allows plenty of time to run.'

The deeper pleasures of running are seldom experienced all at once, nor do they come to those who run only once in a while. To feel the profound changes that running can bring about, you need to run for forty-five minutes or an hour at least four days a week. It takes that much running for its insistent, hypnotic rhythms to induce what some runners describe as a trance-like state, a mental plateau where they feel miraculously purified and at peace with themselves and the world.

Partisan though I am, however, I have to admit that a few people seem simply not to be cut out for running. This has nothing to do with one's body structure; some large-boned people, though they appear to have precisely the wrong build for running, thrive on it. It is a case, I believe, of the cast of mind that will or will not tolerate running's enforced contemplativeness, its meditative aspects. An overweight neighbour of mine in his mid-thirties once asked me to help him get started on a running programme. One weekend afternoon we shuffled through a slow quarter-of-a-mile. Since we had not been more than mildly out of breath at any time, I hoped that his introduction had been pleasant enough to prompt him to stick at it. As it turned out, it had not. 'Never again!' he told me the next day. 'I'm so stiff I can hardly walk. Besides, running is so *boring*.'

If *you* try running and find it worse than a trip to an inept dentist, perhaps you're one of the people whom nature never intended to run. *But you should at least know that many runners don't begin to enjoy the sport until they have been at it for several weeks or even months.* So give it a fair trial. If you don't, you could be missing an extraordinary experience.

Are you cut out to be a runner?

Runners come in all sizes, ages and aptitudes. Yet most of them, especially the ones who stick at it year after year, enjoying all its physical and psychological benefits, share certain characteristics. If you're a non-runner, this rough-and-ready test will give you an idea of whether or not you're long-term running material:

1. Are you ten or more pounds overweight?
2. Do you smoke?
3. Would you like to lose weight?
4. Have you ever worried about someday having a heart attack?
5. Would you like to reduce your risk of heart attack?
6. Do you feel you're not in the shape you once were?
7. Would you like to get back into shape?
8. Would you like to feel better about the amount of exercise you're getting?
9. Would you like to sleep more soundly?
10. Would you like to be able to get along comfortably on less sleep?
11. Would you like to feel more relaxed?
12. Would you rather spend an evening by yourself, or perhaps with one close friend, than go to a big party?
13. At large gatherings do you ever feel like an outsider?
14. Are you usually happy when you're alone?
15. Are you self-assured enough not to mind seeming a little different from other people?

If you would answer YES to twelve or more questions, running is right for you; eight to eleven, you'd probably enjoy it; five to eight, no guarantee, but it's worth a try; four or fewer, the odds are against it.

3 · Why running?

It's not the only sport, but it may be the best

Several years ago I was working in an office in New York. One day at lunchtime a friend invited me to accompany him to a health club of which he was a member. The club had a ping-pong table, a chin bar, a stationary bicycle, a steam room, weights for lifting and a swimming pool. It was frequented mostly by businessmen, and during the hour or so I was there a number of them dropped by to do some training. There was a prescribed programme. The instructor would have a group of members lie on mats, then would put them through a ten minute schedule of sit-ups, leg lifts, push-ups and stretches. Once that was finished, they were free to do whatever else they wanted to—lift weights, ride the stationary bicycle, play ping-pong, swim or sweat off a temporary pound or two in the steam room.

Their time would have been well spent if American health clubs really improved health, but they don't, or not much anyway. They might make you look more muscular, give you a firmer waist-line, and enable you to do more push-ups and lift heavier weights. But in general they cannot make you fundamentally healthier, because for the most part they attack symptoms, not problems. The average participant doesn't do enough swimming, bicycle riding or anything else to improve fitness significantly.

The situation is somewhat better in the United Kingdom, where health clubs or fitness clinics are usually run either by local education authorities or by the Sports Council and are supervised by physical education specialists. None the less, even these are all too likely merely to circle round the problem rather than solve it. Part of the difficulty is that, human nature being what it is, not all participants pursue their programme either with regularity or with zeal. The difficulty lies in the beguiling notion that it is possible to get something for nothing. Fitness in thirty minutes a week, sweatless exercise and drinking men's diets have a mesmerizing appeal. A former high jumper I know has a flat full of springs, weights and exercise devices of all kinds that he has bought over the years whenever he is moved by the recurring impulse to get back into shape. But, he admits sheepishly, he has never stretched or lifted any of them more than once or twice. When we last talked, he had his eye on a $300 treadmill.

The something-for-nothing phenomenon is so widespread that the American Medical Association's Committee on Exercise and Physical Fitness recently issued a formal statement condemning so-called effortless exercisers. 'They do not,' said the Committee, 'provide any hidden benefits or values. Their most serious short-coming is that most of them do little to improve the fitness of the heart and lungs, which are most in need of exercise today.... Real physical fitness results only with regular overloads (in both the intensity and duration) of physical activity.'

There is no lack of information on what various types of physical activity do for our health. Not long ago seven exercise experts were asked to rank popular forms of exercise on the basis of how much they help cardio-respiratory endurance, muscular endurance, muscular strength, flexibility, balance and general well-being. Each panellist was permitted to award a given activity anything from no votes (signifying no benefit) to three (maximum benefit). Thus twenty-one is the best possible score. Their findings for eight selected sports are summarized in the table below.

Eight Sports: How much they help what

	Running	Bicycling	Swimming	Squash	Tennis	Walking	Golf	Bowling
PHYSICAL FITNESS								
Cardio-respiratory endurance	21	19	21	19	16	13	8	5
Muscular endurance	20	18	20	18	16	14	8	5
Muscular strength	17	16	14	15	14	11	9	5
Flexibility	9	9	15	16	14	7	8	7
Balance	17	18	12	17	16	8	8	6
GENERAL WELL-BEING								
Weight control	21	20	15	19	16	13	6	5
Muscle definition	14	15	14	11	13	11	6	5
Digestion	13	12	13	13	12	11	7	7
Sleep	16	15	16	12	11	14	6	6
TOTAL	148	142	140	140	128	102	66	51

Or consider, for the same activities, calorie costs per hour, a direct measure of intensity. (Figures are for a person weighing about 155 lbs):

Running	800–1000
Bicycling (13 mph)	660
Swimming	300–650
Squash	600
Tennis	400–500
Walking briskly (4 mph)	300
Golf	250
Bowling	270
Walking slowly (2 mph)	200

Running, it is clear, is not the only sport that improves health. Bicycling, swimming, and squash all confer worthwhile benefits and may seem pleasanter to some people. In *Sports in America* James Michener writes: 'As one who has jogged many weary miles I personally agree _ that this is one of the world's dullest pastimes.' And William Buckley, Jr, once confessed: 'All I ever managed on those few occasions when I jogged was to concentrate on what a miserable form of self-punishment jogging is.'

None the less, for those who like running's subtle and solitary pleasures, there is no sport like it. But forget the fun of it for a moment and consider only its contributions to physical fitness.

I have already pointed out in Chapter 1 that running can serve as an antidote to many of the hazards of twentieth-century living. Moreover, running appears to confer long-term benefits that are now only beginning to be appreciated. Nathan Pritikin, director of the Longevity Research Institute, told me that in checking *Who's Who in American Sports* he discovered that the average life-span of former football players is fifty-seven years, of boxers and baseball players sixty-one years, and of track competitors seventy-one years. Dr Paul Fardy, a cardiac rehabilitation specialist, reports that in a study of more than 500 people, the hearts of former athletes—runners prominent among them—tended to function better than the hearts of those who had never participated in athletics. He adds, however, that sedentary people who take up a strenuous activity can improve cardiac function markedly, and in many cases perform as well as long-time athletes.

Fardy is one of a growing number of investigators who are discovering that running has distinct advantages over many other sports. In a recent article in the *American Physical Therapy Journal* he wrote: 'Walking and/or jogging is the simplest and probably most popular aerobic activity.' And Dr John Moe wrote in a letter to *The Physician and Sportsmedicine*:

It is hard for me to see how something with such great merit can be so largely ignored by the medical profession. We profess interest in preventive medicine, and we know that arterio-sclerotic diseases, especially of the coronary arteries, account for over 50% of our annual death rate. It has been shown in animal and human studies that endurance-type training increases cardiac perfusion, enhances cardio-pulmonary efficiency, lowers the resting pulse, and reduces blood lipids. Why, then, is it not obvious to more of us that we need to do endurance training ourselves and teach it to our patients?

Even if we grant that there are other sports that are as good for one's health as running, there remain good reasons to choose running. One is the time devoted to it. When I played tennis, I was a member of a regular foursome who played from nine to eleven every Saturday and Sunday. What with time for dressing, showering and driving to and from the courts, I was spending six hours a weekend at tennis. Furthermore, I was burning up at most 2000 calories. Nowadays, unless I am trying to put in high mileage to get ready for a marathon, I run ten miles a day, a total, on a weekend, of about two and a half hours. Thus in less than half the time I get the same 2000 calories' worth of exercise.

An incidental benefit: running widows or widowers, if not unknown, are at least rare. Even a long run can often be tucked away in some unnoticed corner of the day, either early in the morning or at a time when other members of the family are busy with cooking, homework or other activities. All it takes is some foresight and good manners. As one's competitive urges increase, however, such invisible running is likely to become more of a problem. 'One of the biggest problems in Britain with middle distance runners who get married,' a close observer of British athletics told me not long ago, 'is that their wives complain that they spend too much time training. Maybe this is why so many middle distance runners marry girls who compete in similar events.'

The inner spirit of running is also different from that of most other sports. It can be as competitive or non-competitive as you choose to make it. In football, there's no convenient way not to try hard. In tennis, you've got to try to put the ball out of your opponent's reach.

Golfers become so immersed in the game that they tie themselves into tense, tangled knots even during a friendly round. Runners, on the other hand, can run as gently or as hard as they want to. With a stopwatch you can try to run a course faster than you've ever done it before. You can attempt to run your friends into the ground, or you can treat a run as if it were nothing but a romp through the countryside. Even in a race there's no need to run at full throttle if you don't want to. You'll get good exercise even if you run below your top speed.

Many runners, some of them very good ones, never race at all. All they want is fitness and the good feelings that come from a daily run. Jack Gianino is one such runner. He puts in an hour and a half a day and even when acting assignments take him out of town he never misses a training session. But Gianino does not race. 'I tried it and I didn't like all that hard breathing,' he says.

The non-competitiveness of running makes it a perfect family sport. If a man wants to run ten miles, he can run the first two miles with his wife and children, then drop the kids off and run a second loop with his wife alone. When she's had her four-mile run, he can go bashing off through the countryside for a few more miles.

Running is also probably the world's most democratic sport. Runners are almost totally lacking in race, sex, age, or class discrimination. At a recent event in New York City I saw a cardiologist, an orthopaedic surgeon, and a preventive medicine specialist for a major corporation, a foundry worker and a printer, a retired postman and a shoe salesman, a judge, an author, and a film-maker, a business executive and a man who has long been on the dole, along with an assortment of office workers, housewives, students and senior citizens. Running is an egalitarian and distinctly unsnobbish sport.

I would be misleading you if I tried to force upon you the impression that there is nothing wrong with running. You can be frightened into a ditch by a car. You can get *Achilles tendinitis* or a pulled muscle (see Chapter 16). You can find yourself, at five o'clock on a January morning, cursing the moment you first thought of running. (Don't worry; you'll feel fine once you get moving.)

But an even more general, and more serious, charge has been made against running: that it simply isn't good for you, that the harm it does outweighs the benefits. As I write this, one of the most visible proponents of this view is a doctor named J. E. Schmidt. The March

1976 issue of *Playboy* carried an article by Schmidt entitled 'Jogging Can Kill You!' In the spirit of fair play Dr Schmidt starts out by acknowledging that running can help your legs and heart and give you 'that tanned, out-doorsy look'. But his enthusiasm fades quickly. 'The fact is,' he writes, 'that, for both men and women, running or jogging is one of the most wasteful and hazardous forms of exercise. Jogging takes more from the body than it gives back. It exacts a price that no one can afford or should be willing to pay for leg and thigh muscles or for that specious indicator of good health—the tan.' Specifically, Dr Schmidt says, jogging can loosen the linkage between the sacrum and the hip bones, cause slipped discs, contribute to varicose veins, dislodge the uterus from its 'perch', produce droopy breasts and, in men, bring on inguinal hernia. Jogging, he asserts, can even harm the heart by causing it to 'tug' on its blood vessels and shake crusted material loose, inducing heart attack. Furthermore, he says, jogging can cause such architectural anomalies as dropped stomach, loose spleen, floating kidney and fallen arches.

When Dr Schmidt's article came out, it created quite a stir. Although no one I spoke to gave up running because of it, there was concern that beginners might be frightened away. As for me, I simply found the article puzzling. I have been a fairly close student of the medical literature on running, and I thought I had a clear sense of what the hazards were. Although the ones Dr Schmidt cited were not among them, it was, of course, possible that I had missed something.

I talked to Dr George Sheehan about the article. Sheehan, who is one of the world's most widely consulted doctors on the effects of running on the human body, shrugged and told me he knew of no studies that support Schmidt's views. 'He went by what I suppose we would call common sense,' said Sheehan. 'But when you start using common sense where the human body is concerned, you sometimes are brought up short. The body doesn't always operate the way you think it does. These indictments of jogging are done on the basis of *a priori* thinking, but that's not the way to do it. I'm suspicious when people say, "It stands to reason." I think the thing to do is go and find out for yourself whether something does occur.'

Schmidt's criticisms of running nevertheless stuck in my mind, troubling me. If there were any truth in them, no matter how slight, I didn't want to be guilty of ignoring them. So I finally wrote to Schmidt, saying:

... I am puzzled by the fact that none of the physicians most closely identified with running have acknowledged the truth of very much of what you said in the *Playboy* piece, and some have said publicly that there are no studies to support any of it.... I would be most grateful if you could tell me your sources....

Schmidt replied:

... Let me say, first, that I would not be writing an article for *Playboy* in which I rehash well-known medical facts. To do that would be very boring. The understanding of the relationship between running and the traumata I described—plus a few others!—is now in its nascence, but I discovered it through fortuitous medical events more than twenty years ago.

For centuries, scientists held that the earth is flat and that the sun revolves around the earth. You know of the obloquy that fell upon those who first proposed that this is not so! The physicians to whom you refer are unaware of the jogging hazards because they don't suspect jogging. The loving husband is the last to know about the faithlessness of his spouse. To suspect jogging is *outré*.

Alas, I cannot go beyond these meagre generalities, because I expect to do a book of my own on the subject....

A few months after Schmidt's piece appeared, I attended an important conference on the physiological, medical, epidemiological and psychological effects of running. The conference brought together some seventy authorities who for four days, from early morning until far into the night, discussed the results of their studies. Most of the authorities documented the benefits of running, but four or five did mention occasional adverse effects, such as heat-stroke and *Achilles tendinitis*. Schmidt's, however, were not among them.

4 · The longevity factor

Running's effect on how long you'll live

On 11th June, 1958, one of the most extraordinary runners of all time died at the age of seventy. He was Clarence DeMar, and he had been a runner for almost half a century, from 1909, when he came fourth in a college cross-country race, until 1957, when he competed in a nine-mile event. He was twenty-one when he first ran competitively and sixty-nine when he retired. During his 49 years of competition he probably covered as many miles as any athlete in history. He ran in 34 Boston Marathons, winning seven times and finishing in the top ten no fewer than fifteen times. DeMar competed in well over one thousand races in all, more than a hundred of them full length marathons. In an article published after his death he was referred to as 'Mr Marathon'.

Aside from his running, DeMar's history is unremarkable. He was born on a farm in the Midwest of America. When he was eight his father died, and two years later the family (he was one of seven children), moved to Massachusetts. In 1915 DeMar received a degree in applied arts from Harvard, and a few years later a master's degree in education. He taught part-time at a reformatory, worked as a night proof-reader at a newspaper, managed a small farm in his later years, and ran practically every day. On the morning of the Boston Marathon he would come home from his proof-reading job, look after the cows and chickens, sleep for a while, and then get up and head for the starting line.

DeMar's years of running had some profound effects on his body. (In strict logic, of course, it is possible that running had no effect at all on DeMar, that he was an excellent runner because he already had an excellent physique. Most doctors, however, do not believe this was the case.) After his death from cancer, an autopsy was performed. His heart was found to be large, but within normal range. He had some athero-sclerosis, but for his age it was mild. His coronary arteries were two or three times the usual size. In its report on the autopsy the *New England Journal of Medicine* said: 'Strenuous physical effort, so far as is known, does not adversely affect the heart. Few athletes have had such a long period of physical effort during their lifetime as DeMar.' A doctor with whom I discussed the autopsy findings said simply, 'There was no way DeMar could have died of a heart attack. It had to be something else.'

If we judge by the commonly accepted indicators of age, Clarence DeMar was younger than his years. His unusual vigour allowed him to compete in races even after cancer was diagnosed. His coronary arteries were large and allowed a free flow of blood. In his sixties he was capable of athletic feats beyond the ability of most people many decades his junior. In many significant respects DeMar was still a young man. Nor is he the only example among runners of a man with a seemingly delayed ageing process.

But do runners actually live longer than other people? This is not an easy question to answer. If exercised daily, rats, as noted earlier, live as much as 25% longer than their sedentary brethren. But responsible researchers are cautious about relating such findings to human beings. There are also statistical problems. At a recent medical conference Dr Paul Milvy, biophysicist and epidemiologist, warned that it is difficult to prove a causal relationship between exercise and longevity. 'The criteria for demonstrating causality,' he says, 'are quite severe and difficult to satisfy.'

The history of the longevity question is instructive. Hippocrates thought sport contributed to an early death, and such was the force of his opinion that for centuries most people held to this idea. Then in 1873 an iconoclastic doctor, John Morgan, compared the longevity of the average Englishman with that of men who had rowed in the Oxford–Cambridge races between 1829 and 1869. He found that the rowers lived two years longer than insurance tables predicted they should have.

This seemed to settle the question, especially when several subsequent studies of college athletes produced similar findings. In time, however, researchers realized that it might be fallacious to compare the general population with people who had had the advantage of a university education. In 1926, hoping to overcome this possible source of error, J. C. Greenway and I. V. Hiscock compared the life-spans of Yale graduates who had been university athletes and the life-spans of those who had not. Curiously, it now turned out that it was the non-athletes who lived slightly longer.

The results were puzzling but not conclusive, because the Greenway–Hiscock sample had been a small one and thus might have been distorted. Six years later L. I. Dublin used records from the classes of 1870–1905 at eight universities to compare the life-spans of 4976 varsity athletes and 38 269 other graduates. There proved to be a three month difference in life expectancy, in favour, once again, of the non-athletes.

What are we to conclude from this? It is possible, of course, that athletics are simply bad for you, though most investigators do not think so. A more likely possibility is that athletes are more inclined to enter hazardous occupations. Most studies also suggest that to have been an athlete at one time does not confer long-term protection. One must stick to one's sport if it is to continue to do any good.

But the central question still remains unanswered: does running lengthen lives?

Several recent studies shed light on the matter. Two doctors, Arthur Leon and Henry Blackburn, reported recently that thirty to sixty minutes of endurance exercise three or four times a week 'without question can improve health and quality of life for most people ... and perhaps increase longevity'. A cautious appraisal, certainly, but in the context of current research a significant one.

Dr Thomas Bassler, whose comments on loafer's heart and similar ailments were mentioned in Chapter 1, is less cautious. Bassler has made something of a name for himself by his insistence that finishing a marathon in less than four hours gives years of immunity to heart attack. Although not all of Bassler's medical colleagues agree with him, he does have a wide following. Bassler states that simply running the marathon itself does *not* confer the immunity, but that immunity develops from 1) the daily training required and 2) the marathoner's customary life style, which includes, among other factors, no smoking and a diet low in harmful fats such as cholesterol. Studies done in Ecuador, Pakistan and the U.S.S.R. of people who live well past the age of one hundred have shown that a high level of physical activity and low-fat diets are common denominators.

An unusual opportunity for studying the relationship between continued exercise and ageing occurred recently when the World

Masters' Championships, an international track meeting that attracts participants from 30 to over 90 years old, was held in Toronto. Expert doctors examined 128 men and seven women participants. They found, among other things, that the ageing athletes' oxygen-processing ability declined more slowly than it does in the general population, and that heart abnormalities were rarer. Purists will point out, of course, that this conclusion doesn't take into account the self-selection factor. This is true enough. The findings are impressive, nevertheless.

Another relevant study was conducted by Dr Fred Kasch. He began with the hypothesis that a key indicator of ageing is a person's capacity for work, since work capacity is known to decline 35–40% between the ages of 30 and 70. If, therefore, work capacity could somehow be sustained longer than usual, ageing would in effect have been delayed. Kasch signed up 43 middle-aged men, from 45 to 48 years old, for a ten year programme of running and swimming. As the years passed, the results were astonishing. During the course of the study the men's maximum heart rates declined far less than predicted from data on 'normal' men. Their resting heart rates declined because their hearts had become more efficient, and their oxygen-carrying capacity either increased (in the case of the subjects who had been sedentary before the programme began) or remained constant at 36% above average for age and sex (in the case of subjects who had previously been active). Since both heart rate and oxygen-carrying capacity are closely related to age, the programme had acted as a kind of time machine in which the subjects grew old less quickly than their non-exercising contemporaries.

One of the most ambitious efforts to explore this relationship between exercise and longevity was undertaken in Boston in 1965 by Dr Charles Rose. He interviewed the next of kin of five hundred men who died in Boston that year, asking hundreds of questions about diet, drinking habits, recreation, occupation and exercise, both on the job and off. In all, he took into account some two hundred factors. Then, using complex statistical techniques, he sought to discover which were most closely correlated with a long life. One of his findings was odd and significant: physical exertion during leisure hours benefited people more than exertion on the job. Furthermore, exertion off the job, particularly during the decade from 40 to 49, was among the best of all longevity predictors. An even more recent study made public in early 1977 shows, on the other hand, that

San Francisco dockers who work hard have fewer heart attacks than those who do only light work. The conclusion is clear: if you're active, whether on or off the job, the chances are you'll live longer.

PART TWO
The Art of Running

I was convinced each day that I
had strained the limits of human
endurance. Then, gradually, a
strange thing happened....
David Burhans, runner

5 · Getting started

What you need to know as you take your first steps

Running may well turn out to be one of the most significant experiences of your life. Yet it does not always seem fun when you first try it. For one thing, the chances are you're out of shape. Not irreparably, but if you're beyond your teens you're probably not in the best condition. Your muscles are soft. Your joints are stiff. Your heart and lungs aren't used to working hard. As a result, you'll feel slow and awkward when you run and will ache a bit afterwards. But even if you're severely out of condition it only means it will take a bit longer to get back into shape.

I ask you to trust me. The goal, I promise, is worth the struggle. Within a few weeks you'll be covering a mile or two at a time. After a run you'll feel refreshed. You'll have more energy, more zest. You'll take more pleasure in both work and play. You'll sleep more soundly, lose weight if you need to, and feel better than you have in years.

You won't achieve those results on your very first day, but there's no hurry. Running isn't something you do only in the spring in order to look good in a bathing suit. It's best when it's worked into the fabric of your life, as an indispensable part of each day. So start slowly. *If you read a lot about running you'll often come across the phrase 'Train, don't strain'. That could be the most important advice in this book.* You'll improve just as quickly if you take it fairly easy rather than continually flogging yourself to go farther and faster. Furthermore, you won't get injured as often. That's important, for the fewer running days you lose, the easier it is to stay in shape.

Before you run

First, spend a few minutes taking stock of what kind of condition you're in. New runners who are badly out of shape, or who try to do too much too fast, almost always have trouble. Don't let your judgment be warped by wishful thinking. The Royal College of Physicians and the British Cardiac Society advise: 'Most people do not need a medical examination before starting an exercise programme. There are no risks in regular dynamic exercise as long as the programme begins gently and only gradually increases in vigour. Older persons, the obese, and those with a history of cardio-vascular disease or symptoms should first consult their doctor...'

Most authorities, both in Britain and in America, agree. Dr Leroy Getchell directs a popular adult physical fitness class in Indiana. This is his advice for getting started: 'If you're overweight, or have a tendency towards high blood pressure, or have a family history of heart disease, ask a doctor to give you a thorough examination. But if you can walk for a mile or two and not feel discomfort or dizziness, and can then alternately jog for thirty seconds and walk for a minute and still not have any problem, you're probably okay. If you have the slightest doubt about your health, though, I recommend giving the heart an exercise stress test. People under 35 generally need only a check-up or the approval of their family doctor.

'Most people can start out with just a little activity and gradually build it up. If there's a problem, they'll have some indication—chest pains or dizziness or something else. But they shouldn't an hour after a work-out. If they do, that's a sign that it was probably too vigorous for their condition and that they should modify the next day's training.' A few conditions may rule out exercise altogether, if only temporarily. Among them are infectious diseases, recent surgery, kidney diseases, fractures, certain electro-cardiogram abnormalities and extremely high blood pressure.

Some beginners are more comfortable if they have at least a rough idea of what kind of shape they're in before they start. *One of the quickest ways to find out how fit you are is with the Harvard Step Test, which is described in Appendix B.*

How hard you should run, particularly when you're starting, depends on your condition. If you score low on the Harvard Step Test, limit your training for a while. Walk and run alternately, and do it slowly for only a few minutes. Two or three weeks later, when you take the test again, your score will almost certainly have improved. That's the time to start training a little harder, preferably under the direction of a qualified B.A.A.B. (British Amateur Athletics Board) coach who can advise you about the details of training, and work out a programme appropriate to your level of fitness and ability. Physical education specialists at local schools are often good sources of advice, too.

Incidentally, if you're overweight you'll probably score lower than you'd like to. A recent report by Dr Merle Foss and three of his associates shows that extremely overweight people may need as much as eight weeks of training simply to be able to walk a mile. You probably won't have that much trouble getting started, but bear in mind that extra weight will slow your progress.

Warming up

You're wearing the clothes you're planning to run in* and you're ready to start. Don't—not yet, anyway. Your mind may be ready to go, but your body isn't. It has probably been doing nothing all day, and the last thing it wants to do is spring suddenly into action. Before you start running, you've got to prepare it. This is where warming up comes in.

Some people think a warm-up isn't important. (As you become more deeply interested in running you'll find that there are diametrically opposed views about almost every aspect of it.) Vaughan Thomas writes in *Science and Sport* that warming up contains a 'witchcraft element'. It does some good, he implies, but not as much as is popularly believed. 'Physiologically speaking,' he writes, 'more races have been lost due to energy expenditure during warm-up than have been won due to the raising of levels of organic function.' He may be right. Still, warming up does serve some important purposes, so it should never be neglected.

The flexibility warm-up. Running, as discussed in Chapter 3, rates low in promoting flexibility, much lower, for example, than swimming or tennis, and only slightly higher than walking, golf and bowling. Practically all runners develop tight muscles, particularly in the backs of their legs. The reason is that the muscles used in running go through a relatively small range of movement and repeatedly perform the same actions. You can increase their range slightly by doing different kinds of running—fast and slow, uphill and downhill—but you need flexibility exercises, too.

If you have enough time it would be worthwhile to do half an hour or so of flexibility exercises every time you run, since it is desirable to put all the body's major joints through a full range of movement. But

* For sartorial notes and a word or two about shoes, see Chapter 12.

which of us has such time to spare? (I'll confess that when I'm in a hurry I often neglect to stretch because I'd rather spend the time running. I hope you'll be more sensible than I am.) Luckily, you can fit in an abbreviated stretching session in about ten minutes, and this is certainly time well spent. Dr John Williams, co-author of the authoritative book, *Sports Medicine*, told me he thinks five minutes is plenty.

First, for your stomach muscles, do some sit-ups with your knees slightly bent to minimize help from the hip muscles. You needn't do them fast, and fifteen, though you can do more if you want to, is enough. (When you start out, you may find it easier to do sit-ups with your arms stretched out over your head. Later, as your stomach muscles get stronger, do them the hard way, with your hands clasped behind your head.)

Next, to stretch your hamstring and calf muscles, lie on your back with your right knee flexed, foot on the floor, and your left leg straight. Slowly raise your left leg until it's perpendicular to the floor and your toes are pointing straight up. Lower your left leg slowly and repeat the whole sequence with your right leg. Stretch both legs this way three or four times.

Now face a wall or tree, put your palms against it, and slowly shuffle backwards, keeping your feet flat on the ground, until you

Dr Sheehan's leg-limbering exercise

feel the strain in the backs of your legs. Hold that position for twenty or thirty seconds, letting the muscles relax. Repeat the exercise two or three times.

Finally, lie on your back. Keeping your legs together, slowly bring them over your head and, with your knees straight, hold your legs parallel to the floor for twenty or thirty seconds. You should feel the strain in your hamstring muscles.

If you have time, there are still other useful exercises to be done. William Bowerman, who is not only the author of *Jogging* and a former university coach but also the source of some of the wisest advice on running ever uttered, recommends several repetitions of the following exercises to loosen the muscles in the back, abdomen, chest and neck:

1. Roll your head in a wide circle to ease the muscles in the upper spine.
2. Raise your shoulders and roll them forward to loosen the back and chest muscles.
3. Move your shoulders forward as if trying to make them meet. Do the same thing towards the back.
4. While walking, stick out the abdomen. Then suck it in and roll the hips forward.

'A flexible and free-flowing body,' the physical fitness specialist Bob Glover explains, 'is more efficient and tension-free. Proper stretching before and after vigorous exercise will eliminate undue stiffness and fatigue and prevent injuries. It will also increase your athletic efficiency. Runners will increase their stride and fluidity. Less muscle tightness and leg cramping will result.'

If you're over thirty, stretching is especially important. At about that age, muscles start tightening noticeably unless they are stretched frequently, and injuries are likely to be more frequent. Jim Nolan, a marathon runner in his mid-fifties, told me: 'My daughter came home from college for vacation and I went out running with her without stretching first. Next day my muscles really hurt, but hers were fine. Younger people may be able to do without a warm-up, but we old fellows really need it.' Nolan, who is a writer and has a schedule as flexible as he himself is, sometimes puts in as many as ten brief stretching sessions a day.

Incidentally, don't stretch jerkily. When a muscle is pulled suddenly, it fights back and shortens. Only when it is stretched slowly does it lengthen and stay that way.

In Chapter 15 you will find some other useful exercises, but for the time being these will be enough.

The running warm-up. At the Y.M.C.A. where I occasionally run when the winter weather is particularly severe, inexperienced runners sometimes stand beside the track, anxiously watching for an opening. When one appears, they spring into it, sprint two or three laps at top speed, then stop. That's the wrong way to run. First, it isn't nearly enough to do any good. Second, the beneficial physiological changes produced by warming up don't occur in only a minute or two. They take time, six or eight minutes at the very least. That's why it's a good idea to shuffle along slowly for a while when you first start out. I remember watching John Vitale, one of America's top distance runners, warming up before a 10 000-metre race. He was moving so slowly that a toddler would have had little trouble keeping up with him, but later he covered the hilly, winding course at well under five minutes a mile.

After a few minutes of easy running you'll start to sweat. That's a sign that your warm-up is taking effect and that you're ready to move a little faster.

Where to run

At last you're ready to run in earnest. The important thing is to go outside and *do* it. Many people feel they have to have a special place, but actually anywhere that's relatively smooth and safe from traffic will do. For what they're worth, here are a few thoughts on where to run.

I'd be inclined to stay away from tracks, because I find a quarter-mile track one of the world's dreariest places. The chief problem is the treadmill effect. To run a mile you've got to pass the same point four times, and this makes even a short run seem endless.

It's more fun to run in parks or on country roads, even though some authorities argue that too much running on hard surfaces contributes to *Achilles tendinitis*. Not far from my house is a pretty little park with broad grassy areas, a stream and a pond, two gazebos, and a flock of Canada geese. If I'm just coasting, it takes me about eight minutes to run around the circumference; I call it a mile. I never

run for long in the park—the treadmill effect again—but occasionally I'll do a couple of turns there for variety's sake.

Or I go out on the roads, heading either north into hills and
undeveloped country or south towards Long Island Sound with its
shoreline of woods and beaches. It depends on what I feel like
looking at. If you're not fully familiar with the roads and footpaths in
your area, an Ordnance Survey map will help.

You'll find that every course has its own peculiar character. Not
far from my house is a mile-long stretch of pavement, it's called
Laddins Rock Road. Every time I run there I feel sluggish, but as
soon as I'm through it I feel fine again. There's another stretch of
road that always makes me feel good. Even though part of it is uphill,
I can count on feeling fine there.

What about simply staying at home and running on the spot? If for
some reason that's what you want to do, fine. So long as you make
your heart beat fast enough (see below) you'll be getting a measurable training effect whether or not you go anywhere while you're
doing it. But you'll be missing most of the fun of running, the
variations of scenery and seasons, the sun and wind, the pleasure of
running with friends. You may find running on the spot an ideal
form of exercise, but you couldn't pay me to do it.

On not feeling like a fool

Some people feel conspicuous and foolish when they first go out in
public wearing running clothes. I know I did. I used to wait until I
thought nobody was around; then I'd dart out of my back door and
head for places where I was sure no one would see me.

I've discovered that running in secret is unnecessary. First, many
people admire what you're doing. Second, people are generally
wrapped up in their own thoughts, and the sight of a runner scarcely
penetrates their minds. You're just part of the scenery. Furthermore,
the longer you run, the more permanent a part of the environment
you'll become. Where I live I'm just one of the neighbourhood
characters. Children call out cheerfully; adults wave, or if I stray
from my accustomed time, remark, 'Hey, you're early today.' I smile
and wave back and we all get along fine.

Honesty requires me to acknowledge that the foolishness problem
may be more severe in the United Kingdom than in the United
States. A British runner named Roger Smith reports: 'My experience

and that of my friends is that ridicule is common here, particularly
from kids. It is rare to get words of encouragement. I was once so
incensed over this at the end of a seventeen-mile run that I stopped
and harangued my audience. It made no difference; they just
laughed.' As runners become more common, the laughter will no
doubt die down.

The fine, easy art of running

Do you remember the first time you tried to play tennis or golf?
Wasn't it awkward to hold the racket or club the way your instructor
told you to? Running isn't like that. Everybody knows how to run.
Furthermore, the more you run the more efficient your style
becomes.

mistake to imitate anyone else's running style. Just run. Breathe
naturally. Remember that you're running not just for fitness but for
fun. Running is a holiday from everyday chores, a special treat for
your mind and body. If you concentrate on the fun, the fitness and
style will take care of themselves.

How fast?

If you're just beginning, don't think about speed. Move along easily,
letting your body get used to the unaccustomed actions of running.
Stop if you get tired, then run some more. Don't strain. A crash
exercise programme can be just as harmful as a crash diet. You
should be able to carry on a conversation while you run, so don't run
so fast that you couldn't talk comfortably with a friend.

As you get stronger, you'll be able to run faster and sustain a given
pace longer with the same effort. Only then should you think about
how fast you're running.

David Burhans, who took up running in 1970, told me how
pleased he was, after an initial period of difficulty, to see how quickly
he improved: 'I'd like to be able to say that the process was an easy
one. It wasn't. At the end of my daily jaunt I was totally exhausted. I
was convinced each day that I had strained the limits of human
endurance and that no amount of pleading or promises of future
health could possibly move my body any faster. Then, gradually, a
strange thing happened. I began to realize that it was taking me less
and less energy to run a mile. I was beginning to get in shape!'

Adaptation to training depends on the overload principle. If you
ask your body to do more than it can easily perform, it responds by
adjusting itself so that, over a period of time, it comes to perform the
task without strain. To become fitter, simply make use of the overload principle. Calculating how much of an overload you need isn't
hard. Each of us has a maximum heart rate; our hearts are able to beat
just so fast and no faster. It varies from person to person, but your
maximum heart rate is roughly 220 per minute minus your age. If
you're forty years old it's about 180; if you're thirty it's about 190,
and so forth. For most people training should be at resting heart rate
plus 75% of the difference between resting and maximum heart rates.
(In the medical literature you'll usually find it called 'maximal heart
rate'. (*Maximal* is doctors' jargon for maximum; it means exactly the
same thing.)

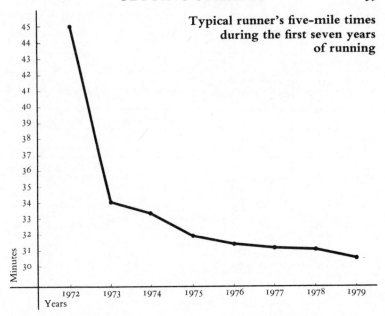

Typical runner's five-mile times during the first seven years of running

To find out how hard you should train, work out your maximum heart rate. Then find your resting heart rate by taking your pulse after you've been sitting still for a few minutes. Subtract your resting heart rate from your maximum, multiply by .75, add that figure to your resting heart rate, and do most of your running at a speed that will make your heart beat about that fast. Use .65 if you smoke or are more than 20 lbs overweight, or if you've recently had surgery or a serious illness. To save yourself the trouble of computing, you can simply refer to the chart on p. 60. It does the same thing as the formula, although of course it does not take into account individual variations in resting heart rate. The figures labelled 'Optimum' are recommended, but it's all right to stay anywhere between 'Minimum' and 'Maximum'.

To take your pulse, use a watch with a second hand. Stop running and check your heartbeat either at your wrist or at your neck just below the angle of your jaw. Count the beats carefully for fifteen seconds and multiply by four.

Don't bother with taking your pulse every time you run. With a little practice you'll learn how fast you have to go to hit that 75%

heart rate. But you should check it every few weeks, since you'll
have to run faster to achieve the same rate as your condition
improves.

The Heartbeat Test: Using your pulse as a training guide

Age	Minimum	Optimum	Maximum
WOMEN			
25	130	157	185
30	126	153	180
35	123	149	175
40	119	145	170
45	116	140	165
50	112	136	160
55	109	132	155
60	105	128	150
65	102	123	145
MEN			
25	137	166	195
30	133	162	190
35	130	157	185
40	126	153	180
45	123	149	175
50	119	145	170
55	116	140	165
60	112	136	160
65	109	132	155

[Source: *The Jogger*]

Don't consider the 75% figure sacrosanct. The maximum heart
rate you'll arrive at by subtracting your age from 220 is merely an
estimate. If yours is lower, you may find yourself tiring as you try to
keep your pulse at 75% of the hypothetical maximum. In that case,
slow down a bit and don't worry about it. Each of us is different. All
we can do is make the best of what we've got.

The reason for the 75% level is that cardio-vascular fitness, the
kind that really counts and, happily, the kind that running gives
us, depends on how efficiently the body uses oxygen. The rate at
which the heart beats is directly related to how much oxygen is being
used. When we make the heart beat faster we are calling the

oxygen-processing mechanism into play and thus strengthening it.

More is not better, incidentally. You won't get faster results by trying for an 85 or 90% heart rate. One doctor I consulted, a specialist in athletic medicine, even goes so far as to argue that the whole heart rate question can be considerably simplified. Just exercise, up to the age of 50, at a pulse rate of 150 per minute.

How far?

The first time you run, don't plan to go far. Try running a couple of hundred yards. If you become tired or winded, walk for a while. When you feel rested do another couple of hundred yards. When you've run a total of half a mile, stop if you don't feel like doing more. *The important thing is to work out at least four times a week. It's the repeated running that brings improvement.*

People in average physical condition can usually cover a total of at least one mile a day, especially if they don't try to go too fast and are content to alternate running and walking. Thereafter it is usually possible to increase the daily run by about one-quarter of a mile per week. But if you find yourself becoming more fatigued than is comfortable, it's perfectly all right to drop back to the previous week's level.

It may take you several months to get to the point where you're running two, three or four miles at a time. Don't be in a hurry. Gradual improvement is safest. If you try to do too much too quickly, you're likely to hurt yourself. When I first started I had all kinds of injuries. I was trying to do too much too fast. Now, even though I run a lot, I almost never push really hard. It's been two or three years since I had an injury that kept me from running.

If you find that your training increments are causing extra fatigue, slow your progress down. It's a good idea not to plan your training too many days in advance. If you're as compulsive as I am, you'll be reluctant to change it. Try to be flexible. It's important to monitor your body closely to see how it's responding. After a while you'll get so that you can fine-tune your work-outs.

On not owning a stopwatch

By this time you've no doubt gathered that I'm fairly relaxed about how fast and far I run. It's more fun that way, and I suspect I improve

almost as much as I would under a more spartan regime. So even
though you may be curious about how fast you can run, don't buy a
stopwatch, not yet, anyway. Stopwatch runners tend to be haunted,
driven souls. What counts most is what one researcher has called
'perceived exertion'. That means nothing more than how strenuous
a run seems to you. If you feel that your training is a good one—not
ridiculously easy but not bone-shattering, either—that's about right.
The beauty of the 'perceived-exertion' formula is that it takes into
account such factors as heat, humidity, terrain and wind. Sometimes
you may fly along; at other times you'll plod. That doesn't matter.
What counts is how you feel.

Watching for your second wind

After you've been running for a few minutes, especially as you begin
to get into shape, a nice thing happens; you get what is known as
second wind. Second wind follows an initial period of breathlessness. When it comes, the breathlessness abates, and you suddenly feel
light, strong and fast.

Over the years there has been a lot of argument about whether
there really is such a thing as second wind. There is. Dr Roy
Shephard reports that when researchers questioned 20 students at
one minute intervals during a hard twenty minute treadmill training
session, eighteen said their breathing improved after a while and
fourteen said their legs felt better. You'll experience a second wind,
too. Watch for it.

On the other hand, if you warm up for ten minutes or so the
beginnings of second wind will occur during that period and you
won't notice it during the run proper.

Weather

In Chapter 13 you'll learn how to run when it's hot, cold, snowy or
rainy. When you're just starting out, there are really only two factors
you have to be cautious about: heat and humidity. Both will slow
you down, so on a mid-August day don't try to run as if it were
April. Heat and humidity can upset your body badly. If it's likely to
be above 80°F (26°C) at midday, try to run early in the morning, or
else wait until after sunset.

After you've been running for a while, heat will be less of a problem because your body eventually gets used to it. It takes a week or two of running in the heat to become fully acclimatized.

After a run

When your run is over, don't stop suddenly. Take time for a cool-down (sometimes called, somewhat illogically, a warm-down). This should consist of a brief, relaxed walk and some stretching of the kind you did before you ran. Stretching after a run is particularly beneficial. Your muscles are warm and supple; they stretch most easily then. Try to devote eight or ten minutes to cooling down in order to help work the metabolic wastes and excess fluid out of your muscles. By the time you stop, your pulse should be within twenty beats of what it is when you aren't exercising.

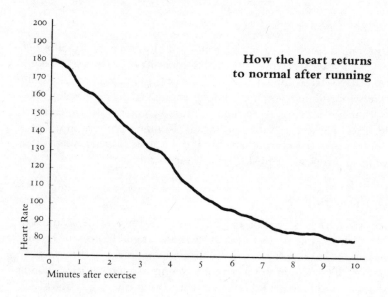

How the heart returns to normal after running

What to do about stiffness

When you first start running, you'll probably get stiff and somewhat painful legs. They're virtually unavoidable. If you have severe pain, you're running too hard or too far. The feeling should be nothing more than a pleasant tingling. It's your body's way of telling you that long-dormant fibres have been asked to do more than they're used to. A hot bath will make you feel better. If the soreness isn't bad, you needn't curtail your running. A slow run the next day, preferably on a cushion of soft grass, will make your muscles feel better.

As you get further into your running programme, you may experience occasional pains that seem to be in the bones and joints. Most such pains are perfectly natural. You're asking your body to do things that it's never been called upon to do—at least not for a long time—and it responds by obligingly restructuring itself to make its various parts more efficient. Small and large pains are therefore bound to crop up from time to time as your body makes adjustments. Most will disappear without any treatment, and very few will make you stop running altogether. A good rule of thumb is: if it feels better when you run, keep running; if it feels worse, take a rest.

Making it a habit

Running, as we have seen, brings not just physical but also a number of psychological benefits. But it does not bring either unless it is done regularly. Make running a habit from the beginning. Set aside a time solely for running, and make it long enough to give yourself plenty of time for dressing, warming up, running, cooling down, taking a leasurely shower and dressing again. Running is more fun if you don't have to dash through it. But if your life is rushed it's far better to fit in a run under pressure than not to run at all.

Getting over setbacks

If for one reason or another you don't run for a while, don't say, 'Well, there goes all my training down the drain.' Unless the lay-off has been a long one, you will still be enjoying some of the effects of your earlier training. It takes about as long to get completely out of shape as it took to get fit. Just get back to your running as quickly as you can. After checking with some light experimental running to see how much of your training has slipped away, start right in again. It won't take you long to get gack to where you were.

The more you run, the fewer excuses you'll make for not running. In the beginning you may miss quite a few days. Later on, you'll hardly ever let a day go by without running. In a recent two year period I missed only five running days, and they were all spent on rocky trails high in the mountains. Any run there might easily have been my last!

So don't worry about setbacks. Just get back on your good behaviour as soon as possible. (Incidentally, you can preserve many of your training benefits during a lay-off by avoiding over-indulgence and weight increase.)

Keeping a diary

Most runners keep a diary in which to record their running experiences. Joe Henderson has kept one for years. It is very detailed, a record not just of miles but of his thoughts along the way. Mine is simpler: 'Wed., Nov. 11—10. Hills.' The '10' means I ran ten miles that day. 'Hills' is a code meaning that I ran my hilly northern course and pushed hard on the upward portions of the hills. Some runners keep records of their diet, weight, how they felt, and so forth. Keep whatever kind of diary you like, but do attempt one, and from time to time record your resting heart rate. That way you'll be able to check your progress from the beginning. You'll find it fun a year from now to look back and say, 'Why, I only ran half a mile at this time last year. Today I did five! And my heart rate is twenty beats slower!'

6 · Getting thin

The mathematics of looking like
a runner

First, the good news. If you run, you'll almost certainly lose weight, whether or not you change your eating habits. Furthermore, this will happen even if your weight is on an upward trend at the moment. Because runners burn significantly more calories than non-runners, women, typically, lose ten to twelve pounds in the first year of running; men lose twenty or more. One woman runner, Kathryn Lance, said: 'Soon after I took up running my body changed completely. All my friends had always been the kind of people who looked good whether they were athletic or not. Not me. I'd been flabby my whole life, even as a teenager. Then I started running and suddenly I wasn't flabby any more. It was a weird experience. I would touch my body and it felt different. My posture improved, too. I lost maybe ten pounds during the first year of running, but I lost inches even more quickly than that. Almost immediately I looked thinner. And my dress size went from fourteen to ten.'

Now, the bad news: unless you're already fairly lean, the weight you lose won't be enough to make you a really good runner. Good runners are startlingly thin. At a recent gathering of marathon runners one observer looked around the room and said in disbelief: 'Some of you people look like the sort of chickens that are only fit to make soup out of.' He was right. A male distance runner in good condition weighs not more than two pounds per inch of height. A male runner is not more than 5 or 10% fat; a female not more than 15 or 20. (The average non-athletic man is about 15% fat, the average non-athletic woman 22 to 35%.) Ted Corbitt, the former Olympic marathoner, says, 'When people tell you how good you look, you can be sure you're not fit. If you don't look gaunt, you're out of shape.' Dr Alan Clark, the same doctor cited in Chapter 2 as an advocate of aerobic exercise instead of tranquillizers, told me that after six months on a running programme, 'friends would approach my wife in private and speak with a concerned air about my gaunt appearance and ask how long I had been ill. Her explanation that I was a long-distance runner would leave them scratching their heads.'

Let's say that according to the life insurance charts you're ten pounds overweight. In clothes you look reasonably trim. It's only when you're undressed or in a bathing suit that you look slightly flabby around the waist. Are those ten pounds anything to worry about? The answer is, unfortunately, yes. After the age of 45, there is an 8% increase in the death rate of people ten pounds overweight. At 20 lbs overweight, the increase is 18%; 30 lbs, 28%; and 50 lbs, 56%. A study conducted a decade ago demonstrated the close relationship between weight and health. Researchers asked 6928 adults a range of questions designed to determine their state of health, past and present, and their eating, sleeping, smoking, drinking and exercise habits. Answers to the two sets of questions were compared. The researchers reported that 'the relationship between overweight, especially the higher degrees of overweight, and poor health is evident.... Men with the best physical health were those less than 5% underweight up to 19.9% overweight; among women, those who were underweight or less than 10% overweight were slightly more healthy than the average.'

The body, complicated as it is, in one respect is remorselessly simple: it is an unfailingly accurate calorie counter. It keeps track of calories (more precisely, kilocalories) in exactly the same way that a bank keeps track of your money. If you put in more calories than you take out, your weight goes up. If you take out more than you put in, your weight decreases. If you want to lose weight you must therefore eat less, exercise more, or do a bit of both.

Curiously, the first possibility is the least effective. In a recent study, Dr Grant Gwinup referred to the futility of treating excess weight by diet alone. As an experiment he therefore decided to try exercise alone. He selected eleven overweight women ranging from 134 lbs to 218 lbs. In some cases they had been overweight all their lives. All eleven had tried dieting with at best only temporary success. Gwinup instructed the women not to make any changes in their diets, but in addition to whatever else they normally did, to walk rapidly for 30 or more minutes each day. Their weight loss in the first year averaged 22 lbs.

Another study had as its subjects 25 women, ranging in age from the mid-twenties to mid-forties, some of whom were as much as 40 lbs overweight. The women were assigned to three groups. Under the study's rules, all three undertook a 500-calorie daily deficit, but they did so in different ways. The first group did it by diet alone, the second by exercise alone, and the third by a combination of diet and exercise. After sixteen weeks the weight loss was 11.7, 10.6 and 12 lbs, respectively. Although the combination group lost more weight, the difference was not statistically significant. What was significant was that the combination group lost more fat and gained proportionately more lean tissue than either of the other two. 'On the basis of this data,' concluded the researchers, 'we recommend that those interested in losing weight should combine a lowered calorie intake with a physical fitness programme.'

Some aspects of losing weight by exercising seem curious and even illogical. For example, running does not increase one's appetite. On the contrary, it usually diminishes it. One researcher says, 'Exercise may be a suppressant rather than a stimulant of appetite.' This finding is borne out by studies in which animals exercised for an hour a day ate less than animals that weren't exercised at all.

It is also curious that your running speed has little effect on the number of calories you burn. A 150 lb person running at an eight-minute-mile pace uses 102 calories during a one-mile run, while the same person running at a twelve-minute pace uses 98 calories. What counts considerably more than your pace is your weight. A 220 lb person running a mile at an eight-minute pace uses 150 calories, while a 120 lb person running the same distance at the same pace uses only 82 calories. The following are the calorie figures for other weights: 130 lbs, 90 calories; 140 lbs, 98 calories; 160 lbs, 110 calories; 170 lbs, 116 calories; 180 lbs, 124 calories; 190 lbs, 130 calories; 200 lbs, 136 calories; 210 lbs, 144 calories.

It's easy to calculate how much you'll lose through running and how quickly you'll do it. Suppose you now weigh 180 lbs and after an initial training period, you regularly run five miles a day. At 180 lbs, you burn 124 calories during every eight-minute mile, so each time you run your five miles you burn 620 calories. The human body requires an intake of 3500 calories to add a pound, and a deficit of 3500 to lose a pound. At your rate of running, therefore, if you don't vary your intake you'll lose a pound every $5\frac{2}{3}$ days, or about five pounds a month. (You'll have to adjust the mathematics slightly from time to time, since as your weight goes down, you'll burn fewer calories per mile.)

Eventually, of course, your weight will stabilize. Exactly where it stabilizes depends on how much you eat and how far you run. When I started running, I lost weight rapidly. Soon I had to take all my clothes to a tailor for alterations. That was wonderful! I was eating and drinking all I wanted, and still losing weight. In my ignorance I supposed this would continue until I was a mere wraith. But soon the rate of loss slowed, and ultimately my weight steadied at 170 lbs. This was about 20 lbs above my ideal weight, 142 lbs.

Something like this will no doubt happen to you, too. You'll lose weight effortlessly for a while, but eventually your weight will stop declining. Then you need to become really clever, and determined. You can, of course, run—and, if you want to, race—even though you're well above your ideal weight, but you'll never perform to the limit of your potential. Not long ago *Runner's World* published an article showing what extra weight does to running times. One example given was a 161 lb runner who had finished a marathon in 3:13.01. The runner reduced his weight to 147 lbs. With no other changes in his training, he finished his next marathon in 3:04.26. In other words, every extra pound costs some 40 seconds.

Extra weight slows you down for several reasons. A given amount of energy carries you less far. Suppose your steps are shortened by only an eighth of an inch. If your feet strike the ground 1000 times per mile, this adds up to a difference of 125 inches—more than ten feet. In a ten mile race, you'll end up 35 yards or so behind a similarly trained runner who isn't carrying extra weight.

Extra weight also means that, since your body obeys Newton's laws, it takes longer every time it shifts from downwards to upwards motion. Watch a fat person run. One reason he or she runs so clumsily is that at each stride the excess weight is still in mid-descent when the rest of the body has begun to move upwards. Fat tends to keep moving in its original direction, and only a fresh expenditure of valuable energy can change its direction. Fat thus acts like an anchor, slowing every step.

Finally, extra weight isn't confined to the outside of your body. Fat lies on the inside, too, lodged in the muscles, where it keeps the fibres from operating efficiently. This is true, incidentally, even if your extra weight is only a temporary increase due to water. For this reason some medical authorities recommend that for two or three days before a competition you should avoid the salty and spicy foods that contribute to water retention.

How, exactly, do you continue to lose weight once it has stabilized? Remember, to lose weight you must use up more calories than you put in. You can eat less, run more, or do a little of both. The chart below shows how this works.

The Runner's Diet: A mathematico-physiological excursus

1 CALORIES REQUIRED PER DAY
   Desired weight (in lbs) _____ $\times$ 15 = _____
   +   *miles run* _____ $\times$ 100 = _____
                                                _____ TOTAL$_1$

2 CALORIES TO BE EATEN PER DAY
   Calories from Normal Diet _____
   +*Calories from Runner's Bonus** _____
                                                _____ TOTAL$_2$

3 CALORIE DEFICIT PER DAY
                                    Total$_1$ _____
                                   $-$ Total$_2$ _____
                                                _____ TOTAL$_3$

4 RATE OF WEIGHT LOSS
   3500 $\div$ _____ *Total$_3$* = _____ *Days to lose 1 lb*

5 TIME REQUIRED TO REACH WEIGHT GOAL
   Days to lose 1 lb _____ $\times$ _____ *lbs to lose* = _____ *days*

* *(Must be less than line 2 under 'Calories Required Per Day')*

Let's say that you'd like to weigh 150 lbs. Since fifteen calories are required to maintain every pound of weight, your proper intake per day, if you were not a runner, would be 2250 calories. Let's assume you run six miles a day. Since the energy cost of running a mile is approximately 100 calories, multiply the number of miles you run by 100. (If your weight is appreciably lower or higher than average, make appropriate adjustments from the calorie-per-mile information given on p. 69.) Call this number the Runner's Bonus, that is, the number of extra calories you're burning every day because you're a runner and not a sedentary person, and add it to your basic calorie requirement.

Now we arrive at the dieting part of the equation. On 'Calories from Normal Diet' enter the figure from 'Desired weight × 15' (in this case 2250). On the next line enter a figure that is less than the Runner's Bonus. Let's make it 100. Add the two together and you get the total number of calories you're going to permit yourself per day. Notice that even though it's less than the number of calories you're burning, it's still enough to provide for an entirely adequate and even filling diet (and, if you balance the budget properly, for such extras as cake or an occasional beer).

We could stop here, for you can be sure that so long as you eat and drink fewer calories than you burn, you'll lose weight. But let's see how *fast* you'll lose. In the example given, Equation 3 shows that you're incurring a deficit of 500 calories a day. Enter that figure in Equation 4 to see how many days it will take you to lose a pound. In this example it's seven days. How long, therefore, will it take you to reach your desired weight of 150 lbs? It depends, of course, on what you weigh now. Let's say you've been running for a while and now weigh not 180 lbs, but 170 lbs. You still want to lose twenty pounds. Thus it will require 7×20, or 140 days, about four and a half months.

Notice that the rate of loss I have cited is not extremely high. It's exactly what many doctors recommend for patients who need to lose weight. A 500-calorie daily deficit is only the equivalent of one container of fruit-flavoured yogurt and two pieces of toast lightly spread with jam. If you want to lose faster, you would probably be able to do so without much trouble.

Furthermore, I have mentioned only one way to unbalance the equation, by eating less. You can also unbalance it by running more. If, for example, you add two and a half miles a day, only an additional twenty minutes or so, you'll burn an extra 7500 calories a month, or better than two pounds' worth. Even if you don't eat a single calorie less than you do now, you'll lose that twenty pounds just as surely as you would by the first method. (If you use both methods simultaneously, eating less and exercising more, your weight will go down that much faster.)

If you want to run well, try not to be satisfied with staying at 'normal' weight. Frank Shorter, who won the 1972 Olympic marathon, is 5 feet 10½ inches and weighs a scrawny 134 lbs. Bill Rodgers is 5 feet 8½ inches and weighs 125 lbs. Jeff Galloway, another top runner, says, 'I'm convinced you run much better the skinnier you are.'

7 · Getting good at it

The techniques of training for speed and endurance

If you've been following the advice in Chapter 5 for a few weeks, you can now probably run a couple of miles without tiring. After a run you feel exhilarated, buoyant. Work is easier and play more fun. Perhaps you're content to leave matters exactly as they stand, running no farther or faster. If so, fine. So long as you cover three miles or so at a moderate pace, you'll stay in decent shape. The only thing you won't do is improve much. When you first take it up, your fitness increases rapidly. Then, as your heart, lungs and muscles, responding to the unaccustomed work, become stronger and more efficient, improvement tapers off. Finally you reach a state of equilibrium; your body is able to perform its appointed tasks fairly easily, but it no longer becomes detectably fitter.

I have already mentioned the first race I ever entered, a five-mile run in which I came in last despite the fact I had been running more or less regularly. It wasn't until I started reading about the sport that I discovered that my slow training shuffle wasn't enough. *In order to achieve the desired responses from my body I needed to run harder some of the time. When you always run slowly, I learned, you aren't teaching yourself to run fast. When you run fast but not far, you aren't building endurance. When you run on flat terrain, you aren't learning to run on hills.* 'We learn what we practise and at the velocity at which we practise it', writes Kenneth Doherty in *Modern Track and Field*.

When we train, a number of adaptations take place in our bodies. Among them are these:

1. We increase our capacity for using oxygen.
2. Our hearts are able to pump more blood at a lower pulse rate and blood pressure.
3. Our lung capacity increases.
4. Our heat-dissipating ability increases.

5. After exercise, our pulse rate and blood pressure return to normal more quickly.

6. We develop greater muscular strength.

7. We produce less lactic acid, a work-limiting substance, for a given amount of work.

8. Our bodies become more efficient mechanically, using less oxygen.

9. We develop greater endurance.

To a limited degree these changes occur even if we do very little running. To produce continuing adaptations we need to train more consistently and purposefully. Probably the most effective way to train is under the eye of a knowledgeable coach. He can tell when you're not working as hard as you could or when you're getting too tired. He knows how to prescribe a training session that will leave you refreshed, or at least appropriately fatigued, rather than exhausted.

This chapter is written on the assumption that you've been running for a while and would now like to become more serious about improving. How much improvement you want is entirely up to you. How you train depends on your goal, but whatever that goal is, four principles are applicable:

Principle 1.   Make running a lifetime activity. It's wasteful to train for just one race and then let all your hard-won conditioning evaporate. Plan to make running a daily habit, or at most skip only two or three days a week. Both your body and mind will benefit.

Principle 2.   Don't expect quick results. If you try to do too much too fast you'll pull muscles or be so tired you'll feel terrible. Gradual improvement is best.

Principle 3.   Alternate hard and easy periods. Beginners often buy a stopwatch and try to run faster than they did the last time every time they run. 'I made many mistakes in that first year,' Tex Maule writes in *Running Scarred*, 'the most painful being a tendency to run the first mile too fast. I began doing that when I got the stop-watch, trying to break my personal record each time I ran, a manifest impossibility.' The hard-easy principle applies to individual training sessions, to successive days of training, and even to entire seasons.

After a tough quarter-mile the body needs a rest; after a hard day, an easy day; after a few weeks of hard training, a period of slower running. Soon after New Year's Day each year I start taking longer and harder runs in preparation for the Boston Marathon in April. Over a three-month period I increase my mileage. While I am doing so I sometimes feel tired, and by the time the marathon is over I'm ready for a rest. For the next few months, particularly during the heat of summer, I run as I feel, seldom pushing myself and treating many of my runs as if they were just walks through the countryside. Under this relaxed regimen, my zest soon returns and almost without realizing it I'm taking an occasional run of fifteen or eighteen miles.

Principle 4.   Increase your weekly running mileage very gradually in order to give your body plenty of time to adapt. Too quick a change produces fatigue and injuries.

Training can be made into a forbiddingly complex matter. Listening to runners' jargon, to their talk of 'intervals' and 'fartlek', is enough to make you want to forget the whole sport and take up golf. But training need not be complicated if you understand that there are really only three ways to do it.

Intervals

Interval training is the most scientific training method. Commonly attributed to Woldemar Gerschler and Hersat Reindell, two German physiologists who are said to have developed it in the 1930s, interval training consists of repeated hard runs over a measured distance, with recovery periods (the intervals) of relaxed running in between. Interval training is a particularly versatile method because, depending on the effect sought, five factors can be varied: the total distance run fast, the duration of each fast run, the number of fast runs, the time between fast runs, and the type of activity between fast runs (walking or slow running). A champion like Olympic marathoner Bill Rodgers might run half a mile, three-quarters of a mile, a mile, and then two miles at a 4:40 pace, with only a four minute interval of slow running between each hard run. Then he may, and in fact often does, repeat the entire set. Less accomplished runners necessarily do lighter running. A little experimenting, with the help of a B.A.A.B. coaching manual, will show what works best for you. Remember, though, that since in interval training you run all the fast portions at the same pace, your first couple of fast runs should not be flat out. If you're planning to do, say, six fast runs, only the last two or three should be really difficult. If your pulse doesn't return to 120 within ninety seconds, you're running too hard.

Interval training produces results, but you pay a price. Since it is typically done on a track, the scenery is monotonous and the runs are repetitious. 'Interval training,' writes Kenneth Doherty in *Modern Track and Field*, 'lends no ears to the singing of the birds. . . . no eyes to the beauties of sand, sea and sky.' Especially if you're doing it alone, it's tempting to slack off and easy to lost interest. One solution is to stay away from tracks and do your training in a park or in the countryside.

Don't, by the way, attempt interval training until you've laid down a solid foundation of long, slow distance. It's hard work and can easily cause injuries unless you're in top shape. Be sure you're fully warmed up before you start an interval session. A mile of slow running is the minimum, and two miles is better. Don't do intervals more than twice a week, and don't let intervals add up to more than 5% of your total mileage. One doctor I spoke to advises that middle-aged runners should not attempt interval training at all except with the advice of a qualified coach.

Since interval training is infinitely variable, I have deliberately not prescribed any specific programmes. One runner I know, a middle-aged marathoner, runs twenty 220s twice a week, doing each in 35 seconds. Rodgers, as we just saw, runs considerably longer distances. You may decide that something in between is right for you. Whatever you choose, be patient; it will take at least three months to get results.

Fartlek

This is a Swedish word meaning 'speed play'. The fartlek method, codified by Gosta Holmer, chief coach of the Swedish 1948 Olympic team, consists of fast untimed runs over varied distances and terrains. Although the alternation of fast and slow runs varies from runner to runner, the goal is always the same: a good training session that is also fun. In *How They Train*, Raoul Mollett offers this description:

Fartlek was perhaps the most alluring discovery since the beginning of the century in the realm of training. . . . A window was opened on the forest, and at the same time an idea of training emerged which one would classify as 'happy'. Fartlek, with its walks, its runs at slow pace through the woods, its short sprints, was able to revolutionize the training of the track world.... There is without doubt not a single irreconcilable sedentary person who would not feel a twinge of nostalgia when faced with the thought of a man running barefoot on springy moss, in a setting of forests and lakes reflecting the sky. Faced with this picture, the track world felt an irresistible rise in spirits.

Fartlek is not intended as a way to avoid working hard, but only as a way to avoid repetition and monotony. It is an effective way to train only if you have the self-discipline to perform a tough training session. One day I ran with the members of a college cross-country team on a ten-mile fartlek session. At the start of the run they carried a couple of tennis balls. One runner would sprint ahead; another would toss the ball to him. There was conversation and laughter. We came to a rutted road deep in mud. We splashed our way through it, we ran through a field of wildflowers, forded a waist-deep stream, vaulted a few fences and finally finished with a fast mile on a country road. It was a hard training session, but it was fun all the way and neatly illustrated one of the special joys of fartlek: you take conditions as you find them. A stream, a muddy road or a snowfall is not an occasion for lamentation but a welcome challenge.

LSD

LSD isn't a drug but a way of training; the initials stand for 'long slow distance'. Its invention is often attributed to Ernst van Aaken, a highly regarded German doctor and coach. In America its chief popularizer has been Joe Henderson. 'LSD isn't just a training method,' Henderson has written. 'It's a whole way of looking at the sport. Those who employ it are saying running is fun—all running, not just the competitive part. Training isn't an exhausting, anxiety-filled means to an end that's barely tolerated. The simple, unhurried, unworried, nearly painless daily tours of the countryside come to be as much fun in their own way as racing.' Running this way offers all the pleasures of walking, but you go seven or eight miles in an hour instead of three or four.

Although it seems paradoxical, a small number of impressively fast runners do all their training by the LSD method. A young lawyer, Frank Handelman, can race six miles in 30 minutes and a few odd seconds, yet he rarely exceeds an eight-minute pace in training. The key, I suspect, is that he competes so often that he gets in enough hard running that way. Most runners and coaches feel that you need to run fast only about 5% of the time, a mere one mile out of every twenty.

In Britain LSD is not held in high repute at present. One reason, no doubt, is that it was much in vogue in the early 1970s, a period when hundreds of runners sought to compile as much as 200 slow miles a week. In running, as elsewhere, fashion is a factor.

Long, fast distance

I mention this method only because some people, under a misapprehension about how our bodies function, try to train this way. There are two reasons why it won't work:

1. The body will eventually rebel and break down. If you're lucky the breakdown will be in the form of a cold or persistent tiredness, but it could be something worse—painful knee trouble or a stress fracture.

2. Long, fast distance conflicts with the physiology of athletic improvement. In training we tire ourselves out in order to let the body become stronger than ever during an ensuing period of rest. Without rest, scientific studies show, repair is severely limited.

Which training scheme is best for you? The only sure way to find out is by experimenting. If you're a highly disciplined person and always accomplish what you set out to do, interval training may work for you. If you like to take it easy, fartlek or LSD may suit you best. Some people do one kind of training during part of the year, another kind during the rest. After a while, as you learn to read your body, and as you come to trust your readings, you'll find out what's best for it.

Not everyone should train the same way. The kind and amount of training you do ought to be based on what you're training for. If you're getting ready for a five-mile race, your training will be different from that of a marathon runner. The reason, as discussed earlier, is that how you train determines how well you'll race. Take two extremes, the quarter-mile and the marathon. The chemical reactions that produce energy require oxygen. When you run a fast quarter-mile you go so fast that during the run itself you get only about 25% of the necessary oxygen. The other 75%, your so-called oxygen debt, has to be made up after you've crossed the finishing line. That's why a quarter-miler has to do a lot of anaerobic training—running in the absence of sufficient oxygen. A marathoner, on the other hand, gets 98 or 99% of his oxygen during the race itself. His is mostly aerobic running, and that's the way he does most of his training. Middle distances require different ratios of aerobic and anaerobic running, 70–30 for the mile, 80–15 for two miles, 90–10 for three miles and so forth.

If the weather is likely to be hot during a race, try to do some training in the heat. If it's cool outside, create your own hothouse by wearing a tracksuit, gloves and a woolly hat. Because it takes only a week or two to become acclimatized to heat, you won't have to put up with the burden of so many clothes for long. Anyway, the slight discomfort will be worth it. At the start of the 1976 Boston Marathon it was 116 °F, 47 °C in the sun. Few runners had supposed it could possibly be so hot on a mid-April day in Massachusetts, so practically nobody had trained properly. As a result, most people's times were terrible. They might have been at least slightly better had they been training in the heat (though of course no one can run really well when it's *that* hot).

The same specificity principle applies to terrain. If you want to do well on a hilly course, you need to get in some hill running beforehand. Running up and down is different from running on flat terrain. Going uphill requires strong quadriceps; coming downhill gives the feet and knees a hard pounding. The only way to do well at hill running is to train for it.

How far should you run when you train? One answer is to run as far as you feel like. Not many years ago I thought six miles was a pleasant distance—enough for a good work-out, but not enough to bring on exhaustion. Now it takes ten miles to satisfy me. (Where it will end I have no idea; I try not to think about it.) If you're preparing for a race, though, you should put in the proper number of training miles to get you safely past the collapse point, the mileage beyond which you simply can't do anything more than what has been called a 'survival shuffle'. Your collapse point is easy to compute. If you never miss a day of running, it's your daily mileage multiplied by three. If you occasionally miss days, calculate your collapse point by adding up your most recent monthly total and dividing by ten.

The collapse point, needless to say, is only a rough guide. Some runners can run farther than theory indicates; a few can run less. Top runners, of course, think about attaining their potential, not about merely avoiding collapse; that's why some of them train twenty miles a day or more. Nor do collapse point computations take speed into account. All they tell you is that if you train enough, you'll probably be able to make it to the finishing line. They don't say what you'll look like when you get there. You'll have to experiment to find *that* out!

There are at least three ways to find out how far you're running. You can drive over your course in a car, checking it with the hodometer. Most hodometers aren't all that accurate (3 per cent one way or the other is common), so your measurement won't be accurate, either, but it will be reasonably close.

Or you can run at your usual pace around a quarter-mile track four times to see how long it takes. Let's say it takes nine minutes. Thereafter, reckon that you cover a mile every nine minutes, if your course is reasonably flat. From time to time, as you improve, check yourself again.

Or, most accurate of all, buy a little mechanical device that counts a bicycle wheel's revolutions. First, to calibrate it, measure off half a mile with a steel tape, put the revolution counter on the front wheel of a bicycle, and ride over the measured half-mile on that bicycle, noting how many revolutions are in half a mile. Then, without adding any air to the tyres (to do so would change the circumference), ride over your intended course and mark each mile with a spot of paint. Put the marks somewhere where cars and pedestrians won't obliterate them. I marked a course nearly a decade ago. The mile markers I sprayed on horizontal surfaces, kerbs and the like, have long since disappeared. The ones I put on vertical surfaces, stone walls, for example, are as good as new.

Once you've run a few races you'll start to notice that you do better at some distances than at others. There are a number of reasons, among them your age, your physique and the type of muscle fibre that predominates in your body. You may want to confine your racing to the distances you're best at—if you do, it will simplify your training—but most people enjoy racing a variety of distances, treating victory and defeat like the impostors Kipling told us they are. If you've trained well, there isn't much point in fretting about bad performances, since research conducted by Dr David

Costill (see Chapter 22) suggests that your basic speed is largely an inborn quality, one that can't be greatly influenced by training. You're either naturally fast or you're not. What you can improve through training is endurance, the ability to run at a given pace for a long time.

Endurance comes with running a great deal. Top runners train two and sometimes three times a day. There's no need for you to do so, though, unless you simply like the idea and have lots of extra time. It may not even do you much good. In a study conducted by Edward Watt, B. A. Plotnicki and Elsworth Buskirk, a number of university distance runners were divided into two groups. For nine weeks both had a training session every afternoon. In addition, one of the groups ran six fairly hard miles every morning. At the end of the experiment the one-mile times of the two groups were indistinguishable. (Differences might, of course, have showed up over a greater distance.)

What appears to be more important than the amount of training per day is regularity over a long period—months, years and even decades. Kenneth Doherty investigated the time it took twenty champion runners to reach their top performances. The average, from the time they first raced until they had their best run, was 10.4 years. (They had trained an average of 5.8 days a week for 10.2 months of the year.)

Some runners and coaches think weight-lifting is essential to good performances. Emil Zatopek, the Czech runner of the 1950s, used to do squats while holding his wife, Dana, on his shoulders. Many runners, however, don't bother with it. They'd rather spend their time running.

Whatever training method you choose, stick with it long enough to evaluate its effects. Some runners impatiently switch from one system to another so often that they never really have a chance to find out whether anything works. The body adapts slowly; some changes occur within days or weeks, but others take years. If you give your body enough time, you may be pleasantly surprised. There's no short cut to experience.

When we train we also are exercising our minds. The indefatigable Ted Corbitt told me of running twelve hours at a time when he was preparing for fifty-mile races; it was as much for his mind, he said, as for his body. Even if you're not planning to run fifty miles, the same principle applies. You need to demonstrate to your brain that certain things are going to be required of it, among other things a toughness that doesn't give way under pressure or fatigue. This is why Zatopek used to hold his breath repeatedly until it hurt. He wanted to teach his mind not to panic if his body didn't get enough oxygen.

When we race, curious things happen to our minds. The stress of fatigue sometimes makes us forget why we wanted to race in the first place. In one of my early marathons I found myself unable to think of a single reason for continuing. Physically and mentally exhausted, I dropped out of the race. Now I won't enter a marathon unless I truly want to finish it. If during the race I can't remember why I wanted to run in it, I tell myself, 'Maybe I can't remember now, but I know I had a good reason when I started.' I've finally learned how to fight back when my brain starts trying to beguile me with tricky arguments.

As a race continues it's also easy to find reasons to slow down: the pain is unbearable, you tell yourself; an old injury is acting up; blisters are coming on; it isn't an important race anyway. Such arguments sound persuasive in the heat of competition. Only later, after you've given in, are you disappointed in yourself. If you're going to race at all, it's only sensible to make a good effort.

This is where mental training comes in. There are several ways to strengthen your mind for running. One is always to run the distance you set out to do. If you plan to cover two miles, do it even if you have to walk part of the way. You'll learn to endure the bad runs and thereby toughen yourself for the occasional discomforts of running. If you give up when training goes badly, you only learn how easy it is to avoid discomfort. When I have a bad run I write 'Ugh' in my training diary. Strangely, a day or two after an 'Ugh' run I almost always have an unexpectedly good one. The reason, I think, is that an 'Ugh' is always slower than usual. It rests me, making a faster and easier run possible the next time.

Another good way to train your mind is to do exactly the type of training you plan, no matter how hard it seems, or how badly you're running. You're bound to have days when everything seems sluggish and ungainly and you'd just as soon not be training at all. That's a good time to persist. As mentioned earlier, studies show that the effort an athlete feels he is putting into a work-out is very close to the actual effort as measured by such criteria as heartbeat and oxygen consumption. So even if you're moving a lot more slowly than you'd like, the chances are you're getting in a decent training session. At the same time, your body is getting some rest.

A third way to train your mind is occasionally to run an unusually long distance. Instead of running three miles a day on two successive days, run a mile on the first day and five on the next in order to accustom yourself to running for long periods. When you train in this way, after a while even marathons don't seem intolerably long.

Another way to train your brain is by rehearsing in your imagination what you hope to do. Richard Suinn recently described his work with Olympic skiers. Suinn found that if they first imagined themselves skiing down a course, their performance on the slope improved. In addition, he found that not just their minds but also their muscles were helped, that true learning apparently took place:

I recorded the electromyograph responses of an Alpine ski racer as he summoned up the moment-by-moment imagery of a downhill race. Almost instantly, the recording needles stirred into action. Two muscle bursts appeared as the skier hit jumps. Further muscle bursts duplicated the effort of a rough section of the course, and the needles settled during the easy sections. By the time he finished this psychological rehearsal of the downhill race, his EMG recordings almost mirrored the course itself. There was even a final burst of muscle activity after he had passed the finishing line, a mystery to me until I remembered how hard it is to come to a skidding stop after racing downhill at more than 40 miles an hour.

Other athletic researchers confirm Suinn's belief that mental training is as important as physical. A psychologist named Robert Nideffer found that mental rehearsal significantly improves performance in nearly all sports. Similarly, in *Sports Psyching* Thomas Tutko and Umberto Tosi write: 'The psychological factors are the most important yet the most neglected in our approach to sports. . . . Most great athletes acknowledge state of mind as the key to success.'

Mental rehearsal is particularly helpful when applied to relaxation, a crucial aspect of running. You can't run well unless you're relaxed. The reason is that every muscle used in running has an opposing muscle; if both are tensed at the same time, movement is necessarily slowed. For example, the quadriceps is used to swing the leg forwards. If its antagonist, at the back of the upper leg, is relaxed, the leg can move quickly and easily. If it is tensed, the action of the quadriceps is inhibited. Mentally rehearsing a proper running style makes relaxation easier when you get tired and your legs want to tighten up.

A runner named John Hale uses a related relaxation technique. In the late stages of a race, when staying loose is difficult, he ticks off a mental check list of the various parts of his body, urging each one to relax. 'Relax, ears,' he will say. 'Relax, mouth ... head ... neck. ...' and so forth. I've tried it while running with Hale. It works.

To talk about such things as fatigue, blisters and pain might seem to suggest that training may be nothing but drudgery. It doesn't need to be this at all. Sometimes it's hard work, but because you have a worthwhile goal in mind it's not only tolerable but fun. If you find that it's becoming more work than fun, ease up. After all, we run chiefly for pleasure, not for pain.

One thing that will add to the pleasure of training is occasionally to run with a friend. Having a companion makes the time pass easily and takes your mind off incidental discomforts. Another is to run different courses for the sake of variety, or run by the time rather than the distance. Sometimes, wearing a watch, I simply go out and run, wandering wherever I want to and exploring new places. If I feel I'm running at about an eight-minute pace, I'll call an hour's run seven and a half miles. I may be wrong by a few hundred yards, but it doesn't make much difference.

Some people seem to become more bored with running than I do. They're the ones who carry transistor radios. If you need Bach or the Beach Boys to get you through a training session by all means take your radio along. I've even seen runners carrying them while competing in marathons. Most people soon discover, though, that running is entertainment enough.

After a few months of conscientious training you'll find that you run more easily, cover the same distance in less time, and, if you race, beat people who used to beat you. When these things happen, you may be so encouraged that you'll be tempted to step up your training. That's the time to be wary. For just as you can do too little training, you can also do too much. Your body needs time for repairs after a hard training session. Rest periods are an essential part of training.

How good do you want to be?

The Road Runners Clubs of England and America have established standards of excellence (in hours, minutes and seconds) for races of ten miles and more.

MEN	World Class	Champion Class	First Class	Second Class	Forty & Over	Fifty & Over
10 Miles	0:49.10	0:50.30	0:53.00	1:01.00	1:03.00	1:10.00
15 Miles	1:14.25	1:17.30	1:23.00	1:37.00	1:40.00	1:50.00
20 Miles	1:41.40	1:47.00	1:54.00	2:16.00	2:20.00	2:30.00
Marathon	2:15.00	2:23.00	2:35.00	3:04.00	3:10.00	3:25.00

WOMEN	World Class	Champion Class	Class A	Class B	Class C
10 Miles	0:56.16	1:00.25	1:05.14	1:10.54	1:17.37
13.1 Miles	1:14.51	1:20.25	1:26.52	1:34.26	1:43.05
20 Miles	1:57.38	2:06.27	2:16.41	2:28.44	2:43.06
Marathon	2:37.57	2:49.53	3:03.45	3:20.04	3:39.35

8 · The mythology of the woman runner

Why she usually gets more out of running than she expects

It was an early September day, cool and bright and just right for running, and I was in the first few miles of a 10½-mile race over a course booby-trapped with steep, exhausting hills. Still, I felt rested and springy; despite the hills it was going to be a fine run.

Just ahead of me was Peggy Mimno, a teacher. She, too, was running easily, moving along efficiently at my speed. The pace felt comfortable, so I decided to stay where I was; why bother to concentrate on pace when she was setting such a nice one? I'd overtake her later on when she tired.

So I tucked in behind her. The course headed north for five miles, wandered west for a hilly mile, then turned south again along a winding road. The race was getting tougher. We had four miles left and already it was beginning to be real work. I was breathing hard, and my legs were turning to jelly.

Peggy overtook a young male runner. Apparently she knew him, for they exchanged a few cheerful words as she passed him. Their exchange worried me. You don't chat during a race unless you are feeling good, and Peggy plainly was. There was still a discernible bounce in her stride. Whatever resilience I'd once possessed had long since left me. But I was close enough to overtake her if she tired, so I didn't give up hope completely. We were approaching a long, punishing hill now and that would be the test. We were a mile from the finishing line. Whatever happened on the hill would almost certainly determine who crossed it first.

    As I moved up the hill, working hard, my attention wandered for a few minutes. When I looked up, Peggy was moving away. First five yards, then ten, then more. Finally it was clear that there was no hope of catching her. She beat me decisively.

    There is an important lesson in that race. Much of what you read about running makes a sharp distinction between the sexes. Women are assumed to be weaker, slower and not nearly as adept athletically. (For example, women are always being told how to place their feet and hold their arms; the assumption is that any man simply knows such things.) Yet as Peggy Mimno so clearly demonstrated, the similarities between male and female runners are more important than the differences. I have run with a number of women, both in training and in competition, and I can testify that it is often hard work. As I was gathering information for this book I took a seven mile run with Nina Kuscsik, the 1972 Boston Marathon women's division winner, thinking that I would interview her as we ran. I finally became so breathless I had to abandon my questions until we finished.

Men in general are faster than women in general, but that's only part of the story. Far from being inferior to men as runners, there are certain ways in which women clearly excel. Their running style is likely to be tidier and more economical. 'Women seem to run with greater ease than men,' writes Thaddeus Kostrubala in *The Joy of Running*. 'Their style is easy. The natural style of most twelve-to-fourteen-year-old girls is almost perfect. . . . They roll their feet, their pelvises move. They look at ease and ready to play; in fact, they are playing. Is all this because they have not been the victim of male cultural expectation—that of competition?'

Kostrubala's impressions about women's running style are borne out by a study conducted by Dr Richard Nelson and Christine Brooks. Comparing 42 top runners, both male and female, they found that women had longer strides compared to their height, took more strides per minute and were in contact with the ground less. The clear conclusion is that women shouldn't try to mimic the running style of men; their own is every bit as good.

One important exception manifests itself when previously unathletic women let their style be influenced by mistaken notions about running. A knowledgeable woman runner told me: 'I maintain that women do *not* run as well as most men without some training tips. Maybe if all men and women had the same sort of athletic background, women would have some kind of advantage because of their pelvic build or whatever, but I notice a lot of common mistakes in almost all new (and some experienced) women runners. Most of these mistakes I made myself and had to correct. The most common is running daintily, on the toes. I think this is because women have observed sprinters running this way and also because women have greatly shortened Achilles tendons as a result of wearing high heels. Another mistake is shuffling. Another, carrying the arms too high, almost at the shoulder. Another, too much swivelling from the pelvis, or throwing the feet out too much to the side. I think these faults are common because few women have had a chance to engage in sports where a lot of running is involved, and so have had no opportunity to observe correct running form or to be corrected as men are.'

Contrary to the old wives' tales, women are no more prone to injuries than men. After gathering data from 361 schools, more than 125 athletic trainers and all manner of published reports, Dr Christine Haycock and Joan Gillette concluded that well-trained women are no more likely to be hurt in athletics than are well-trained men. The one exception is that because women's joints are looser, their knees are slightly more subject to injury.

Furthermore, women derive just as much benefit from training as men do. In a comparison of males and females during a carefully controlled programme, according to a report in the *Archives of Physical Medicine and Rehabilitation*, women's physical condition improved just as much as men's did. It is simply a myth that men need and can benefit from exercise while women don't and can't. (This idea is particularly dangerous after the menopause, when women's partial immunity to heart attack disappears and they become just as susceptible to heart trouble as men.)

Why, then, are women so commonly treated as second-class athletic citizens, despite the numbers of them that can be seen in races, both in the United Kingdom and elsewhere?

The chief reason appears to be cultural. Kathryn Lance has not only thought deeply about the subject, but has put many of her conclusions into a practical and wise book entitled *Running for Health and Beauty*. When I talked with her, she spoke with feeling about the way society conspires to keep women from discovering the pleasures of athletics.

'Women know they're too sedentary,' she said. 'But no one tells them to go out and learn a sport, the way men are supposed to do. Women are told to get their exercise by bending over daintily while they're doing housework. If you're a woman, people are always giving you silly exercises to do at home or at the office or on the way to the market. This is the result of cultural bias.'

Joan Ullyot, a doctor and marathon runner, has described how, sitting in a park some years ago with a friend, she was watching her husband run on the grass. Suddenly she was startled by a thought: 'Maybe I can do that.' She recalled later: 'It was a revolutionary idea. I'd never seen a woman running. The whole concept was foreign to me.'

Nina Kuscsik told me of feeling 'cheated' by not having been offered a chance to enjoy the benefits of running when she was growing up. And in *Against Our Will* Susan Brownmiller writes with passion of the same phenomenon: 'There are important lessons to be learned from sports competition, among them that winning is the result of hard, sustained, serious training, cool, clever strategy that includes the use of tricks and bluffs, and a positive mind-set that puts all reflex systems on "go". This knowledge, and the chance to put it into practice, is precisely what women have been conditioned to abjure.'

Sport and Society, an even-handed treatment written and edited by two males, John Talamini and Charles Page, puts it succinctly: 'To note [sport's] emergence as a two-sex activity . . . should not obscure the persistence in sport of male domination, male prejudice, and discrimination against girls and women.' Today such discrimination remains more evident in Britain. In America women runners have become so ubiquitous as to be quite unremarkable. A regular London runner named Linette Singer told me that while living in California for several years she was repeatedly encouraged to take up running and, once she did, was praised for doing it. When she returned to England, however, she found attitudes markedly different. 'In London I just run along with my eyes down,' she said. 'I'm certain people are looking at me as some sort of freak.' But times are clearly changing. 'Most of the people I know admire me for running,' says Amanda Crouch, who runs every day in Hyde Park. 'Only one friend has told me I'm mad!'

But a bad situation is not necessarily a hopeless one. Although at this point only a small percentage of race participants are women, their numbers are growing rapidly. Bruce Ogilvie, a clinical psychologist, recently offered some relevant advice at a sports seminar. 'Women,' he said, 'have no lack of natural ability; they are merely subject to cultural prejudices. Cultural pressures are created by what people think a woman should be,' he said. 'Remember the old saying, "horses sweat, men perspire, women glow". The woman who wants to turn to athletics must therefore make a leap—a psychological leap. She has to have the courage to redefine herself as a human being.'

Women runners I have spoken with agree with Ogilvie about the need for determination. 'When I first began to run I found it tremendously exciting to feel so good,' said one. 'Girls practically never have that experience in our society the way boys do. But it did take courage.' Another said, 'Sister joggers should each get a medal just for breaking out of the cast-iron stereotype.'

More and more women are breaking out. In my own family, my sister runs regularly and occasionally competes in races. My wife, Alice, runs two or three miles a day. Women are now accepted in road races and marathons in the United Kingdom, and there are numerous women's cross-country leagues. Women are beginning to take part in fell races and they already play a major role in orienteering. One happy result of their relatively small numbers is that women take away a goodly share of the prizes. In the 1978 Shaftesbury Ten-Mile road race, for example, some 500 men competed, but there were only five women. Thus, if you were a woman, your chances were vastly better of winning the first-place prize in your division.

Most female runners find their way into the sport as part of a search for physical fitness. Dr Ullyot recalled what she had felt like at the age of 29. 'My body, like all of ours after about the age of twelve, started going downhill because I wasn't keeping fit. I lost my endurance, if I'd ever had any. If you looked at my list of physical complaints, not just absence of good health, but actual complaints, I had insomnia, constipation, migraine headaches twice a month like clockwork that would last a couple of days. I was rather ill-tempered and tense. Looking back, I think I was never really alive.'

Kathryn Lance started running for another reason: 'I had this job where I was under enormous pressure. I was smoking a lot and I was overweight. Then I got high blood pressure. I got really scared. I had this idiot doctor who said, "Stop worrying. Don't eat any salt, and if your blood pressure's still elevated in a few months we'll put you on pills." I had read about those blood-pressure pills, how they make you depressed and have weird side effects, and once you're on them you may have to stay on them for the rest of your life. I didn't want to start taking them. I had heard that jogging can lower your blood pressure, so I went out and bought Dr Cooper's book *Aerobics* and read it and started jogging.' Today Ms Lance's blood pressure is normal, *low* normal, in fact, and like most women runners she reports a number of beneficial side effects. (More about these later.)

How should a woman start running? The principles outlined elsewhere in this book are applicable for the most part to both sexes. There are, however, a few differences dictated by women's anatomy and physiology, as well as by certain hazards more common to the female than to the male.

Women sometimes have more trouble than men when they try to buy running shoes. Although it is perfectly all right to wear men's shoes if they fit, women with small feet are likely to find that the shoes they want don't come in small enough sizes. The short-range solution is simply to keep looking until you find a shoe that feels right. The long-range solution is to complain, loudly and long. Eventually, word of the general discontent will find its way back to the manufacturers and they will mend their ways.

The Great Bra Controversy is probably a good subject for a man to stay out of. Yet I would be remiss if I didn't mention that some women insist you need a bra when you run, others say you needn't bother, while others even specify certain brands. Nina Kuscsik takes a no-nonsense approach: 'Women need a firm bra, not one of the flimsy all-elastic ones. That's especially true if you have large breasts. Otherwise they'll bounce and you'll always be waiting for them to come down before you take the next step. Also, you can get abrasions from the skin rubbing repeatedly against either skin or clothing.' Most women feel that you're not going to injure yourself if you wear a loose bra, or even if you don't wear one, so it's safe to experiment to see what works best for you.

Some women worry about damage to their bodies. Some time ago (see Chapter 3), J. E. Schmidt wrote in *Playboy* that jogging is one of the most hazardous forms of exercise. In the case of women, he said, it can displace the uterus and 'snap' ligaments in the breast, causing it to droop 'like a partly deflated balloon'. Every one of the numerous doctors I have talked with about these hazards has been puzzled. There seems to be no evidence in medical literature to justify such conclusions. On the contrary, women report that on taking up running their breasts become firmer, probably because the action of the arms strengthens the pectoral muscles. Nor has any female runner I have spoken to reported any problem with her uterus.

Many women are afraid of becoming muscle-bound. The fact is that women runners don't become any more muscle-bound than men runners do. The next time you see a woman running, look at her legs; you'll see long, supple, nicely shaped muscles, not lumpy ones. Furthermore, they'll stay that way no matter how hard or long or fast her exercise programme is.

Some women do weight-lifting to improve their running. Jack Wilmore of the U.S. National Athletic Health Institute points out that it's not true that strong muscles have to be big ones. 'Contrary to the misconceptions created by the comic books,' he says, 'the skinny kid on the beach might be as strong or stronger than the thick-necked ruffian who kicks sand in his face.' Wilmore, who is well-known for his work with women athletes, says women have increased their strength by as much as 44% with almost no increase in muscle size. One British observer told me, 'Women runners in the U.K. use weights a lot. I don't think you can say they're exactly Amazons.'

In fact, the odds are that if you're a woman who runs you'll lose both weight and girth even if you don't change your eating habits. As noted in Chapter 6, many women report that in the first year of running they lose ten pounds or more. Furthermore, they do it painlessly and with no recourse to will-power because running doesn't make you any hungrier than usual. After a few months of running, Kathryn Lance writes in *Running for Health and Beauty*, 'I had the spooky feeling that I was dressed up in somebody else's body.'

Louise Foottit, the London secretary who was introduced in Chapter 2, recalls that before she started running she was extremely unfit. 'I suddenly realized I had let myself get into terrible condition,' she told me. 'The only thing I was doing all day was sitting at my desk. Then one day I noticed that I couldn't even go up a flight of stairs without puffing. That's when I decided I needed to do something about it. I started running. Now I feel wonderful again.'

Far from experiencing difficulties as a result of having taken up running, most women report that their lives become pleasanter and easier. Dr Ullyot's testimony reflects what many women say: 'All my physical problems have disappeared now that I run. I've gone from a size fourteen to a size ten dress. My pulse is down to 45–50 from 70–75. I haven't had one migraine in five years. . . . I have no problems with constipation. And I sleep like a log the minute my head hits the pillow.'

Dr Kenneth Cooper, one of the gurus of the running movement, may underestimate the benefits of running for women. 'Women suffering from dysmenorrhea [the medical term for painful or difficult menstruation] find exercise extremely uncomfortable,' he writes in *The New Aerobics*. 'Common sense alone tells them to skip exercise during those days.' Not every woman agrees. In *The Jogger* Natalie Browne wrote: 'I have found jogging during my period beneficial for two reasons: first, it cuts down on the severity of the pains (perhaps because I am in better physical shape). Secondly, if I jog at the time my pains are particularly intense, they dissipate.'

Marge Albohm, head women's trainer at the Indiana University, maintains that most women feel better during their periods if they run. She also reports that 'physical performances are not dramatically altered by the menstrual cycle. Some phases of the cycle may put the female in a condition more conducive to efficient performance, principally the phase following menstruation, when water retention and therefore weight is lowest. But the differences have been found to be so slight in average daily performance that they are unnoticeable. . . . Full participation in athletics should be allowed at all phases of the menstrual cycle.'

Other investigators report that cramps are by no means the only menstrual condition that is helped by exercise. In one study Dr G. J. Erdelyi points out that 'athletes had the fewest symptoms of pre-menstrual tension, especially headaches and dysmenorrhea'.

Dr Evalyn Gendel goes even further, reporting that women who are in top physical condition not only experience less menstrual discomfort but also have less fatigue and fewer backaches, digestive disorders, colds and allergies. Once they have taken up running, most women are pleasantly surprised by their increase in stamina. A runner named June Cheek tells of having to wake up three times a night to nurse her newborn baby: 'I would begin to drag in the mid-afternoon. By six I was ready to take a nap instead of preparing dinner. Jogging changed all that. I couldn't believe how much better I felt.'

The moral would seem to be that during your period, keep running even if you don't much feel like it. You may be pleased with the results. If you aren't, you can always stop.

What about running during pregnancy? Most doctors say that this isn't a good time to start. If you're already running there's no reason not to keep on—unless, that is, your doctor says you shouldn't. You'll not only feel better, but after delivery you'll return to your normal shape more quickly. Carol Dilfer tells of running following the birth of her second child, Erin: 'I kept it up until Erin was born, sensing that there was some intrinsic value in this whole business of jogging during pregnancy. After I delivered Erin, I *knew* that exercise during my pregnancy had been a tremendous help. I went into a long labour which began at one a.m. after a week-long bout of flu. I expected to be totally exhausted. Instead, I felt great, took a shower an hour after delivery, chatted with my friends, and never did experience that terrible fatigue that frequently follows childbirth. My recovery was very rapid, my stamina inexhaustible, my sense of well-being tremendous. To top things off, I was able, the very day I brought Erin home, to wear clothing that I hadn't been able to squeeze into for six months after my first child was born.'

Lisa Veijalainen won the world orienteering championship in Scotland when she was three months pregnant. Sandra Davis finished one marathon when she was four weeks pregnant and another when she was eight weeks pregnant. Trina Hosmer went out for a four mile run two hours before her first son was born. (She had miscalculated the date he was due and didn't realize that her feeling of malaise came from being in labour.)

Running performance need not suffer after childbirth. 'There are many examples that women do as well after pregnancy and delivery as before,' Dr Erdelyi said recently. 'Some of these top-ranking athletes have been Olympic champions after having children. The only thing that could happen is that the children might keep an athlete away from the proper training, and then her performance might drop for lack of preparation.'

Women well beyond childbearing age have also been helped by running. And even the condition known as idiopathic osteoporosis, in which older people's bones become brittle because of calcium loss, can be reversed through exercise, according to one study.

By far the most spectacular alterations, in women as in men, are those described in Chapter 2—the psychological changes. 'It was the first time,' Nina Kuscsik reports, 'that I had experienced any confidence in myself. I knew I had disciplined myself, that running was my own doing, that no one had pushed me to do it, I knew that I was able to accomplish what I had because I had worked on it. It was very clear-cut.'

One woman told me how running helped her during her divorce. 'Even with all the emotional trauma, I began to run better and better. I wondered, How can this be? My insides were in such a turmoil that I thought that sooner or later this would take its toll. I ran a marathon four days before my divorce. I was on tranquillizers, and I don't know how I did it. But I knew the running would be good for me physically, and that the end result would be good emotionally. Running helped me through that time, and I came out of it healthy.'

Where running is concerned, women, unlike men, are only at the beginning. Little more than a decade ago it was thought that no female could possibly run a marathon. Women who applied were refused entries on the grounds that they 'couldn't run that far'. In 1966, however, the Boston Marathon was finally overcome by Roberta Gibb, who hid in the bushes until the gun sounded, slipped into the race unnoticed and covered the whole distance. A year later Kathy Switzer became the first woman to run while wearing an official number (see Chapter 19). But not until 1972 were women allowed to compete officially. In Britain they were not permitted to run marathons until six years later.

The women's marathon record, improving year by year, reflects the change in attitude. In 1967, it was three hours and seven minutes. By 1978 it was two hours and thirty-two minutes, far faster than most men will ever run the distance, and it was recently estimated on the basis of scientific analysis that one day a woman will cover the course in two hours and twenty-three minutes. Records at other distances are also falling fast. There is no doubt that as more women take up running, thereby increasing the odds that some really gifted ones will enter the lists, spectacular performances will occur. For women, it's an interesting time to be running, perhaps the best of times.

9 · When you're over forty

You'll actually start looking forward to your birthdays

After the Boston Marathon a few years ago, I went to a party given by some participants in their hotel suite. No one is more at ease than a runner in the company of other runners after a hard race, so it was a cheerful and convivial gathering, with people busily review-ing—and no doubt embellishing—their performances. Eventually I fell into conversation with a white-haired man named Norman Bright. Bright was nearly sixty-five years old then, yet had run the race that day in an astonishing 2:59.59 and had finished in 615th place, thereby defeating two-thirds of the field. Many of the younger runners at the party, exhausted by the race, were seated or lay sprawled on the carpet, but Bright stood and talked with animation. He was planning to go abroad soon for some races in Europe, he told me, and was looking forward to the change of scenery. Opening an orange knapsack he had stowed in a corner of the room, he began showing me the maps, brochures and entry forms he had gathered in preparation for his trip. He was as enthusiastic as a teenager.

Norman Bright is unusual chiefly because he is an American. In the United States, and in Britain too, we have some odd ideas about how older people, even those barely into their forties, ought to behave. Europeans have few such preconceptions. In West Germany, the Deutscher Sportbund has formed more than 40 000 athletic clubs, many of them with programmes for elderly people. In Italy some 4000 senior citizens were among the 33 000 participants in a recent Stramilano, the fifteen mile race held each spring in Milan, and 150 Italians over 60 entered a 43-mile ski race. Though exercising isn't likely to displace wine drinking as the French national pastime, several thousand Frenchmen over 60 turn out weekly for physical training. And in the Soviet Union the state-run *Gotov k truduy oboronye* ('ready for labour and defence') sponsors cross-country runs and ski meetings. In the winter it adds ice swims that are said to be good for the nerves, metabolism and will-power.

All this is in contrast to what is expected of older people in Britain and the United States. 'Our attitude is one of over-protection,' says Dr Theodore Klumpp, a New York cardiologist. 'Our middle-aged and older people are encouraged and virtually compelled to reduce their physical activities to the point where atrophy sets in, with damaging if not disastrous results.' As recently as a generation ago there was serious debate about exercise for middle-aged people. In 1950, in a book called *How to Stop Killing Yourself*, P. J. Steincrohn wrote: 'Exercise is a state of mind. Like sheep we follow the leader. We have been told that "exercise is good for you"; we have accepted this dictum without reason, and have subjected creaking joints and protesting muscles to unnecessary strain simply because we think exercise is a necessary adjunct to proper living. Remember: *you don't have to exercise.*'

Yet at long last there are some harbingers of change. A growing number of men and women over 40 have taken up running. One current estimate puts over-40 runners in Britain at 15% of the total. One club alone, the Veterans Athletic Club of London, has some 600 members, I was told by Sylvester Stein, publisher of *Jogging* and the current over-55 British sprint champion. In America a report from the National Running Data Centre showed that of 18 466 runners who entered official races in one recent year, nearly 10% were 40 or over. Furthermore, many of these men and women train as hard and race as well as runners decades younger. In races where contestants are divided into five-year groupings, it is not unusual for the winner of, say, the 50–54 year-old category to cover the course faster than the winner of the next younger group. At a race not long ago I met Percy Perry, a 72 year-old runner who started in his sixties after his doctor told him he ought to get more exercise. Today, as a member of an organization called the Old Guard Club, Perry runs six miles a day and can outrun many people half his age. 'The doctor says I'm good for another 50 years,' he told me.

As mentioned in Chapter 4, Dr Fred Kasch has demonstrated that several of the chief physical changes associated with ageing can be arrested and even reversed by exercise. In a study of women 52 to 79 years old, Dr Herbert deVries and Gene Adams, whose work was noted briefly in Chapter 2, showed that as little as three months on an exercise programme can significantly improve the cardio-vascular system and lower the resting heart rate. Scientists have also demonstrated that previously sedentary middle-aged women benefit from a conditioning programme exactly as men do, and are no more susceptible to injury. Finally, researchers have shown that through a programme of running and other exercise faithfully carried out for a year, men in their eighties can lower their blood pressure, body fat and nervous tension levels while significantly increasing their strength. In short, you can improve no matter how late you start.

Probably the biggest benefit to older people, however, is not health as such but the fact that they simply feel better and have more fun when they're in good condition. This, more than dry statistical measures of improved health, accounts for the large numbers of people over 40 who are entering the ranks of runners these days. Whatever you do, whether it's work, a hobby, or something as pedestrian as carrying out the rubbish, it's pleasanter to do it without having to breathe hard. Conversely, few things are more discouraging than being unable to do what practically everyone else your age can do. 'Disuse is the mortal enemy of the human body,' says the American Administration on Ageing. 'We know today that how a person lives, not how long he lives, is responsible for many of the physical problems normally associated with advanced age.' One doctor put it another way: 'Most of us don't wear out. We rust out.'

Fifteen years ago, at a publishing house where I worked, I met a trim young editor in his mid-twenties whose name was Ted. He was a person of formidable intelligence, and we enjoyed each other's company. Eventually we both left the publishing house and lost track of each other. A year or two ago, Ted called and we had lunch together. I hardly recognized him. He was 40 lbs heavier and had developed a double chin that bounced as he talked. He asked me how I managed to stay thin, and I told him about running. A worried look came over his face. 'But is it really a good thing for a person your age to do something like that?' he asked me with concern. 'I'm 40 years old, you know, and I try to take it as easy as I can.'

So does most of the population, but by no means all of it. In 1935 a 27 year-old runner named John Kelley won the Boston Marathon.

Ten years later he won it again, covering the course faster than in his first victory. Today, in his seventies, Kelley still competes in the marathon, to the appreciative cheers of a crowd that regards him as a permanent fixture at the event. And in San Francisco, Larry Lewis was still running six miles a day—and working full-time as a waiter—when he was over a hundred.

The remarkable and wonderful thing about the world of running is that people like Lewis, Kelley, Bright and Perry are in no sense looked upon as intruders, or even as curiosities. They run in the same races as 20 year-olds and receive equal respect for their accomplishments. They have their own magazines, including an excellent one called *Veteris*, their own organization, the Association of Veteran Athletes, and even their own annual International Senior Olympics. It is no wonder that far from dreading their birthdays, many runners actually look forward to them, reckoning they'll be that much tougher to beat in the next age group.

There is usually little difference in the training of serious young runners and serious old ones. Many of the latter cover as many miles as their juniors, and in some cases even more. 'Just because you're getting older doesn't mean you should do less,' Ted Corbitt says. 'If you step up from five mile races to marathons you require more mileage.' John Kelley runs an hour every day, much of it hard. Jim McDonagh, a top runner in his fifties, once did a 65-mile workout in preparation for the famous 52½-mile London-to-Brighton race, and Corbitt himself has been known to go out early in the morning and simply run all day long.

If you're an older runner, your training will necessarily be governed by two factors: the distance you're training for, and how much work you can tolerate. As Corbitt indicates, a middle-aged marathoner needs to run as many miles as a younger one—probably nine or ten a day at a minimum, and more if he hopes to do really well. But if he's going to run only an occasional casual race of five or six miles, then three or four miles a day is plenty. Many runners have no interest in racing, and for them, a total of twenty miles a week will confer the fitness and sense of well-being they're looking for.

Older runners may run just as far as young ones, but they do not, except in rare instances, run as fast. The reason, of course, is that the human body slows down as it ages. As we get older our muscle strength, co-ordination, maximum heart rate and ability to use oxygen all decrease. So does our ability to adapt to heat. One study showed that men from 39 to 45 work up a sweat only half as fast as men from 19 to 31, and that when they're through exercising it takes them longer to stop sweating. Furthermore, older people get hurt more easily and recover more slowly.

There are compensations, though. For one, athletic ability declines slowly up to the age of sixty. Physical strength, as the graph indicates, rises from early childhood to the age of 20, then starts an extremely shallow decline. It is not until the age of sixty or so that the decline shows any steepening. Moreover, even though older people are more susceptible to injury, they compensate by being more careful. Young people, especially those who do hard interval training, are forever pulling muscles, wrenching knees and bruising heels.

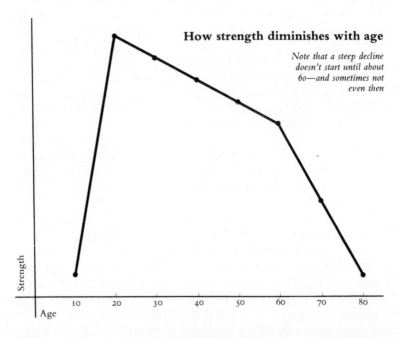

How strength diminishes with age

Note that a steep decline doesn't start until about 60—and sometimes not even then

Strength

Age

10   20   30   40   50   60   70   80

If you're over 40 and want to take up running, see a doctor first. Thereafter, the most important thing, and probably the most difficult, is to be content with slow improvement. The admonition 'Train, don't strain' is especially pertinent. If you put on a pair of running shoes and start sprinting after a twenty-year layoff, you may improve for a while, but sooner or later you're sure to hurt yourself.

Muscles and tendons accustomed to years of disuse need lots of time before they can readjust to a more vigorous regimen. During my first two or three years of running I suffered from lots of injuries. Then, mysteriously, the pains went away. Today, more than a decade later, it is only infrequently that I feel even the faintest twinge of discomfort—and then a good run usually cures it.

Dr Getchell's programme at Ball State University, which meets from 6.15 to 6.45 four mornings a week, is a good model for an adult who wants to start running. Men and women train together. (There's no point in depriving yourself of companionship just because you've decided to take up running.) After some warm-up exercise, participants run fast enough to raise their heart rates to 75% of the difference between their resting and maximum rates, added to the resting figure, the same method described on pp. 58–9.

Even in older people, exercise, in particular running, can do a lot to reverse the long-term effects of smoking, drinking and overeating, the salient hazards of twentieth-century living. Studies have shown that sedentary old people who start training can become as fit as long-time athletes. Dr deVries has demonstrated that through exercise, even octogenarians can increase their physical capacities enormously. His research has also revealed that people over 60 derive benefits from exercise so mild that it would have little effect on younger people. Even walking produces measurable results.

In the town where I live, a group of runners gathers at a quarter-mile track once a week during the summer for short races. There are no entry fees and no formalities, and the participants range from college competitors to one-mile-a-day housewives and children. During the past couple of summers a muscular white-haired man in his seventies has been coming to the track. Wearing shorts and tennis shoes, he runs slowly in an outside lane while we race. One night I talked to him. He told me that his wife had recently died, that he lives alone now, and that he started running to see if it would make him feel better. When I asked him whether it had, he grinned like a kid and said, 'You couldn't *pay* me to miss a day.'

10 · Kids

They're faster—and tougher— than you think

One-upmanship starts early in my family. One Sunday when my son John was ten or eleven years old we entered a five-mile race. I ran well, so I received the second-place trophy for contestants of my age. A few minutes later, John's name was called; his trophy was for being the youngest finisher, and to his delight and my chagrin it was twice as big as mine.

A few days later, hearing about John's award, a friend asked, 'But is it *good* for someone that young to run so far?' I realized that I didn't really know. I was aware that plenty of children, some of them much younger than John, run, and that many even compete in marathons. I also had heard of one boy, the son of a marathon runner, who'd had open-heart surgery and whose parents encouraged him to run long distances, presumably on medical advice. Still, I didn't know exactly what effect running had on kids and whether it was beneficial, so I started asking questions. If running was going to hurt John, I didn't want him to continue, no matter how big his trophies. For all I knew, running might have quite different effects from those of football or tennis. In those sports, while there are bursts of flat-out heart-thumping effort, there are also occasions for rest. But in running, especially competitive running, it's flat-out continually. The heart pounds, the legs ache, breathing is laboured. What might happen to a child?

As I pursued the question, pieces of evidence started to fall into place. Studies show, for example, that early signs of atherosclerosis (blockage of the arteries) are detectable in an alarming number of young children. Since aerobic exercise, especially if accompanied by a diet low in saturated fats, can arrest and, in the view of some doctors, even reverse atherosclerosis in adults, it seemed possible that running might also help children. I raised the question with Dr Elsworth Buskirk, the distinguished director of the Noll Laboratory for Human Performance Research. His answer confirmed my hunch. 'Evidence in the literature,' he said, 'suggests that primary prevention programmes should start with the very young.'

A second support came from three researchers, William McCafferty, Arthur Cosmas, and Dr Dee Edington, who reported not long ago on a study they did which was designed to clarify aspects of the relationship between exercise and longevity. They wanted to find out whether exercise begun late in life might help people live longer. They used rats, so the results cannot be related directly to human beings. None the less, they have a significance. McCafferty, Cosmas and Edington started with four groups of rats ranging in age from four to 20 months and exercised them on a treadmill for 20 minutes a day until they were three years old. The earlier the rats started training the better their survival rate. 'It appears,' said the researchers, 'that there may be a threshold age above which an exercise programme may not be beneficial. ... It is reasonable to assume that exercise programmes begun early in life (before a hypothetical threshold age) and continued into old age promote longevity more than an exercise programme begun late in life.'

Dr Harry Tomason of the University of Salford Human Performance Laboratory agrees on the value of starting exercise early. 'On balance,' he writes, 'the small risk of cardiac complications from strenuous exercise seems to be far outweighed by the benefits, provided that regular exercise becomes a way of life at an early age.'

Another good reason for a child to start exercising early is that he or she is less likely to become fat. Obesity, reported Dr Nathan Smith at a meeting of the American College of Sports Medicine, is not a dieting problem at all, but one of activity; usually it is too little exercise rather than too much eating that causes fatness.

Young people benefit just as much as adults from the psychological changes running produces. Knowing at an early age that you can cover ground faster than all but a few people is a powerful stimulus to self-confidence. To run in a race as a teenager and, with a hundred yards to go, sprint past a fit-looking 25 year-old is to enjoy a rare sense of equality. Sir Roger Bannister has written: 'Adolescence can often be a time of conflict and bewilderment, and these years can be weathered more successfully if a boy develops some demanding activity that tests to the limit his body as well as his mind.' (Bannister made the observation more than a decade ago. Were he writing now, he would, I suspect, include girls as well as boys.)

Even the period before adolescence is a good time for running. One autumn day I went to watch the National Age Group Cross-

Country Championships. There, 3429 boys and girls, some of them only six years old, competed on a 1½-mile course around the perimeter of a broad, grassy field. Divided into two year age groups, they ran in wave after stampeding wave, first six- and seven-year-old girls, then eight- and nine-year-old girls, and so on to boys sixteen- and seventeen-years-old. The results were astonishing. A girl in the youngest category ran the course at a pace well under seven and a half minutes a mile. A boy in the same category ran a 10:48, that is just over seven minutes a mile, and far faster than many adults will ever do it. But what was even more remarkable than their times was the spirit of the occasion. As the children fought for position in the last few yards, their faces wore the same agonized expressions you see on the faces of international runners, but once they crossed the finishing line they were again grinning kids on a day's outing.

Such all-children's races, incidentally, are the kind many authorities recommend. In many races children are simply not allowed to compete against adults, although special children's races are sometimes held at the same time. Despite such precautions against overcompetitiveness, some parents worry that children will hurt themselves by running hard. Since I have children of my own, I've asked doctors and physiologists for their views. Most recommend caution—don't urge your four-year-old to run a marathon, for example—but not one has mentioned any way in which a child, however young, can hurt himself permanently by running. What it comes down to is simply being sensible. You don't want your child to return from a training session so exhausted he or she can hardly crawl, any more than you yourself would want to. But if you don't push him to perform beyond his capacities, this isn't likely to happen. No matter what their age, most people have sense enough to slow down when they start hurting too much.

Most, but not all. Young people are less inclined than adults to ease up when the going gets too tough—as, for example, on a sweltering summer day. On such a day I've seen children and teenagers in races, too proud to drop out, staggering dazedly from heat exhaustion or running on painful blisters. That's silly. There's always another race. Like the rest of us, young people should think of running as a long-term sport, not as something to be conquered in a single season.

It doesn't matter if young people don't race; that's just a bonus if they want it. What counts most is the continuity. There's a special pleasure in running every day in all sorts of weather, and young people are as receptive to it as the rest of us. Running is also something children and adults can do together, an occasion not simply for training together but communicating with each other both verbally and through their bodies. There's nothing quite like two or even three different generations running together, forgetting the differences that originally divided them. David Burhans, who was introduced in Chapter 5, spoke of the joys of running with his children: 'The pleasure of running was greatly enhanced for me by the fact that right from the beginning four of my six children ran along with me. I bought them all inexpensive running shoes and university track shirts just like Daddy's, and we soon had the makings of a family track team. Fortunately, one of the rules of our daily run was that "nobody is permitted to run faster than Daddy", so they patiently trotted along beside me as I gradually got into condition to run the kinds of distances and times that they could have

managed much sooner. We have since run nine miles—on my daughter's ninth birthday!'

Young people will find most of the principles scattered through this book just as applicable to them as to older people. However, there are a few points that warrant emphasis.

Children's bodies adapt more quickly to training than older people's do, and because improvement comes so fast, it's tempting to push hard and try more than you can manage. Under a grinding regimen, everything will probably go fine for a while, but eventually the young runner will acquire an over-use injury, or if he's lucky, just a nasty stale feeling. Staleness goes away after a few days' rest, but a muscle or tendon injury takes longer than that. It's important, therefore, to start training slowly, building the 'base' before making any effort to increase speed. In early training, the emphasis should be on learning to cover distance, no matter how slowly.

Unfortunately, in many track and cross-country programmes, such a leisurely approach isn't possible. At the start of the season runners turn up untrained. Within a few weeks they're expected to compete in a race, so the hard training starts right away. The shrewd runner has an antidote: several weeks of slow pre-season training on his own. Then when his coach starts cracking the whip, he's ready for anything.

This is especially true if the runner has been eating a proper athlete's diet. Most of the nutritional principles in Chapter 14 are applicable to young runners, yet many young people find it hard to apply them consistently. They're tempted to fill up with crisps, soft drinks and junk foods and to skip breakfast in the morning rush. If you're a young athlete, try to avoid developing such habits. Unwholesome foods don't give fair value for the calories, and skipping breakfast leaves you without energy when you need it. Nutritionists say that a third of one's calories should be eaten in the morning.

If you're a girl, foods rich in iron are important to make up for the iron lost in menstruation. Liver and dark-green leafy vegetables are convenient ways to take this nutrient. It's also important for girls to stick undeviatingly to sound eating habits. *In Nutrition and the Athlete* Joseph Morella and Richard Turchetti write: 'Males reach their maximum natural fitness during their late teens and early twenties; females on the other hand reach their peaks during puberty and the middle teens. There is a steady fitness decline from these ages onwards, unless it is maintained through proper exercise and diet.'

While it is generally agreed that an adult runner's diet during the hours immediately preceding competition makes little physiological difference, in the case of young athletes, there is less certainty on this score. Some authorities say that children fifteen and younger shouldn't eat for four hours or so before competition. Others dispute this. Among the dissenters is Dr Robert Craig. Recently he wrote: 'As any parent knows, youngsters seem to be eating constantly.

Many of them are undergoing their growth spurt. If they are deprived of food for periods of four hours prior to a game, it is my impression that the second half of the game provides the setting for extreme fatigue or lack of co-ordination. Six hours is too long for this age group to be without food.'

Much depends, I suspect, on the individual child. If a young athlete feels weak and tired after four hours without food, it's probably a reliable sign that he or she needs to eat more often. As with much else in running, a little personal experimenting often yields answers that can't be found even in the most authoritative medical textbooks.

If you're a young athlete who eats properly, trains wisely and toughens your mind for the rigours of competition, are you assured of going to the top? Unfortunately, no. An Israeli doctor, Dr Oded Bar-Or, has made a study of the early indications of athletic excellence and reports that such unchangeable factors as height, bone structure and reaction time are crucially important. As the Swedish researcher Per-Olaf Åstrand has said, 'I am convinced that anyone interested in winning Olympic medals must select his or her parents very carefully.' They must also have the champion's peculiar psychological make-up, which permits him to keep trying to improve, even when he is already out-performing his fellows. 'If you have natural talent,' says Dr John Williams, 'you may get to 80% of your potential and then lose interest. It's very easy to become bored with the rituals of training.'

There are, however, a good many elements that science can't foresee, at least not so far. It can't take into account motivation, learning ability or willingness to endure discomfort, which is why a person with all the right genetic equipment may be beaten by someone who looks too clumsy to cover a hundred yards without tripping over his own feet. This is also why young runners are so full of fascinating surprises, and why you're in for some fun if you're one of them.

11 · Fitting it into your life

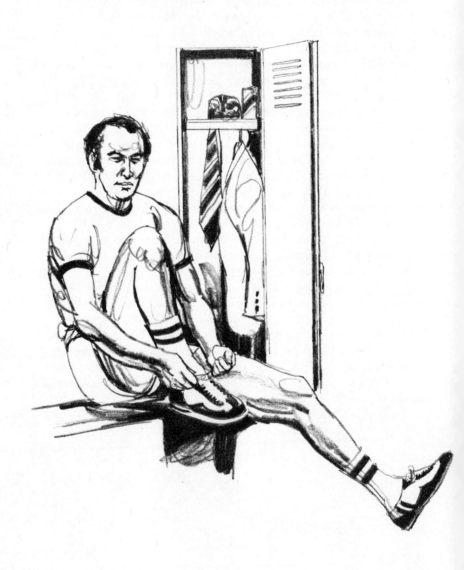

Thoughts on the problem of finding time

Jerry Noah (which is not, for reasons that will become clear, his real name) is an important Manhattan advertising executive with a big flat in the city, a summer place at a fashionable seaside resort, two cars, a dog and children in good schools. Manhattan advertising executives, especially important ones, work hard. To outsiders it may sometimes appear as if they aren't working at all, but that's because outsiders don't understand what they're doing. The main thing outsiders notice are the three-hour lunches. What they don't realize is that this is where much of the work gets done. The three-hour lunches are not a luxury or indulgence; without them, there could be no advertising business as the civilized world knows it.

Thus Jerry Noah attracts only perfunctory attention as he leaves his big corner office each weekday at noon, not to return until three. He has been doing it for years and will be doing it for many more to come, if his luck holds. For Jerry Noah does not in truth eat lunch at all. Instead he takes a cab to the West Side Y.M.C.A. and changes into running clothes. In a few minutes he is joined by a maker of documentary films, a magazine editor and a man who works for a big accounting firm. Their stories are much like Jerry Noah's.

These are the secret runners, and there are many of them. Once you know what to look for, the secret runner is easily identifiable. He (or she, for many are women) has a windburned look all year long. He becomes restless, even downright twitchy, if a late morning meeting threatens to last beyond its allotted time. He invariably carries a commodious briefcase of sweatproof construction. Above all, he exhibits a vagueness akin to amnesia when anyone asks about his lunchtime activities. (In most business offices it is perfectly all right to come back from lunch with your brains so shrivelled by martinis that you can hardly find your own desk, but it is considered frivolous to spend an hour in a tracksuit.)

Even world-class runners have problems with those who do not understand their love for the sport. Bill Rodgers, who set a course record in winning the 1975 Boston Marathon, was once a school-teacher. He was devoted to his students and often gave them souvenirs such as shoes and T-shirts that he had worn in important races. But he was also devoted to his training, and customarily ran during his lunch hour. 'One day,' Rodgers told me, 'my headmaster took me aside and said, "Isn't it about time you started giving as much attention to your vocation as you do to your avocation?"' The comment hurt, Rodgers said, but he knew that if he eliminated the noon run he'd soon be far back in the pack. Not long afterwards he left teaching to go into the sporting goods business.

Cindy Bremser, a nurse and a top-ranked runner at 1500 and 3000 metres, has had similar difficulties. A matron once remarked, 'She's going to have to make up her mind about what is more important to her—nursing or sports.'

These cases illuminate a problem common to us all: how to find time for running. I have a friend named Wolfgang, a tall, handsome publisher in his late thirties. He knows he is out of shape. He used to ski at weekends and, when he had time, run in a park near his home, but in recent years the pressures of a volatile business have kept him from exercising. Lamenting the condition he has fallen into, he once asked me what I thought he might do about it. When I suggested that he set aside half an hour a day for running a pained expression came over his face. 'I just don't have the time,' he sighed.

Whatever Wolfgang thinks, time isn't hard to find if you know where to look. Many busy and successful people run regularly. One thinks of the thousands of doctors, executives, financiers, lawyers, judges and others in posts of responsibility who would no more omit their daily run than neglect to brush their teeth. The trick lies in knowing where to ferret out the time. Each of us has a different schedule. It may be impossible to run at one time of day, much easier at another. The first step, therefore, is to make an honest appraisal of your day.

What if no part of your day is perfect for running? In this case, sacrifices are necessary—giving up part of the cocktail hour, perhaps, or getting up earlier than you really want to. You'll find that any inconveniences are thoroughly compensated for by the pleasure of running.

Most people, however, can easily avoid being seriously inconvenienced. Simply settle on the right time of day and then summon the will-power to get out of the door. Or pick different times from day to day, depending on your schedule. You're luckiest if you're a student. Just choose any time after lectures. For most of us, though, more planning is necessary.

The easiest time of day for running, the time least likely to be disrupted by unexpected intrusions, is early morning. All that's needed is to rise a bit earlier than usual. Even in winter there's a special joy in being out of doors at dawn, a peaceful sense of privacy found at no other time.

Some people, it goes without saying, don't like to get up early, not even for running. (Moreover some authorities feel that it's physiologically better to run later in the day.) If you're in that category, try to fit it in at lunchtime. Changing clothes in your office or car may be inconvenient, but it's nothing compared with the greater inconvenience of not running at all.

Running after work has distinct advantages, and is my favourite time. It's the best time to sweep the day's tensions away. Furthermore, as mentioned in Chapter 6, exercise diminishes your appetite and keeps you from eating too much dinner. There's no reason, by the way, not to run in the dark as long as the footing is good and you wear clothing that can easily be seen by motorists.

Or if your office is a convenient distance from your house, why not run to and from work? Many people fit in their running this way. Given the slowness of rush-hour traffic, it can take practically no extra time. Jerry Mahrer, a schoolteacher, runs the five miles from his home to his job and back again. Ted Corbitt, the former Olympic marathoner, runs to and from his office. 'I've adjusted my route to make it as traffic-free as possible,' he says; 'to cut down on pollution I pick the streets that have the least traffic.'

Another way to fit running into your life is by being alert to every opportunity for it. When you take your car in for servicing, for example, run home from the garage. Run to and from the post office as well, or when you pay a casual visit on a friend. Bill Rodgers wears running shoes much of the time so that he can break into a run whenever he wants to. So do I.

If you're responsible for the daily care of young children, finding time for running is likely to be especially difficult, but it's seldom impossible. 'It is common,' writes Kathryn Lance, 'for women runners to stop running altogether, or to cut back considerably on their time or mileage, as soon as they become mothers.' Try not to. Perhaps you can run when it's convenient for your husband to look after the children. Or hire a babysitter; it's worth the cost. Or search out another runner and take turns looking after the children. Martin Hyman told me, 'I once called on a friend to go for a woodland interval session, but his wife had gone out and left him babysitting. So we took the baby with us to do interval circuit training alternately while the other watched the baby.'

Certain circumstances put a special strain on even the most dedicated runners. Business trips are one. When you're away from home it sometimes seems as if there's no time for even a short run. If, as sometimes happens, you find yourself being entertained far into the night, to face an early-morning alarm clock isn't appealing. I've found, though, that there's one period of the day when I can usually slip a run invisibly into my schedule—the hour or so before dinner. Meetings tend to break up about five o'clock and dinner is commonly scheduled for seven. Some people go to their rooms for a bath and a rest; others gather for a drink or two. That's the time to go running. The chances are that you won't even be missed, but if your disappearance will be noticed and commented upon, don't hesitate to announce, 'Well, time for a little jog.' People will admire you for it.

An incidental semantic point: although for convenience we have agreed in this book to call all running, no matter at what speed, running rather than jogging, it's more tactful to refer to it as jogging when you're with non-runners. 'Jogging' sounds less arrogant. Even if you've just returned from a two-hour bout of interval training that has turned your legs to tapioca, refer to it as a 'little jog'. Why rile people for no reason?

On holidays, running is both a pleasure and a problem. First of all, it is a way of doing some sightseeing. But fitting in a run when you're on holiday can be difficult, especially if you wait until the end of the day. You're likely to be tired then, and eager to settle down in a warm bath or pub. Furthermore, unknown footing may make it hazardous to run in the dark. The best solution is to run early in the day. It's always possible to be surprised. In England one of the pleasantest runs I ever had was after dark in Weston-super-Mare. My wife and I had been driving all day and I felt tired. Our hotel, a vast Victorian place of towers and turrets, was on the waterfront. Outside our window, to my delight, was a two-mile-long lighted promenade. I got into my running clothes and went out. It was a mild evening and the scent of salt-water hung in the air. Suddenly I felt better, and I ran lightly and easily. A dentist from Scotland, who had recently established an office in Weston-super-Mare, was also running, and we ran together for a while. In an hour I was my old self.

Don't always wait until nightfall, though, because you can't count on being as lucky as I was that time. If you have any doubt about what the day is going to be like, run early.

12 · Gear

What to wear,
no matter what the weather

One of the nicest bonuses in running is that you need so little equipment. A pair of shoes and the right clothes to keep you warm when it's cold, and cool when it's hot, are practically all you need. Yet dressing properly is more involved than it may seem at first because there's a lot to learn about the body's behaviour under varying conditions. I had been running for five or six years before I finally learned how to dress in winter, and I made the discovery by accident after someone gave me a paper-thin nylon jacket that repels wind better than all the sweaters, coats and track-suits I had ever tried.

This illustrated probably the most important lesson in dressing for running: common sense doesn't necessarily help. For example, in winter you'll feel comfortable if you dress more lightly than common sense would suggest. (The heat your body generates is the equivalent of a lot of heavy clothing.) Hence, even though you've been choosing your clothes for most of your life and doing very well at it, the notes in this chapter may spare you years of trial and error.

The main principles are simple. To start with, it doesn't matter what you look like. Dress as expensively or as cheaply as you like. Cut-off jeans and an old sweater are fine. The only important point is to surround your body with as hospitable an environment as possible. Think of one of those wonderful spring days when the temperature is 55°F or so, a light breeze is playing with the leaves, the sun is out to warm you, and the young grass is springy underfoot. On such a day the best way to run would be naked. There's nothing that clothes could provide that nature hasn't already given you. On a cooler day, however, you need to give nature some help. And always, cold or hot, you need to have the right shoes on your feet.

Because running is such an individual matter, what works for 99% of the people may not work for you. So treat the observations that follow as guidelines, not gospel. If one suggestion seems sensible, try it. If it doesn't work, or doesn't work as well as you'd like, try something else. When I started running, I saw a lot of runners wearing sweatbands, so after sweat had dripped into my eyes a few times I went out and bought one. I didn't like it. I couldn't get over the feeling that my head was in an iron maiden, so I stopped wearing it, reasoning that I'd rather get sweat in my eyes than have my brains squeezed. Sweat bothers me only part of the time; the sweatband bothered me all the time.

Here, then, from the ground up, is a primer on running gear. All but a few of its suggestions are applicable to women as well as to men.

Shoes

Think what you are asking your feet to do when you run. In fact, the remarkable thing is that you can run at all. Each shoe lands on the ground 1000 or so times a mile. In a ten-mile run, that's 10 000 times. That's quite a pounding, and it doesn't stop at your feet, either. The impact of those 10 000 jolts is carried through your feet to your ankles, knees, hips and spine. If you're not wearing the right shoes, your chances of having trouble, either with your feet or somewhere else, are greatly increased.

Tennis or basketball shoes aren't sturdy enough and don't give your feet enough support. If I didn't have any *bona fide* running shoes and wanted to go out right now, I wouldn't hesitate to run a mile or two in tennis shoes, or even, for that matter, in street shoes, but I wouldn't do it regularly. It's worth the expense—anywhere from £5 to £25—to own real running shoes. First, they treat your feet properly. Second, lacing on your running shoes brings a welcome psychological lift. Even if you feel sluggish, putting on a familiar pair of shoes makes you feel like running. It may sound strange, but it works.

For training, that is, for everyday running rather than racing, most runners like shoes with well-padded soles. The cushioning shouldn't be too soft, though. If you can compress it easily with gentle pressure, it's not firm enough. If, on the other hand, a shoe is stiff and feels unyielding when you stamp on the floor, the padding is too hard. Look for padding that's firm but gives a little. The shoes I've found best have a fairly hard sole with a layer of soft cushioning between it and the foot.

A running shoe should be flexible, especially at the ball of the foot where it bends as you push off with each stride. If it doesn't flex easily enough you'll be using unnecessary effort and putting needless stress on your legs. Before you buy a shoe, bend it. If it takes a lot of pressure, choose another pair. If you already own shoes that are too stiff, you can limber them up by cutting three or four slits across the soles where you want them to bend.

A stable heel is important. Look for one that's wide enough to provide a good foundation when your foot lands, though one doctor I know suggests avoiding the widely-flared heels that have recently become fashionable. Compare shoes, and don't buy any that have noticeably narrow heels. Also, most runners feel that the heel should be built up somewhat higher than the ball of the foot since that's the way street shoes are made. The theory is that you don't want to strain your feet, in particular the Achilles tendons, by putting them into something radically different. I'm not so sure; I wear running shoes that have practically no heels. But I usually wear fairly flat street shoes, so maybe my feet are used to them.

Don't worry about the weight of a training shoe. A couple of ounces one way or the other aren't going to make much difference. What is important is that your feet be protected from road shock. Some people wear heavy shoes when they train and lighter ones when they race, in order to cut down on weight when they're looking for speed, but many runners wear the same shoe for both training and racing.

A few years ago most running shoes were made of leather. Now almost all of them consist mainly of nylon, which dries quickly and doesn't need much breaking in. If you choose a nylon shoe, be sure to buy one that's firm where it grips your heel; that's where support and rigidity are particularly necessary.

Good shoes are made by all the major manufacturers: Adidas, Gola, Laws, New Balance, Tiger, Reebok, Puma and so forth. But don't just take a salesman's word about what you need; carefully check any shoe you're thinking of buying.

Many brands of running shoes have become absurdly expensive. You can save money by shopping around. For example, a shoe called Inter, made in Taiwan, can be bought for half the price of one leading brand. And shops such as Lillywhites in Piccadilly Circus have a wide range of running shoes at a similarly wide range of prices. The Sweat Shop, in Teddington, not only stocks all the chief brands of shoe but has its own strip of tartan track so you can see how yours will feel when you run in them.

If you must save money, do so by wearing cut-off blue jeans instead of running shorts, or a worn-out shirt with the sleeves cut off instead of a T-shirt. But please *don't try to save money on shoes.*

Pay particular attention to how the shoe fits. Running shoes should be a bit snugger than street shoes, but they shouldn't pinch or cramp your toes and shouldn't let your foot slide forward so your toes can jam against the front. And it goes without saying that if you're going to be wearing socks when you run (see below), you should wear them when you try shoes on. The Dr Moe mentioned earlier has passed along a clever trick for making shoes fit well. 'I take a short pair of laces,' he says, 'and lace up the toe of the shoe for maybe four sets of eyelets, and tie that. Then I take another short pair and go up the rest of the way. I can then adjust the fit of the toes as loosely as I want to, while using the upper set of laces to clamp the foot firmly. I've been lacing my shoes this way for over a year with good success.' An English doctor told me he thought this a particularly good idea since it allows shoes to be, in effect, custom-fit.

No matter how well running shoes fit, break them in before you race or take a long run in them. I always start wearing a new pair before the old ones are completely worn out. In this way I can shift over gradually from one to the other. The first time I wear a pair of new shoes I run only three or four miles; then I switch back to my old ones for a day or two. Soon I start taking longer runs in the new pair and wearing the old ones less. By the time the old shoes are close to tatters, the new ones are well broken in and my feet are used to them. Such a cautious introduction may not be necessary if you don't run more than a mile or so a day, but if you're going to be running further, especially in anything like a marathon, it is essential.

The care of shoes isn't complicated. If they get wet, let them dry slowly (not over heat) with crumpled newspaper in them. If, after a few hundred miles of running, your nylon shoes begin to smell, just toss them into the washing machine. If the uppers are all leather, you're stuck with the smell; but washing doesn't seem to hurt the little incidental patches of leather on nylon shoes. They get a bit stiff when they dry, but they limber up as soon as you run in them.

A note on spikes: not long after I started running I bought a pair of shoes with spikes, thinking they'd make me faster when I ran on cinder tracks. They didn't. Unless you specialize in the 100-metre sprint, the only thing spikes will do is make it more probable that your foot will catch on something and cause an injury.

Socks

Some runners wear socks; others don't. One tireless theoretician of our sport, Charles Steinmetz, thinks running sockless is better because of the weight it saves when your feet get wet, but you should do whatever is most comfortable. For what it's worth, I like the feeling of having my feet in direct touch with my shoes, although the advantage may be entirely in my mind. Whatever the truth of the matter, I've run dozens of marathons sockless and haven't had any trouble. The only exception is in warm, sunny weather when dark pavements become blisteringly hot. If the heat is intense enough—and in Britain this isn't often—it comes right through the soles of your shoes and makes you uncomfortable. In such a situation, running through a stream or puddle, if you're lucky enough to find one, helps, although some runners think wet feet are more likely to cause blisters.

If you decide to wear socks, choose cotton or wool ones. Nylon can tear your skin. If you want to keep weight to a minimum, tennis anklets, which are made of cotton, are a good idea. One runner I know advocates the use of cushion-sole socks advertised as 'golf socks'.

Shorts

I find nylon shorts, the kind that are slit up the side, best in hot weather. They're light and cool, and they dry quickly when they get wet. I know runners who insist on cotton because it absorbs sweat and allows for evaporation. In weather that is cool but not brisk enough for long trousers, cotton shorts will give you a touch of warmth. But compared to nylon shorts, they seem to me both stiff and heavy. Some runners sew a little three-by-three-inch pocket on the front of their shorts for carrying toilet paper and so forth.

Long trousers

When it gets really cold, you need something to protect your legs. You'll be surprised, though, at how cold it can get before you have to switch from shorts to long trousers. I run in shorts until it gets close to the freezing point. Then I wear a pair of black leotards under my cotton shorts. These cut the force of the wind and keep out some of the cold; furthermore, the dark colour helps soak up any available sunshine. It's a good idea to avoid track-suit trousers whenever you can. They're heavy, bulky and floppy and will do nothing for your running, especially if they get wet. Wear them only as a last resort in the worst weather. When conditions are severe but not truly terrible, an orienteering suit is a good compromise; it's so light you won't even notice it.

Supports

If you're a woman you don't have this problem, but if you're a man you have to decide whether to wear a jockstrap or jockey shorts. Try jockey shorts first. If they don't give enough support, switch to a jockstrap. If you decide on a jockstrap, pick one with as narrow a waistband as possible to prevent curling—an inch is about right—and choose nylon; it dries faster than cotton.

Shirts

When the temperature is about 21°C (70°F) the shirt question is simple for men: don't wear one. You'll keep cooler and feel more comfortable without a shirt. (There's nothing like a soaked T-shirt clinging to your skin to make you wish you were doing something else.) If you don't feel right going out in public with no shirt on, try wearing a string vest, the kind with just straps instead of sleeves. High-quality ones are available at sports shops, but you can find perfectly good ones in the underwear sections of most department stores. To make them cooler some people cut lots of holes in their running shirts or snip off the bottom part. A specially designed I.A.A.F.-approved string vest is also available, and the Sweat Shop sells an excellent lightweight garment called a 'Lifa' T-shirt. It comes from Norway and is used by Scandinavian athletes.

As the temperature gets cooler, you'll want to put more on your upper body. The secret is to dress in several layers. When it gets really cold, a light jacket will keep you warm no matter what the weather outside. I have an old wool sweater that I put on over my T-shirt when conditions become severe. With a track-suit top over it and my nylon outshirt over that, I have four layers on, each with its cushion of warm air. Some runners recommend turtleneck sweaters because they minimize heat loss from the carotid arteries.

Gloves

During my first winter of running I bought a pair of leather ski mittens, reckoning to put an impermeable barrier between my hands and the cold air. My idea didn't work. After a few minutes of running my hands were swimming in sweat because there was no way for moisture to get out. What I needed was something that would breathe. Wool gloves or mittens are fine, but I like white cotton gardening gloves best; when they're dirty toss them into the washing machine along with your other clothes. (Wash all your running clothes often and thoroughly. Nothing will chap you faster than dirty, sweat-soaked clothes.) Some people are convinced that mittens or old socks keep you warmer than gloves, but I haven't noticed any difference.

Hats

Quite a bit of body heat escapes through your head, so what you wear there matters. In the summer some runners wear a painter's cap for protection. This may be a good idea if you're bald or your hair is thin, but if you have plenty of hair I think it's better not to wear anything. After all, you want to let the heat escape from your head as easily as possible, and a cap doesn't help.

When it's really cold, hats serve a different purpose; they help keep your body heat in. Then they're essential, especially if you're going to be running for a long time. What I've found best is a simple wool hat, the kind sailors call a watch cap. If it's not very cold you can wear it turned up and let your ears stick out. When it's really freezing, you just roll it down and feel snug.

When it's sunny some runners wear sunglasses or visors, the kind that are held on by a headband. To me, visors don't seem necessary, though they do keep the sun out of your eyes and prevent long hair from flopping around.

Masks

I once met a runner who insisted we all ought to wear masks to filter dirt particles out of the air. He wore one whenever he ran, and he used to delight in showing people how dirty it got. What was caught by the mask, he pointed out, didn't get into his lungs. Somehow the idea has never caught on, but if you run in a particularly polluted area you might consider it.

Night running

If you run at night it's important to be seen easily, so don't wear dark clothes. After you're dressed, put a white T-shirt on over everything else, or get a reflective vest; they are available from sports shops that deal in running equipment.

Some runners attach strips of reflective tape to their shoes to catch the attention of motorists. As you try different techniques to make yourself more visible, you'll quickly learn which works best. Cars will swerve the moment drivers spot you, and how early they swerve indicates how clearly you are being seen. If they don't swerve until they're five yards away, you need a different wardrobe and up-to-date insurance. *But whatever you wear, run facing traffic so you'll be able to see cars coming and take evasive action.*

Other equipment

One of the few other things you may eventually want is a stopwatch. Every once in a while it's interesting to time yourself over a familiar course. You don't have to run at top speed; simply run the course a bit harder than usual. With training your times will come down.

A watch is also useful if you do a lot of running in unfamiliar places, on business trips, say, or while you're on holiday. With a watch, you'll have some idea of how far you've gone.

You can, of course, use an ordinary wristwatch, but if you're racing it's helpful to have what's known as a chronograph. A chronograph has a regular watch dial and two or three small ones that together keep track of elapsed time. It's the only practical way of computing your pace accurately at mile checkpoints. Calculating becomes increasingly difficult as you get tired, as you will in a long race, but with a little practice you'll be able to multiply 17 by $7\frac{1}{2}$ right up to the moment of exhaustion.

Some runners always take along a few sheets of toilet paper for emergency use. And it's a good idea, too, to have a coin in case you pull a muscle and have to phone home.

There's one other category of equipment you'll need from time to time: medical gear such as elastoplast, Vaseline, skin toughener and liniment. But there's no need to stock them in advance; wait till you need them.

13 · Coping

What to do about rain, hail, snow, cars, dogs and other vexations

In the high reaches of some mountain ranges, where the air is so cold that few animals can survive, specially adapted species of insects live in a micro-environment, a thin layer of sun-warmed air that covers their rocky dwelling-place like a skin. A quarter of an inch above those balmy rocks they would perish, but within that warmed skin they live as contentedly as tourists in the Bahamas. Some of the special pleasures of running come when we, too, inhabit our own micro-environment. It is a joy to run in bracing cold, wind, snow, and rain in comfort. Part of the pleasure comes from being out in weather that has driven the faint-hearted indoors. Part also comes from learning how, in foul weather, to create a micro-environment that makes conditions next to your skin no more blustery than those in your living-room.

Running is most fun when you do it every day, or with only an occasional day off. There is a feeling of self-mastery in setting forth no matter what the weather. One's spirits receive a particular lift when ingenuity has been required. Some people are easily dissuaded from running. Nightfall, cold, heat, rain or a few snowflakes dissolve their will-power. Yet there are few conditions under which it is impossible to run in comfort. Where I live the winters are harsh. Once I ran in a blizzard so severe I could hardly push my door open against the wind. I was nearly blown off my feet on the icy roads. Yet within a few minutes, despite icicles on my eyebrows, I was sweating pleasantly and feeling fine. It was fun knowing that though an improperly dressed person would quickly have developed frostbite, my tracksuit, wool hat, gloves and nylon jacket turned the air next to my skin into a balmy summer day.

Cold

Although it sometimes seems unpleasant, even extreme cold isn't much of a problem. With a little experience and some attention to the suggestions in Chapter 12 you'll find it easy to dress comfortably in any weather. In fact, the chief problem is to avoid *over*-dressing. When a blizzard is howling it's hard to restrain yourself from putting on an extra sweatshirt or a pair of heavy ski mittens. If you dress lightly you may, it's true, feel chilly when you first step out of doors, but within a few minutes you'll find yourself sweating as if you were in a tropical rain forest. Experiments by Canada's National Research Council show that the amount of clothing needed to keep a resting person comfortably warm at 70°F (21°C) will keep a runner warm at −5°.

The key to winter dressing, therefore, is to wear as little as you can—just enough to keep you pleasantly warm. After a while you'll be surprised to discover how few clothes you need. This is a good thing, too, because extra clothes weigh you down and make running more difficult. But be careful on days when the weather may worsen during your run. If it turns cold when you're a long way from home you may be in for some real discomfort. Stephen Richardson suggests that in changeable weather you take along a nylon jacket. Such garments are light enough to be stowed in a pocket or tied around your waist, yet can give a lot of protection.

To minimize the effect of evaporative cooling, plan your run so that you're running to windward as you start and downwind as you finish. Even in extremely cold weather it's astonishing how pleasantly warm you can feel while running downwind, and (see the table on page 137 how cold you can feel when you're running into the wind.

Dressing for winter running is easy if you understand how the body protects itself from the cold. The first priority of its regulating mechanisms is to keep the head and torso warm. If excessive cooling there becomes a problem, your body sends these parts of your anatomy extra heat, even at the expense of your fingers and toes. If, on the other hand, all's well with your head and torso, any spare heat will be available to be sent elsewhere. The lesson is clear: always dress so that your head and torso are warm. Wear a heavy wool hat and enough clothes to protect your chest, stomach and back.

Dr William Kaufman of the University of Wisconsin conducted an experiment that neatly demonstrated the body's system of priorities. When he exposed volunteers to cold he found that as long as their torsos were warm enough, no matter how cold their fingers and toes became, they didn't shiver. But when he kept their fingers and toes warm and let their torsoes get cold, they started shivering. This is the body's way of forcing itself to work, burn calories, and thereby create heat.

Rain

One day while I was running it began to pour. It was a warm day, and even though I was quickly soaked I was happy and comfortable. A car pulled up alongside me and the driver rolled a window down. 'Want a lift?' he called. I thanked him and waved him on. 'You'll get soaked!' he insisted. When I finally explained that I enjoyed the rain, he shook his head and drove off.

Rain is not usually a difficulty. On a hot day you'll be grateful for it. It's only when the temperature drops below 55°F (13°C) or so that you'll want to protect yourself from it. A light rain jacket is usually enough.

Snow

Running in the snow is a wonderful experience. When there's a thin sprinkling on the ground you'll feel as if you're running in a Christmas card. It's only when the snow gets deeper that it will bother you, and then only because you won't be able to maintain your usual pace. Don't try; accept conditions as they are. Because you'll be working harder you'll get just as much exercise going slowly. Instead of counting miles, count minutes. If you ordinarily run for half an hour, do that and no more. What does it matter if you don't cover as much ground?

Ice

Running on ice is tricky. Especially on wet ice, it's easy to slip and pull a muscle. Avoid it if you can. If there's ice on the roads in the morning, wait for cars to wear it away; it may be gone by later in the day. Better still, find a place that isn't icy, perhaps a snowy path or field. I've never tried it myself, but I've heard of people running along the covered pavements of shopping centres. I recently talked with a runner who sometimes wore crampons of the type used by mountain climbers, and I once met a woman who said she used spiked running shoes when it was icy. The trouble with such devices is that when you come to bare road they jar your legs and set up an annoying clatter. Probably the best solution is to use an indoor track until the weather eases up.

Hail

If it begins to hail while you're running, common sense is the most reliable guide. When hailstones are small and don't threaten your life, health or equanimity, press on. When they get big enough to hurt you, take cover. Fortunately, hailstones of that size are rare. I've been in perhaps a dozen hailstorms and have never had to stop running, though I've come close to it.

Wind

You'll be aware of wind whenever it's blowing at eight to ten miles an hour. If you're running against it, it will slow you down and make you feel sluggish. Don't let it bother you. Act exactly as you do when you're slowed by snow; simply accept the fact that you can't move as fast as usual. Put your head down, lean into it, work your arms energetically and make the best of it. If you're in a race, you can console yourself with the thought that everyone else is running under the same handicap. (But for a way to minimize the effect of wind, see Chapter 17.)

If the wind is at your back, enjoy it. It will make running easier, lengthen your stride and feel like a friendly hand pushing you along. The 1975 Boston Marathon was run in a blustery tail-wind, and all of us, including the winner, Bill Rodgers, were cheered on by it.

Wind is a problem only in low temperatures. Because of the wind-chill factor, a given temperature feels colder than in still weather. In a 20-mile-an-hour wind, for example, a temperature of 13°C feels like zero. When it's windy, the severity of cold increases more than you might imagine. The table shows how winds of various speeds lower the apparent temperature.

Air temperature °F	Apparent temperature at given wind speeds			
	10 mph	20 mph	30 mph	40 mph
+50°	40°	32°	28°	26°
+30°	18°	4°	−2°	−6°
+20°	4°	−10°	−18°	−21°
+10°	−9°	−25°	−33°	−37°
0°	−21°	−30°	−48°	−53°
−10°	−33°	−53°	−63°	−69°
−20°	−46°	−67°	−79°	−85°

Heat

Of all the circumstances under which you'll run, hot weather is the most hazardous. This is particularly true in Britain, where runners have little experience with extreme heat and where the most experienced runners sometimes dress too heavily. Even in cool weather a runner generates enormous quantities of heat as a by-product of his metabolism—up to 30 times the amount produced at rest. This is easily dissipated through the skin when the surrounding air is cool. But running in hot weather is different. Because heat does not leave the body as easily, your body temperature increases, and there is the possibility, especially if you persist in running hard, that it will rise to the danger point—104°F (40°C) or so.

Fortunately, because the body operates best within a narrow temperature range, it goes to great lengths to maintain the correct balance of heat and cold. Experiments have shown that an unclothed person who is relaxing feels most comfortable at a temperature of 85°F (30°C) or so. If the temperature rises three or four degrees above this, the body activates its heat-regulating mechanisms. First, the skin's blood vessels enlarge in order to allow warm blood to flow from the interior and thus let heat escape into the air. (This accounts for the flushed look people sometimes get in warm weather.) Second, the heart rate and blood flow increase, turning the skin's blood vessels into more effective radiators.

If those mechanisms are enough to keep the body temperature stable, nothing more happens. But assume that the air temperature continues to rise. Now the body calls upon its reserves: sweat. The sweat glands wet the body with as much as three quarts an hour in extreme heat, and under most circumstances this evaporation is enough to keep body temperature within its proper range.

But not always. A person exercising heavily, as in running, has special problems in hot weather. If the body's thermo-regulatory mechanisms can't keep the temperature low enough two conditions may result. In order of seriousness they are:

1. **Heat Exhaustion.** This is brought on partly by fluid loss (the result of sweating), and partly by the fact that the body's cooling system has sent so much of its blood supply to the skin. The correspondingly decreased flow of blood to the brain can produce confusion or even unconsciousness. Heat exhaustion thus acts much like a circuit-breaker, usually preventing the second, more serious stage.

2. **Heat stroke.** In heat stroke the body's temperature is extremely high—commonly 110°F (43°C)—and the skin is usually (though not always) hot and dry. Other symptoms are dizziness,

vomiting, diarrhoea and confusion. Immediate attention by a doctor
is extremely important.

For heat exhaustion, administer salt water, half a glass every fifteen
minutes for an hour; lie the sufferer down and raise his feet eight to
twelve inches; loosen his clothing; and cool his body with wet cloths
and by fanning. In the event of heat stroke, call for an ambulance at
once. Body temperature must immediately be lowered with cool
water or rubbing alcohol, or by putting the victim into a tub of cold
water. Prompt medical care is imperative, followed probably by
hospitalization.

Another heat-related problem, **dehydration**, is dangerous because
the body is so dependent on water. Its chemical reactions take place
in water. The substances bound for the body's various parts are
water-borne, and water is crucial in keeping body temperature stable
in hot weather. If exercise doesn't last long, dehydration isn't
normally a problem. If exercise continues, however, it can cause 1) a
loss of water from the bloodstream; 2) a disturbance in the concentration of certain substances in the blood and cells; 3) heat exhaustion.

There are several steps you can take to minimize the likelihood of
developing the foregoing problems.
  First, wait until you're used to the heat before training hard. It
takes from seven to fourteen days to become acclimatized to hot
weather. During this time the heart rate decreases, sweating increases
but becomes less salty and starts earlier. The most effective way to
acclimatize yourself to heat is gradually to train more intensively
each day. Once you're used to running in the heat, acclimatization
lasts about two weeks.
  Drink lots of water while you're exercising. It used to be considered unwise to drink while training. Recent studies have shown
that athletes, including runners, function best when allowed to drink
whenever they want to. A 5% drop in body weight can reduce
efficiency by 15%, and 6% is about the maximum you can comfortably tolerate. To compensate in advance for fluid losses, some
authorities recommend drinking *before* you train. The reason is that
our bodies can absorb liquids only half as fast as we sweat them out
on a hot day.
  Dress lightly. (Even a T-shirt covers some 40% of the body.) Wear
light-coloured clothes to reflect the sun.

Help your sweating mechanism by dousing yourself with water whenever you can. On warm days I often run along a river. If I feel hot I stop and wet myself down. In a race, if you're handed more water than you can drink at once, drink what you can and pour the rest on your body. If you do, you'll notice an immediate improvement in your running ability, although some runners find that if their feet get wet they are more susceptible to blisters. Dr R. P. Clark of the National Institute for Medical Research in London has found that of all parts of a runner's body the thighs heat up the most.

Warm up as briefly as possible. As pointed out previously, warming up increases the body's heat, and extra heat is certainly not what you need. (One study showed, incidentally, that long hair, even as long as shoulder-length, doesn't affect an athlete's ability either to withstand heat or to recover from its effects.)

A brief but comprehensive summary of these suggestions is sent to competitors in the Boston Marathon, which starts at noon. Part of a sheet entitled 'Medical Facts You Should Know' reads as follows:

Heat Problems: These occur when it is hot or muggy or both and result from dehydration, loss of salt, and rise in body temperature to dangerous levels. To prevent this, try to train for a week in warm weather; on the day of the race salt your breakfast heavily and/or have a cup or two of very salty broth *no later than 10.00 a.m.* (salt tablets prior to competition can induce nausea). Drink about two or three ounces of water at every refreshment station along the race course. *Don't* wait until you're thirsty because then may be too late.

Not all people are equally troubled by heat. Some runners seem to have a sort of immunity to it and run well even in midsummer, while others are slowed appreciably on the first warm day. Your ability to tolerate heat depends partly on your size. A heavy person is at a disadvantage in heat because, pound for pound, the skin has less heat-dissipating surface.

Humidity

Humidity compounds the difficulties runners experience in heat. When the relative humidity is 100%, no sweat evaporation occurs. Under such circumstances the body will heat up badly. You can use a wet-bulb thermometer to tell how severe a problem humidity is; a reading above 70° means that competition will be difficult. A wet-bulb temperature of 80° is pretty much the upper limit for athletic activity, however light.

Lightning

Once in a while you'll get caught in a thunderstorm. If you can, get inside a building or a car. If you can't, stay away from water, ridges and solitary trees, and don't touch metal. Get into a hollow or ditch and crouch down, under cover if possible—unless it's wet there. If

your hair stands on end, an electrical charge is building up nearby and there's danger of a lightning strike. The best thing to do, according to the latest word from the International Commission on Atmospheric Electricity, is to kneel down, press your knees and feet together, put your hands on your knees, and bend far forward to make your body as unlike a lightning rod as possible.

And, perhaps the commission should have added, Pray. Once, near the summit of a mountain, my wife and children and I were caught in a thunderstorm as we hiked on a trail that snaked its way along a ridge. At one point our hair stood on end and Saint Elmo's fire danced on the metal frames of our rucksacks. We got off the ridge in a hurry.

Sand, Slush and Mud

All three will slow you down. As there's not much you can do about them, be stoical.

Sand is annoying when it gets into your shoes. If you're running on a beach, you may be more comfortable running barefoot; it's no trouble to carry your shoes, one in each hand. Whenever you can, land on patches of seaweed (watching out for jellyfish); you'll sink in less and have more secure traction.

As for slush, it's chiefly a nuisance, not a danger. When you run your feet keep working so hard that even severe cold usually won't hurt them. They may feel numb for a while after you get back home, but soon they'll come tingling back to life, ready to take you dancing all night. The chief problem with slush is the cars that splash it all over your body. There's nothing like a faceful of the stuff to take the fun out of a winter's day.

I find it hard to say anything good about mud. It makes you slip, gets your clothes dirty, and, should you fall down in it, subjects you to the merry laughter of your companions. Stay out of it if you can, and be careful if you can't. For running over the muddy English countryside, especially in winter, you'll find studded running shoes a great help.

Rough terrain

Uneven ground—forest trails and rocky paths, for example—are no problem if you don't run on them for too long at a time. If you put in a lot of mileage on uneven ground, the stabilizing muscles of your legs tire, and this increases the chances that you'll twist an ankle or fall. Take rough terrain in small doses. Be particularly careful not to step in a hole, trip on a fallen branch, stub your toe against a rock, or slip on wet leaves. One doctor I spoke with recommends having a tetanus injection to preclude the possibility of contracting tetanus should you fall.

Hills

When I first started running I considered hills my enemy. They were hard to run, made me slow down and shorten my stride, and left me winded. But it finally occurred to me that if hills were hard to run on, they might be doing me some good. And so they were. Running uphill strengthens the quadriceps, increases cardio-respiratory capacity and makes it easier to run uphill the next time. You can't, of

course, run uphill as fast as you can downhill; that's simply one of the things runners learn to accept.

When you come to a hill, start climbing at a pace you think you can sustain. (It's discouraging to start out fast, then have to fade to a walk.) Lean forward, shorten your steps and swing your arms parallel to your direction of movement as if you were a steam locomotive, rather than across your body. Think of uphill running as changing gears. You want to cultivate an efficient style, one that gives plenty of power for overcoming gravity; speed can wait until you reach the top. Then you can celebrate by letting yourself fly. In a race, however, don't go downhill at a flat-out pace. You'll tire more than you think, and be half dead when you reach the bottom.

Darkness

Most of us do at least some of our running in the dark, either in the early morning or at the end of the day. There's nothing to it if you observe a few simple rules:

1. Run facing the traffic and stay close to the edge of the road. If a car should look threatening, simply step off the road. Of course, there are hazards in leaving the road for the dark unknown—ankles have been broken this way—but it's an easy choice, considering the alternative.

2. Wear a reflective vest or at least light clothing. If you forget and go out in a dark-blue tracksuit, you'll notice a disturbing difference in how soon the cars veer away.

3. Run on roads you know well. Before you venture on to a road in the dark, survey it carefully to make sure it has no potholes or other booby traps.

4. Don't look directly at headlights: bright light temporarily blinds you. If, as frequently happens, a driver neglects to lower his lights, try to catch a glimpse of the road ahead and memorize its contours. Looking slightly away from light also helps to bring into play your less light-sensitive peripheral vision.

Fog

Running in fog is much like running in the dark, except that it rarely gets so thick you have trouble seeing the road ahead. But remember that in fog motorists can't see as well as usual, even in daylight.

Furthermore, because they're concentrating on driving, they may not be ready for the sudden materialization of a runner. Try to run on roads without much traffic, or on paths or pavements.

Don't wear grey in fog; you'll be invisible. Red and orange contrast well with fog.

Remember, too, that fog, especially near industrial plants, can be a distinct health hazard by contributing to respiratory disease. This is particularly true in middle-age.

Cars

Night or day, cars deserve caution. Few drivers will go out of their way to maim you—though it's not unknown*—but some seem to have only a vague sense of where they are on the road. As mentioned a moment ago, it's always important to face traffic but there is one exception to this: a sharp bend. On the inside of such a bend drivers can't see far ahead, so always run on the outside of it. The risk from traffic on the blind bend is greater than the risk from traffic behind you. Both dangers are minimized if you stay away from narrow roads.

Another automotive risk is breathing exhaust fumes. Harry Daniell has pointed out that carbon monoxide attaches itself to the blood's haemoglobin even more tightly than oxygen, and that, unlike carbon dioxide, it does not readily disappear but circulates in the bloodstream for some time. If, therefore, you run in an atmosphere heavy with carbon monoxide, the concentration in your blood increases. Furthermore, during a full eight hours of sleep only half the carbon monoxide in your body is expelled.

The moral is clear: run where there are as few exhaust fumes as possible. Even in cities you can usually find lightly travelled streets.

Dogs

Every runner has at least one dog story. Frances Goulart tells of a dog that bit her while she was running. The owner laughed and remarked, 'He only nipped you.' 'Nipped me!' said Mrs Goulart.

* One theory, enunciated persuasively by George Sheehan, is that runners are seen as a threat to society's prevailing values. Once you've had a beer can or two tossed in your direction it's difficult not to suspect that Sheehan is on to something.

'Look at my stomach! I'm bleeding.' Whereupon the owner laughed again. 'He was just playing,' he said.

Mrs Goulart's story illustrates a peculiarity of dog owners—their belief that a dog, no matter now murderous, is incapable of doing wrong. A few years ago I had some bad moments with a Great Dane in a public park near my house. In alarm I picked up a stick in order to hold the beast at bay. Its owner rushed over and ordered me to drop the stick.

'You're frightening my dog,' he said.

'Your dog is frightening me,' I replied, none too pleasantly. I was not at my cheerful best.

'Well, do your practising somewhere else,' he said. 'Tiny has as much right to be here as you have.'

In short, you can expect little sympathy from dog owners. Instead, you must learn to fend for yourself. There are several theories about how to do it. Over the years I have probably tried them all, and have discussed the subject with innumerable other runners and even with a running vet who offered some insights into canine psychology. Here, then, are the principal ways runners customarily deal with dogs:

The 'nice doggie' gambit.   In the belief that love really does conquer all, some runners try Christian charity by attempting to make friends with dogs. All that Christian charity does, I am sorry to say, is make an animal wonder what's wrong with you.

The Richardson riposte.   Stephen Richardson, a dog owner and close student of dogs, relies on an authoritative 'NO!' or 'GO HOME!' He says this always works, but then he's six foot three. I suspect that anything works when you look like Richardson.

The no-doggie ploy.   This one consists of simply ignoring the beast, and it doesn't work well. When a dog goes to the trouble of barking at you, it wants attention. It will become more menacing until it gets the audience reaction it feels it deserves.

The mad runner caper.   To execute this one, wait until a dog is close to you. Until this strategic moment, run as usual. When the dog is nearly upon you, turn, make a blood-curdling noise and flail your arms as if demented. Even a dog seriously bent on mischief will think twice about pursuing a relationship with so unpredictable a soul.

The bluff. Dogs naturally don't like to have things thrown at them. If, therefore, you bend down as if to pick up a rock—there doesn't actually have to be one handy—all but the boldest animal will retreat. If the menacing dog is one you pass often, tossing a real rock in its direction from time to time will suggest who's boss. It may continue to bark at you but will probably keep its distance. One runner I consulted takes even more extreme measures. He told me, 'I find that if you pretend to ignore dogs until the last moment—when they leap at you—and then kick them as hard as possible on the nose they will run away. A cool nerve and great accuracy are required, but this technique is effective.' Runners who have found it ineffective are, I suspect, not around to tell the tale.

My vet was able to shed some light on the reason for canine aggression. Dogs, he explained, are assiduous defenders of turf. They quickly learn their territorial limits and zealously guard their borders. If a passing runner shows no sign of threatening these borders, a dog will usually content itself with some harmless warning barks. Upon sighting a dog, the prudent runner should cross the street in order to avoid hallowed ground. But try not to act afraid. Dogs are extremely responsive to fear and only become more aggressive.

14 · Eating to run

Good news if you really love food

A few years ago, soon after I had started running, I yielded to temptation one day and ate an enormous lunch; two hamburgers, chips, and a milk shake. On the way home from work I cursed my lack of will power. I felt leaden and dreaded the terrible, plodding run I was sure I would have that evening. If I got through it at all, it would be on sheer doggedness; I was sure there would be no joy in it. Instead, it turned out to be one of the best runs I've ever had. My feet were feathers, in swift and subtle communion with asphalt, sand and grass.

Now consider another run. This time I was starved. I was training for a marathon and wanted to be light and lean. Even before setting out, I felt weak. Furthermore, the day was hot (in the nineties) and I remembered with no relish my last two runs in the same heat. Yet as I jogged down my drive searching for rhythm, I suddenly knew that this too was to be an extraordinary day. Unbothered by the heat, I moved easily along the sticky asphalt roads, feeling light, powerful, tireless. At a wooded seaside park three miles from my home I stopped for a drink of water, then went on, enjoying the sight of geese, rabbits and pheasants, and keeping an eye on the progress of a yacht making its way down the channel, parallel to my path. In the hills at the end of the run I finally tired a bit but felt no need to slow down.

One lesson to be drawn from these two almost identical runs in which my nutritional preparation was so different is that our bodies work in mysterious ways. Another is that nutrition isn't everything. You can try to improve your running by eating sensibly, and in the long run you'll probably have some success, but eating properly is no guarantee that any particular run or race is going to be a good one. There are too many other variables in the equation.

Even professional nutritionists find it hard to agree on matters you might suppose would be beyond debate. For example, is fasting a good idea for a runner? This would seem to be a fairly fundamental question, one long since answered, yet in *Food for Sport*, Dr Nathan Smith says: 'Now and then a question arises regarding the advantages of periodic fasting. Fasting limited to 24 or 48 hours need not be damaging to a healthy individual, but an athlete cannot expect to compete effectively if he is deprived of energy sources for such periods during his training. There is no evidence to suggest that periodic fasting provides any competitive advantage.' By contrast, *Food for Fitness* gives quite a different view: 'Many people undertaking fasts of several weeks or more mention feeling 'strong as steel', even increasing in strength during the late stages of not eating.' Plainly the truth is difficult to sort out. Dr John Williams, impatient with the whole fasting controversy, disposes of fasting for athletes with the single word: 'Rubbish.'

Two individuals may even respond differently to the same regimen, so each of us must discover how his or her own body works. Sir Roger Bannister, who ought to know, once said, 'What applies to one person doesn't necessarily apply to another. It's easy to build a whole mystique about diet and the pharmaceutical side of sport. There's no proof that special foods or extra vitamin supplements are necessary as long as people eat a normal, balanced diet. I think the essence of good performance is doing it the natural way.'

Yet in spite of all these caveats, there do seem to be a few general principles worth heeding, particularly in view of the fact that dietary deficiencies are surprisingly common.

Eating and drinking can be made into enterprises of incredible complexity, and this is particularly true of sports nutrition. Not long ago a group of researchers gathered in Leningrad for an international symposium on the nutrition of athletes. They came from England, Eastern Europe, Japan, Brazil, Cuba, the United States and many other countries. On and off the dais, they argued endlessly about nutritional matters so minute that you and I would consider them insignificant. But George Mann, a doctor who attended the conference, explained, 'When many competitors are very good and almost equal, attention turns to training factors that will give some small advantage.'

Average runners, and even most runners who are better than average, need no such knowledge of nutritional minutiae. We simply want some general information about how to eat sensibly. Since we're going to make so many deliberate mistakes anyway—a glass of beer here, a piece of cake there—it hardly makes sense to become fanatical about the subject. Hence, this chapter will only examine some of the generally accepted principles of athletic nutrition. It is written on the assumption that you have already been exposed to, or can easily find out about, everyday nutritional rules. After all, you got this far on your own.

To start with, one notion should be cleared out of the way. Some people persist in thinking there are certain 'miracle foods'. There aren't. *Nutrition and Physical Fitness*, a classic in the field, by Jean Bogert and others, puts it this way: 'A good diet—one based on meat, milk, fish, poultry and eggs, whole grain cereals, legumes and nuts, leafy green vegetables, and other vegetables and fruits—will meet all the nutritional requirements of athletes. Vitamin pills and special supplements are not needed and should not be relied upon because they may lull the individual into thinking he has met his nutritional needs when in reality he may still be lacking in protein and minerals.' Dr Thomas Bassler of the American Medical Joggers Association says, 'We do not endorse the use of any specific foods or diet supplements. Avoiding highly refined foods is recommended; sucrose, starch, saturated fats, and distilled alcohol.' Otherwise, Bassler says, a normal, well-balanced diet containing fresh fruit, raw vegetables and not too much meat is best.

Not every athlete agrees. Some top British long-distance runners, Ron Hill and Jos Naylor among them, are advocates of the notorious 'jam butty' diet—a high concentration of refined sugar in the jam and plenty of white flour in the bread. They have, it is true, at least a partial nutritional justification for the practice, for there are not, of course, really any such thing as 'health foods' even though we label some foods thus. A container of fruit-flavoured yogurt, for example, often considered a health food, contains some 250 calories, as many as you'd find in the same amount of ice cream. Still, if it makes you feel better to buy food at so-called health food stores, there's no reason not to. There's probably something to be said for avoiding the pesticides, herbicides and fungicides that go into so much of what we eat nowadays. But in a nutritional sense health foods and ordinary foods work in exactly the same way.

For many years it was thought that athletes needed more protein than other people. Nutritionists now agree that they don't. What you *do* need more of, particularly before a run lasting over an hour, is carbohydrates. The reason lies in the body's way of converting the chemical energy in food into mechanical energy. The process is somewhat complicated—complicated enough, in fact, that if you think about its details while running you're likely to worry yourself into inertia beside the road. Whole books have been written on the subject. (One of the briefest and best is E. C. Frederick's *The Running Body*.) For practical purposes you'll know enough if you simply remember that protein, important as it is for other reasons, doesn't count for much in energy production. Studies have shown that diets low in carbohydrates and high in fats markedly reduce energy, while the opposite diet—high carbohydrate, low fat—increases energy. One reason is that about 10% less oxygen is needed to metabolize a given unit of carbohydrate energy. Another is that a high carbohydrate diet can pack the muscles with more than their customary amount of glycogen, the substance which, once the body converts it into glucose, is oxidized and turned to energy.

All this doesn't mean that you will gain anything but weight by *over*eating carbohydrates. What it does mean is that when you are choosing food, it's better to lean towards carbohydrates than fats. One day I stopped at Bob Glover's office to say hello. It was a Wednesday, and Glover was planning to run a fifty-mile race on Saturday. As we sat talking, he broke pieces off a succession of raisin biscuits and popped them into his mouth. To a non-athlete such a diet would have looked insane, but Glover knew what he was up to. (He came fifth in the race and felt fine practically all the way.)

What Glover was doing is exactly what most top athletes do before a race of 10 000 metres or more. The process is called 'carbohydrate loading', or in more scientific terminology, 'supercompensation'. Researchers have discovered that if the body is deprived of carbohydrates for a few days, then fed large amounts, the energy-producing glycogen in muscles can be increased by as much as 300%. The results are two-fold: first, you have more energy; second, you may postpone, and perhaps avoid altogether, the dread moment known as 'hitting the wall', when your energy stores are exhausted and the ability to work declines greatly.

Carbohydrate loading is a fairly recent development. 'Only ten years ago, we all ate a steak the night before a race,' says Paul Fetscher, an accomplished marathoner. 'Now we're busy packing away pasta.' The process was developed by a Swedish physiologist named Eric Hultman. It takes a week, though the optimum time varies from person to person. On the first day you take a long, exhausting run. Then for three days you train normally while eating a diet extremely low in carbohydrates and high in protein and fat. During the last three days you eat more carbohydrates than usual—bread, spaghetti, cake and so forth—and cut down on protein. Thus nourished, the muscles soak up all the glycogen they can hold. ('Loading' is a slightly misleading term. It doesn't mean stuffing yourself. You should eat about the same amount you normally do but alter the proportions.)

Studies of marathoners indicate that those who observe the routine do better than those who don't. Still, not every marathoner is a party-line carbohydrate loader. Frank Shorter follows the second part (high carbohydrates) but not the first (low carbohydrates), in the belief that when he's training hard every run is glycogen-depleting. He doesn't feel there's any need to rid his body of glycogen; it's already gone. Moreover, many runners feel they have got better results by altering the depletion and loading periods. I know one marathoner who undergoes a two day depletion phase followed by a four day loading phase.

Not all nutritional researchers think carbohydrate loading is a sound or even effective practice, especially for middle-aged runners. For one thing, since every gram of glycogen is chemically associated with three grams of water, the additional weight in the muscles may interfere with performance.

Apart from carbohydrate loading, most runners eat much as other people do. Indications are that runners don't even need extra vitamins, no matter how hard you're training, although some doctors recommend them as a precautionary measure. But you should be careful to eat green and yellow vegetables and fresh fruits; they're important sources of the vitamins needed to metabolize carbohydrates and fats.

Remember, too, that what you eat on the day of a race isn't going to contribute much to your energy; it's too late for that. All it's going to do is keep you from feeling hungry. In a study conducted at Oklahoma State University, 68 of the university's football players were divided into four groups. One group ate a steak breakfast, another pancakes, a third oatmeal, and the fourth no breakfast at all. Later in the day all four groups ran two miles, and there was no difference in their performance. In other words, it doesn't seem to matter what you eat before you run, or even whether you eat at all, since even non-athletes have enough glycogen in storage to last for about an hour of heavy exercise. The average distance runner, because of a diet higher in carbohydrates, and also perhaps because of metabolic changes induced by training, may store as much as two hours' worth of glycogen. An athlete on the carbohydrate loading diet may store a three hour supply. Some runners find that exercising on an empty stomach causes cramps and even vomiting. For such runners, eating may be a necessary antidote.

People have long thought it unwise to try to store up extra energy by eating sugar before or during a run. Sugar can produce cramps, nausea and in some cases an over-reaction that leaves you with a lower blood sugar level than normal. At a recent conference, however, a Stockholm doctor and researcher named John Wahren presented evidence that taking sugar *during* a run may increase energy. But there's no point in trying to eat anything else in the middle of a race; you won't be able to digest it. Your body is too busy moving blood and oxygen and attending to complex chemical reactions to digest food. No matter how hungry you feel (and the chances are you won't feel hungry at all), you're not going to starve—even during a marathon.

What you *do* need to be concerned about is liquids. A loss of as little as a quart can slow you down, and losing twice this amount can do real damage. It's important, therefore, to replace fluids promptly. Coaches, as noted earlier, used to think it was good to sweat but bad to drink during training; the discomfort of thirst was thought to toughen an athlete. Research has shown this to be untrue. The body works best when fluids are replaced, preferably with something cool (but not ice-cold), as soon as they are lost. Research shows that a drink containing up to 4% glucose is beneficial in a run lasting over two hours.

After a race you won't feel hungry for a while. Your body is busy getting itself back to normal. If you eat too soon, you may feel nauseated or have cramps. A reliable guide, I've found, is to wait until your body tells you it's ready. Trust it. *It knows.* Until then, just sip liquids. Rudy Oehm, a cardiologist and marathoner, suggests drinking a variety of liquids: soup, water, fruit juices, soft drinks, perhaps some beer. Because the body loses various kinds of minerals as well as water when you run, he explains, no single drink is exactly right for making up the loss. Give your body a cafeteria-like choice, he says, and it will find what it needs.

What about alcohol? Many serious runners enjoy an occasional beer. Few of them are heavy drinkers, though one runner, a man of considerable distinction, is said to drink nine or ten bottles of beer every day, and one top marathoner drinks a crate or more a week. (I don't know how they manage it; both of them remain elfin in size.)

As for me, after a long, hot run I find that there is nothing like the taste of a cold beer. It cancels out the calories lost during a whole mile of running, but that's a small price to pay. The inventive Dr Bassler has even come up with a sound medical reason for drinking beer; the dehydration of long-distance running, he points out, may cause kidney stones, especially if you are training in a hot, dry climate. Water, he says, quenches your thirst before you've drunk enough for your kidneys. Beer doesn't work that way, since, as every beer drinker knows, it goes more directly to the kidneys.

Some runners have developed specialized theories about the relationship of beer and running. Martin Hyman, for example, told me, 'The first time I ran in the New Year's Eve race in Sao Paolo, Brazil, I drank the local beer—ugh!—and finished third. The second time I took along some English beer, and that year I won.'

Hyman, who is something of a student of the beer-drinking proclivities of athletes, likes to tell the story of a top British runner who was widely known for his prodigious capacity. Once, on the way to an important international race, he was seen entering a pub. The rumours began circulating and, as time went by, growing. After the runner had won his event, a team-mate finally confronted him: 'They're saying you had eight pints of beer and a pork pie in there. Is it true?' 'Absolutely not,' replied the champion. 'I never touched a pork pie.'

If you want to become really serious about running, you may decide to stay away from alcohol altogether. After all, it does add weight. And in addition to impairing co-ordination, it decreases your ability to process oxygen, it reduces muscle strength, and it has, as noted earlier, an adverse effect on your tolerance to heat. Indeed, studies have shown that even a single bottle of beer can reduce your ability to run in hot weather, and that the effect lasts for as long as two days.

Nevertheless, if it were a question of deciding between giving up drinking or smoking, I'd unhesitatingly stay with the drinking. One doctor points out that smoking has much the same effect as breathing carbon monoxide—hardly the regimen an athlete would choose if he wanted to improve performance. In fact, I don't know of a single even semi-serious runner who smokes, and I suspect that there is none. One of the special pleasures of post-race banquets is being in a roomful of two or three hundred people and realizing that not one of them is smoking.

Nor are marijuana and other drugs held in very high regard by most runners. While I know of a number of runners, some of them quite accomplished, who occasionally smoke marijuana, I have heard of none who do so when they are in serious training. 'Marijuana and good running just don't mix,' one marathoner told me.

What about coffee and tea? Caffeine, which is found in both, stimulates the central nervous system, promoting wakefulness, increased mental activity and the release of the stimulant epinephrine, the natural form of adrenalin. There has been a great deal of controversy over whether it should be considered a drug in athletic competition. (It was once on the International Olympic Committee's dope list, but was withdrawn.) I like coffee and tea and suffer no discernible ill effects from them, so I'll probably go on drinking them. Most runners do.

Because of a symptom called 'cotton mouth', runners sometimes worry about drinking milk. I've never suffered from it, but one writer describes it as 'a condition of dryness and discomfort in the mouth.' It is commonly thought to be caused by milk, but this isn't so. Research has found that cotton mouth is caused by too little fluid, not too much milk.

You may want to dig more deeply into nutritional lore, and certainly there is much to be learned. But whatever regimen you decide on, no matter how standard or bizarre, be wary of simply adopting it unquestioningly. Remember that your body isn't exactly like anyone else's. Don't be afraid to try something different.

There is one way of eating that claims enough support among runners to make it worth close scrutiny, and that is vegetarianism. I remember lying on a cool patch of grass after a long, hot race in Connecticut, and listening as Amby Burfoot, a lean, bearded schoolteacher who won the Boston Marathon in 1968, quietly explained his vegetarian regimen to several other runners. I had been running for a long time before I realized how many vegetarian brethren Burfoot had, and why.

One reason the discovery was so slow in coming is that the vegetarian generally does not proselytize. I had, I confess, always thought of vegetarians as part of the vast eccentric fringe, and I assumed that they would tend to be as wild-eyed and vocal as other true believers. But they go their own gastronomical way, living quietly on fruits, vegetables and nuts, and not caring whether you or I join them. Many of them are very good runners indeed.

Vegetarians do claim that their way of eating gives them more energy. They like to cite the case of the swimmer Murray Rose, who won two Olympic gold medals in 1956, of the distinguished Australian runners Herb Elliott and John Landy, and of Johnny Weissmuller, who became a vegetarian and went on to set six world swimming records.

Of course these people could simply be flukes who did well in spite of their diets. (I talked to one British doctor who insisted the human body needs meat in order to obtain certain important amino acids.) But if the scientific research cited by vegetarians is to be believed, they are nothing of the kind. One of their most oft-quoted studies, undertaken as long ago as 1907, compared the physical endurance of fifteen meat-eaters and 34 vegetarians. When asked to stretch their arms out horizontally for as long as they could, only two of the meat-eaters were able to do so for fifteen minutes, and none could do it for 30 minutes. Of the vegetarians, 22 did it for fifteen minutes and fifteen for 30 minutes or more. One is said to have held the pose for three hours.

Still, the case for vegetarianism is not based only on the energy factor. It rests on a number of others, too, some of which seem to be fairly persuasive.

There is, for example, the physiological argument. Mankind, vegetarians say, was never designed to eat meat, which is the reason some people choke on it and die—the so-called 'café coronary'. Unlike the wolf, which uses its spike-like teeth to tear meat into large chunks and then, swallows them whole, human beings have teeth that were meant first to cut and then to grind. They are, it is said, ideal for eating a banana, or a carrot, but by no means right for *filet mignon*. This, argue vegetarians, is why we tolerate cholesterol so poorly, and why, according to one study, strict vegetarians have only one-sixth as many heart attacks as the rest of us. We were never intended to eat so much cholesterol in the first place, if indeed any at all. (Eskimos, on the other hand, eat great quantities of meat yet rarely suffer from heart attacks.)

Vegetarians claim that meat isn't good for you. It's high in fats and contributes to heart disease and—in laboratory animals, at any rate—to cancer. It's a breeding ground for bacteria, and it isn't digested as easily as plant foods. Furthermore, the kind of meat most cf us like to eat is really partly putrefied. (Just reading some of the more vivid vegetarian tracts is enough to turn you away from the stuff, the validity of their arguments aside.)

No less a person than Pythagoras is considered to be the founder of vegetarianism and other notable advocates are Socrates, Plato, Aristotle, Milton, Newton, Voltaire, Rousseau, Thoreau, Tolstoy and St Francis of Assissi.

Hoping to find out more about athlete vegetarians, I paid a visit one day on Frances Goulart (who, you will recall from Chapter 13, was bitten by a dog). Mrs Goulart, who is in her late thirties and weighs all of 85 lbs, is the author of three books on vegetarianism. The first, *Bum Steers*, is a collection of non-meat recipes, with considerable discussion of the nutritional justification for them. *The Ecological Eclair* is about non-sugar desserts, and *Bone Appetit!* examines—I swear I'm not making this up—natural foods you can serve your pets.

Mrs Goulart lives with her husband, Ron, a prolific writer of science fiction, and their two sons. She runs nine or ten miles a day and also bicycles, swims and plays tennis.

'The things I eat might be repellant to some people,' she said. 'For one thing, meat has stimulants in it, and you miss them when you first stop eating meat. It takes a while to get used to being a vegetarian.'

There are, Mrs Goulart explained, three kinds of vegetarians: the 100% vegetarian, sometimes called a vegan; the lactovegetarian, who uses milk, as well as products made from it; and the lacto-ovo-vegetarian, who consumes both milk and eggs. Mrs Goulart is a lacto-ovo-vegetarian.

'You drift into these things little by little,' she said. 'Ron was doing some writing about food, and I decided I'd try going without meat for a while. I felt better right away. I didn't seem to require it. For one thing, your body doesn't have to work as hard to digest fruits and grains, so you run better. It stands to reason that you've got more energy for running if your body isn't busy doing something else.'

Mrs Goulart is a racer as well as a runner. She has set a number of course records for women and has a collection of trophies. Since she attributes much of her running success to what she eats, she is eager to share her knowledge. She gave me a number of books, articles and pamphlets on vegetarianism. Reading them, I came to see that vegetarianism means more than the simple avoidance of meat; it is also concerned with the search for pure and wholesome foods in general. For example most vegetarians do not favour either white sugar or white flour. Sugar has been suspected as a factor in atherosclerosis, gout, vitamin B deficiencies and even cancer, and of course its role in tooth decay has been thoroughly documented. 'You can undo a week of training in just five minutes,' says Bob Hoffman, a former Olympic weightlifter, speaking of the effects of sugar. As for refined flour, one source says it is so lacking in nourishment that even insects stay away from it.

Vegetarians also tend to cook less than other people because, they say, heat destroys enzymes, minerals and amino acids. One night when my wife and I had dinner with the Goularts, the *hors d'oeuvres* consisted of celery, tomatoes and cheese, and dessert was simply fresh fruit.

If you decide you'd like to try vegetarianism, how do you begin? Most vegetarian authorities urge you to proceed slowly in order to give your body—and your mind—a chance to adjust. They recommend a changeover period of a week or two. During this time eat progressively smaller amounts of meat and larger amounts of plant protein. Vegetarians recommend using different kinds of beans in combination. This improves their protein value, since they tend to complement one another.

Many people think that without meat they won't get enough protein, but plants provide plenty. Cereals are 10% protein. Common varieties of bean are 25%, and soya beans 40% protein. There's only one essential nutrient you can't get from plants: Vitamin B_{12}. For that you need some sort of supplement.

All of which would seem to be a small price to pay for being as fit as Mexico's renowned Tarahumara Indians, who not only live extremely long lives, but also run up to 200 miles a day in mountainous terrain. They do this on corn, beans and practically no milk, meat or eggs—a diet very similar to the one our own vegetarians advocate.

15 · Preventive maintenance

How to keep everything working right

By itself, a good diet won't guarantee you trouble-free running. Running can jar the body, tire it, change its structure and some of its functions, and alter its chemical behaviour. Any one of these effects can, if severe, interrupt or curtail your running. Most interruptions, however, need not occur. All but a few injuries are preventable.

The typical runner learns mainly by experience, sometimes bitter. A few cautionary tales do, it is true, come our way from friends and from magazines such as *Athletics Weekly* and *R.A.C.E.*, but it's hard to take much interest in some awful-sounding malady like chondromalacia patellae until we're suffering from it ourselves. So we muddle along, learning chiefly by trial and error how to avoid or treat injuries. The suggestions and warnings in this chapter may save you years of having to discover them the hard—and painful—way.

Don't strain

After you've been running for a while it's tempting to imagine that you've become indestructible. Day after day you put more effort into your running, and a sort of continuing miracle occurs: nothing falls apart. So you take this as a licence to run faster and longer. Sooner or later something *does* break down, a muscle, perhaps, or a tendon, or a bone, or your good disposition, because you simply can't run harder continually unless you do so in extremely small increments.

How small? Much depends on how fast your body recovers from a training session. Some people can put in two days of hard training and then after only one easy day feel rested. Most of us, however, need more rest, perhaps two or even three easy days between the hard ones. The main point is to give your body time to repair through rest what you've torn down through exercise. Fatigue results from, among other things, too little blood sugar, too much lactic acid, too little water, too few electrolytes, too little glycogen, too much heat and too many metabolic wastes. Recovery from all this cannot be instantaneous.

If you don't take it easy occasionally, you won't improve. You can easily tell how much rest you need if you pay attention to how you feel. Sometimes, for no apparent reason, you'll feel sluggish or lazy. On those days, once you start running you'll discover that you're not really tired at all. You'll feel springy, and in no time your laziness will vanish. Sometimes, though, even after a thorough warm-up your legs will feel heavy and you just won't want to run; if so, don't push yourself. Run slowly and patiently, keeping in mind that better days will come. The antidote for staleness is rest. You simply can't 'run through' it.

Fatigue isn't the result of speed and distance in themselves, but of running at a speed and over a distance greater than you can comfortably handle. I may tire after half a mile; you may be able to run 20 miles easily. If you tire yourself day after day, fatigue accumulates. One of the first signs of the fatigue-on-fatigue effect is an out-of-sorts feeling. For no good reason you're touchy, ill-tempered, and impatient. Routine tasks seem formidable. Among other signs of cumulative fatigue are these:

1. Pain in the joints, muscles or tendons, especially if it's more severe than usual.
2. Local muscle tenderness and trembling of the muscles.
3. Trouble falling asleep or staying asleep.
4. More colds, mouth ulcers and runny noses than usual.
5. Continual thirst (a result of dehydration.)
6. A tired feeling, especially if you still have it after a night's sleep.

If you have only one of these symptoms, it's nothing to worry about, but if you have two or more, it's almost certainly a sign you're overtired. The remedy is to ease up for a while. Miss a day's running, or cut your mileage in half for two or three days, or even longer. Above all, don't do any fast running. Wait for your energy and zest to come back, and only then resume normal running.

If you race, particularly long distances, you'll have residual fatigue for several days after a competition. You may think you feel fine, but the tiredness is lurking inside you, waiting to fell you with a cold or a pulled muscle.

Probably the chief enemy of sound training is dogmatism. Once we have planned our regimen, we're reluctant to change it. We feel weak-minded, for example, if we set out on a two mile run and end up doing only a mile. But when we have learned to listen to our bodies we will know what is a lack of will power and what is a sensible decision to head for home or to cut our pace.

Run efficiently

Later, in Chapter 20, I describe a run with Bill Rodgers. Watching him run is like seeing a beautifully designed piece of machinery; every component is synchronized and in harmony. Although this is a wonderful way to run, for you or me to try to imitate Rodgers would be silly. We're not built the way he is. If we were to try to imitate Rodgers's style or anyone else's we'd be working against our own bodies and increasing the risk of injury. The only sensible way to run is your own way, no matter how much it deviates from textbook style. Only don't try to land on the balls of your feet like a sprinter. If you do, you'll almost certainly hurt your Achilles tendons. Land on your heels, roll forwards, and push off with your toes.

Most beginners hold their arms too high. When they finally try positioning them lower, with the forearms roughly parallel to the ground, they usually find that they feel more co-ordinated. Try various arm positions until you find the one that seems most natural. Once you discover the right spot, there's no need for any more experimenting. Like your voice and fingerprints, your style is something you can't do much about. Fortunately, there isn't any need to, since a natural and relaxed style—the one that comes most easily—is the best way to minimize injuries.

Wear good shoes

Don't try to save money on shoes. Good shoes do at least three things that inadequate ones don't. Because they fit properly, they minimize blisters. Because they're well padded they cushion shocks. Because they have a stable heel, they keep lateral sway to a minimum and reduce wear and tear on leg muscles. (See the SHOES section in Chapter 12.)

Take care of your feet

The sole of each of your running shoes has some 30 square inches of surface, but only a few of these touch the ground at one time. Thus the repeated impact of your weight is concentrated on an area not much larger than a puppy's paw. It's no wonder feet give runners trouble—blisters, blackened toenails, aches, pains and occasionally even broken bones. Happily, many if not most of these injuries are preventable, primarily by wearing the proper shoes.

A couple of other routine maintenance procedures are also impor-tant. Keep your toenails closely trimmed. When your foot lands, it tends to keep moving inside its shoe. The result is that the toes move towards the front. If the nails are too long, they take the brunt of the impact, are loosened, bleed and turn black underneath, eventually falling off. It doesn't feel as bad as it sounds, but when your feet are in this condition they'll never win a beauty contest.

Take care of blisters as they develop, and try to catch them while they're small. They need not keep you from running, but they do require attention. Cover small ones with antiseptic cream and Elas-toplast and leave the Elastoplast there for five or six days; they'll heal with no further trouble. Once you've discovered the spots where you usually get blisters, toughen the skin there with Friar's Balsam. Using different running shoes on alternate days helps, too.

Stretch before you run

Chapter 5 described some simple warm-up exercises for beginners. After you've been running for a few weeks, strengthened muscles need a more comprehensive set of exercises. The reason is two-fold. First, running does little to improve flexibility and the extensibility of muscles and tendons; runners therefore require stretching exer-cises more than most athletes do. Second, running strengthens some muscles but leaves their antagonists—the muscles that oppose their efforts—weak. To prevent imbalances that can cause injury, the antagonists must be strengthened.

The best all-round set of exercises are six that have been popularised by Dr George Sheehan. Notice that the first three are specifically designed to improve *extensibility* (as opposed to mere flexibility of the joints), for it is extensibility of the muscles and tendons that creates a smooth, free-flowing running style. Sheehan recommends the following:

1. To stretch your calf muscles and Achilles tendons, stand about three feet from a wall or tree. With your feet flat on the ground, lean in until your legs hurt slightly. Hold this position for ten seconds, then relax. Repeat five or six times.

2. To stretch your hamstrings (the muscles at the back of your upper leg), keep both legs straight and put one foot up on a waist-high table, or something lower if you can't reach that high. Bend your head towards your knee until you feel strain. Hold this position for ten seconds, gripping your leg or foot to steady yourself if you like, then relax. Repeat the exercise five or six times with each leg. (Ted Corbitt says he thinks this exercise is even more effective: keeping your knees bent, bend over and touch the floor. Then with your fingers on the floor, push upwards until you feel your hamstrings pulling hard. After a few seconds, bring your hands up off the floor and slowly straighten up, vertebra by vertebra until you are standing upright. Repeat this exercise five or six times.)

3. To stretch the lower back and also the hamstrings, lie on your back, arms down by your sides, and bring your legs, with the knees straight, over your head. Lower them as far as you can, touching the floor behind you if possible. Stay in this position for ten seconds, relax, and repeat five or six times.

4. To strengthen your shin muscles, sit on the edge of a table and hang a 5 lb weight on the lower part of the foot just above the toes. (A paint tin with stones in it will do.) Raise your toes slowly. Keep them up for a few seconds, and repeat the exercise until you're tired.

5. To strengthen your quadriceps (usually referred to simply as 'quads'), sit on the table again and hang the weight over the toes of one foot, so it rests on the floor (to avoid stretching the knee ligaments.) This time raise the weight by straightening your knee. Hold it up for a few seconds, lower and repeat the exercise five or six times with each leg. To get much the same results without using weights, simply step up on to a bench and down again repeatedly.

6. Finally, to strengthen your stomach muscles, the antagonists of the powerful back muscles, do 20 or so sit-ups with your knees bent as before. Your hands can be either clasped behind your head (the hardest way) or extended over your head. Whatever way you do them, sit-ups should be begun by tucking in the chin and curling the

body up from the floor in order to maximize use of the stomach muscles.

Some authorities also recommend exercising the spinal extensor muscles, since backache, a common problem in middle distance runners, can be alleviated by increasing the strength and flexibility of these muscles. One knowledgeable doctor, a marathoner himself, recommends squatting while bending the trunk of the body as far forwards as possible, or else bending over frontwards while standing. A growing number of runners stretch by using yoga exercises. The 'Salute to the Sun', described in most books on yoga, is a particularly good all-round routine. If you use yoga exercises for stretching, you should use the strengthening routines described above as well.

Get enough sleep

Runners need plenty of sleep. Fatigue tends to accumulate quickly if you don't sleep enough, leaving you listless, unenthusiastic, and susceptible to colds. Sometimes job and family responsibilities, late-night television and a daily running programme make it hard to find time for enough sleep. If you can bring yourself to do it, turning the set off half an hour earlier works wonders.

Eat properly

For scientific guidelines, see the preceding chapter. Some rules, though, are just common sense. Don't eat for several hours before a run. If you do, you'll only feel heavy since fluid enters the stomach during the digestive process. Don't stuff yourself with so-called convenience foods. They may fill you up, but they don't give a fair return in energy. Use fat sparingly; fats are digested more slowly than proteins or carbohydrates. Don't eat too many fresh fruits, prunes and the like; they'll force you to interrupt your run when you least want to.

Stay thin

There are two reasons for becoming as thin as possible. First, you'll run better that way. The less weight you carry around, the faster you'll go. Second, the lighter you are, the less strain there is on the body's cartilages, joints and muscles. A simple calculation will show why. Your feet strike the ground about 2000 times per mile. If you weigh 175 lbs, that's a cumulative impact of 350 000 lbs. If you reduce your weight to 150 lbs the cumulative impact has been pared to 300 000 lbs—a saving of about 25 tons per mile.

Avoid chapping

A runner quickly learns where chapping usually occurs. The most common sites are the lips, nipples, crotch and underarms. A few good-sized smears of Vaseline before starting out will usually prevent chapping. Putting Elastoplast on your nipples—especially before a long run like a marathon, where rubbing is going to be sustained—will prevent painful wear. (Incidentally, chapping is equally common in summer and winter; a damp tracksuit almost precisely duplicates the effects of a humid summer day.)

Prevent frostbite

Suggestions for cold-weather dressing are found in Chapter 12. If they are scrupulously followed, cold should be no problem. However, since your face is usually exposed no matter how cold it is, be on guard against frostbite when it's windy and severe. Coat your face with Vaseline. Some runners carry a ski mask for use when running upwind in freezing weather. When the wind is coming from behind you, the mask can be stowed in a pocket or tucked into your waistband.

16 · If, despite everything, something goes wrong

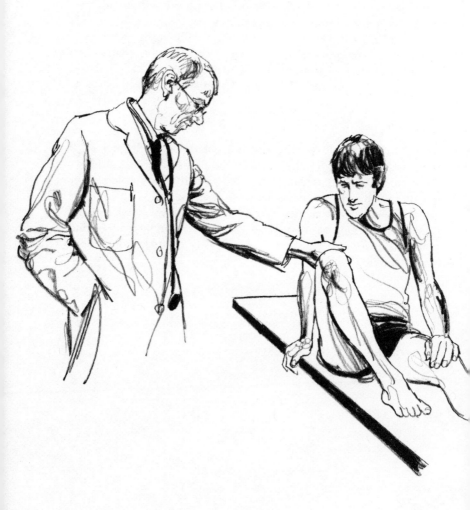

A medical paradox and what to do about it

There is a curious medical paradox about running. The very activity that improves our hearts and lungs, protecting us from heart attack, stroke and other ailments common to our times, brings its own special maladies—what one doctor has called the diseases of excellence. These come chiefly in the form of sore feet and legs, but they sometimes include other problems as well. I am afraid you will frequently find, when these injuries do appear, that many doctors can do little to mend them.

What follows is a catalogue of the runner's most common ailments, with some remedies.

Runner's knee

This is more properly known as chondromalacia patellae, a linguistic hybrid from the Greek words for 'cartilage' and 'softness' and the Latin word for 'a small plate' (i.e., the knee cap.) Common among runners, it is usually brought on either by injury or by a mechanical fault such as knock-knee. Its chief symptom is pain that is felt after exercise or while sitting for a long time with the knee bent. Occasionally pain is felt, too, while going up or down stairs.

To cure chondromalacia, many doctors recommend that you stop running. Runners who are prone to injury, and who are not lucky enough to have a doctor sympathetic to their problems, frequently encounter this all-purpose advice. Tom Talbott, a runner in his mid-forties, went to a doctor for a back problem. On being questioned, he said that the injury hurt most after running. Not surprisingly, the doctor then recommended that his patient stop running.

Talbott, who has been running, and competing, for a quarter of a century, replied, 'You don't understand. I don't consider myself well unless I'm able to run.' The doctor replied, 'That puts an entirely different light on things'—and set about finding an acceptable alternative. Talbott was more fortunate than many athletes. Dr P. N. Sperryn, consultant to the Farnham Park Rehabilitation Centre and co-editor of the widely respected work *Sports Medicine*, has written, 'The demand from sportsmen for advice and help with all aspects of general medical care and preparation is insatiable, and the response of the medical profession has in the past failed almost totally to meet this challenge.'

Runner's knee is often relieved simply by cutting down temporarily on mileage, doing strengthening exercises for the quadriceps muscles and running on a surface that slopes downwards towards the injured side—a road with a high camber, for example. (For chondromalacia of the right knee, run against traffic; for chondromalacia of the left knee, with it.) Chondromalacia often disappears after a runner starts wearing inserts—sometimes called orthotics—that change the foot's support patterns and thus shift the relationship of the knee-cap and femur.

Foot problems

Since the feet contain 214 ligaments, 38 muscles and 52 bones (a fourth of all the bones in the body), it's hardly surprising that something occasionally goes wrong with them. The foot problems of runners fall mainly into the following five categories:

Blisters.   Prevention, as noted in the preceding chapter, is the best cure. Choose the right shoes. When a blister does form, there are several remedies. If it's small, simply treat it as described earlier. If, on the other hand, it's so big that it hurts, puncture it with a sterilized needle and squeeze out the fluid, then cover it with antiseptic cream and a moleskin plaster, or else methylated spirits or iodine. Usually you'll find that you can go on running with no trouble. It's only if an infection develops that you may need to see a doctor.

Stress Fractures.   A stress fracture is a minor change in a bone's structure caused by strain or jolting. Generally these don't require casts or taping and will disappear with rest, but they are frequently mistaken for shin splints or bruised feet. (Diagnosis is tricky, even for a doctor who knows what to look for, because they don't always show up on an X-ray.) Stress fractures occur most often in the longest foot-bones (the metatarsals) and the two bones of the lower leg (the tibia and fibula.) As a result of the current trend towards high mileage training, some authorities say they are more common today than they were once. Stress fractures almost always disappear in six weeks or so if training is reduced to the point where you can run in comfort. Staying on a soft, yielding surface also helps.

Bone Bruises. To the layman's ear, the medical name for this condition—calcaneal periostitis—suggests some dread disease. Actually, it's nothing more than an inflammation of the heel caused by repeated pounding. Heel cups, available at sports shops that deal in running equipment, relieve the pain while the injury heals.

Plantar Fasciitis. This is an inflammation that occurs where ligaments in the sole of the foot join the heel, and its chief symptom is pain in the heel. It results from muscle weakness and can be alleviated by physiotherapy and exercise.

Heel Spur. Without an X-ray, it is difficult to distinguish this, a bony growth on the heelbone, from plantar fasciitis. Nor is there usually any need to, since it too is often relieved by heel cups. Only in stubborn cases will a doctor recommend surgical removal of the growth.

Ankle problems

Ankles sometimes become painful either from too much wear or from too much running on uneven surfaces. As I write this, my friend Charles Steinmetz has had a sore ankle for two weeks as a result of having run hard enough in a marathon to beat his own best time. But Steinmetz, a specialist in preventive medicine, says he isn't discouraged. He knows that minor injuries are occasionally the price of athletic accomplishment. Besides, the ankle is healing steadily. Such injuries are easy to accept and deal with.

What is less easy to bear, and certainly less easy to cure, is the most vexing ankle injury runners are subject to: Achilles tendinitis. (It's spelled with an *i* because the Latin root is spelled that way.) This is an inflammation of the sheath within which the tendon at the back of the ankle slides. Hundreds of thousands of words have been written about the treatment of Achilles tendinitis, and the recommendations from both lay people and doctors range from exercise to surgery. There is something of a consensus about several points.

Since Achilles tendinitis feels worse when the tendon is irritated, shoes with well-padded heels (and an added heel lift if necessary) usually relieve the pain. Taping with an elastic bandage sometimes helps.

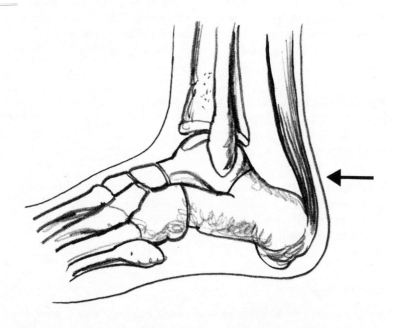

It is essential to curtail your running until the inflammation disappears. Confining your training sessions to flat, unyielding surfaces also helps. So does avoiding uphill running, which stretches the tendon.

If you should get Achilles tendinitis, you'll probably conclude that it's worth avoiding a recurrence no matter how much trouble it requires. Stretching the calf muscles and tendons as described in the preceding chapter, both before and after running, is the key preventive measure.

Don't treat Achilles tendinitis casually. Once you've got it, don't try to prove how tough you are. If you run too far or too fast, it can develop into a partial or complete tear of the tendon. When this happens, you've got real trouble.

Shin splints

Shin splints are usually the result of inflammation but may also be the symptoms of stress fractures. Although they most often occur in beginners, they sometimes develop in advanced runners after an increase in training intensity. Shin splints range greatly in severity; sometimes they are nothing but a dull ache, while at others they make running impossible. They are caused mainly by jolts, by running too high on your toes, by some other error in running style, or by training in shoes that are too stiff. Wearing flexible, well-padded shoes and landing on your heels usually helps, but one British doctor told me shin splints can never be fully eliminated unless one's running style is greatly improved.

Muscle soreness

Avoiding sore muscles altogether isn't possible or even desirable, since training necessarily overworks the muscles, but you can minimize the pain. Sore muscles result from metabolic waste products cast off during exercise, from infinitesimal tears and from an increase of fluid that causes stiffness. Soreness is lessened if you continue to exercise mildly for a few minutes after a training session; this will flush the waste products from your muscles. Increasing the intensity of exercise gradually over a period of weeks rather than days suddenly also helps. Once you have sore muscles, there isn't much you can do about them except take a sauna and wait for the pain to go away.

Cramps

When you decide to contract a voluntary muscle, a calf muscle, say, your brain sends a message through your body's nerve network.

Once the message reaches the nerve ends, it releases a chemical that contracts the muscle. When contraction is complete, a second chemical neutralises the effect of the first. According to one theory, cramping occurs when this biochemical mechanism goes awry. A simpler, though not contradictory theory, is that cramps are the result of a salt, calcium, potassium, magnesium or vitamin B deficiency. Some authorities even say that cramps are caused simply by fatigue, but of course this begs the question of what produces them. Whatever the fact of the matter, cramps can usually be relieved by stretching, kneading and walking. (If you sit down, they may come straight back.) A knowledgeable British doctor told me, 'If you get cramps in a muscle you can usually stop it by moving your body in such a way as to stretch the muscle as far as it will go. For a cramp in the calf muscle, for example, raise the toe as far as it will go.' Runners who frequently get cramps might first try increasing the salt in their diets and then, one by one, the other chemicals.

Bloody urine

Blood is occasionally seen in the urine after an exhausting training session, especially by the best competitive runners (Frank Shorter among others). It can have several causes—the destruction of minute amounts of muscle, for example—and doesn't indicate any problem. Still, it's a good idea to take a urine specimen to your doctor. Try to catch it right away, though; the next time you urinate it may not recur.

Runner's blahs

Sometimes, for no clear reason, a runner will feel lackadaisical, uninterested in life around him and depressed. When this happens, the cause is almost always training too hard and too often for full recovery to occur. Easing up on running and getting more sleep is the cure.

Side stitch

A side stitch almost always occurs while you're running hard enough to require deep breathing for a long time, and it will quickly disappear when you run more slowly. Some runners seem to be more susceptible than others, but everyone is helped by training and by making an effort to breathe from the diaphragm. It is in fact rare to get a stitch when you're in good condition. Thus the symptom can be minimized, and perhaps eliminated altogether, by increasing your fitness and by not running for several hours after meals. If you do get a stitch, breathe deeply using your stomach muscles, and run more slowly. If you're in a race at the time, the second suggestion won't seem a very reasonable one; then it's just a question of how much discomfort you're willing to tolerate. No one has ever died of side stitch.

17 · Racing

Notes on the competitive spirit

Some runners never race. I know people who faithfully put in ten miles or more every day but never go near a starting line. Some, perhaps, don't like the idea of winning at someone else's expense; others simply don't enjoy all that hard breathing and discomfort.

But for many of us a race is a special treat, a chance to compete primarily against ourselves and to see how much faster we can go than we have before. It's fine if we happen to pass someone or surprise a rival inches from the finishing line, but those aren't the main pleasures of a Saturday outing. That's why there's such camaraderie at races. Other racers aren't your chief competitors; you are.

Still, there's no rule that every runner must race, so don't feel obliged to. If you're not interested in competing, skip this chapter for now, but remember that it's here. Later, as your running improves and you find yourself occasionally reaching a state of buoyant and tireless strength, it may be that you'll want to try some racing.

Finding and entering a race is no problem. Simply buy a copy of *Athletics Weekly*, scan the ads. for races until you find one near your home, and send in your entry fee (which will be approximately 30p.) Or you can ask the secretary of a local running club about races in your area. Once you've joined a club, you're eligible to join the Road Runners Club, which publishes its own fixture list each year. Not long ago I had a chance to talk with the R.R.C.'s general secretary, Peter Goodsell. A former athlete himself, Goodsell told me that the R.R.C. not only acts as a forum for long-distance running enthusiasts but supervises the measurement of courses, organizes several races (including the London-to-Brighton race each autumn), and publishes an informative thrice-yearly newsletter. At a membership fee of £1 a year, it's one of running's best bargains.

Don't be intimidated by fear that you'll make a fool of yourself by being the slowest person in a race. While the majority of racers are fairly serious runners, anyone is welcome.

One of the pleasures of racing is the almost infinite variety of competition. In the United Kingdom runners typically run cross-country during the winter and compete on the track in the summer. In addition, on most winter weekends it's easy to find road races that range in distance from three miles upwards. For spice, if you don't mind hard work, you can toss in an occasional marathon.

Of course, following the advice in this chapter is no guarantee that you'll do well in competition. One of the deepest mysteries in athletics is what causes good and bad runs. There are times when you feel wonderful, yet run dreadfully, other days when you feel terrible, yet unaccountably have a fine run. A doctor with whom I discussed this told me he thinks the phenomenon has to do with the body's biological tides and rhythms, as well as with the subtle interactions of factors like diet and training. When you run poorly it's also possible that you are harbouring a cold or other infection, one not severe enough to produce detectable symptoms but enough to lower your strength.

A top runner faces a different competitive problem. As soon as a champion has set a record or won an Olympic medal, he or she has less incentive to improve. Henry Ryder, Harry Jay Carr and Paul Herget have convincingly demonstrated that the chief restraints on world-class athletes are not physical but psychological.

There's not much that can be done about such imponderables but there are many things we can control, and it is these that we pay close attention to in racing. It's one thing to finish badly because your body won't move any faster, quite another to do so because you're wearing the wrong clothes or because someone passed you while you were day-dreaming.

The physical and the mental aspects of racing are inseparable. No matter how fit you are you won't run a good race unless your mind is on what you're doing. That's why this chapter is concerned not just with tactics but with psychology. Let's examine briefly how your mind can help and hurt you in a race.

A race starts long before the gun goes off, sometimes months, or even years before. As you read this, runners are preparing themselves for the next Olympics. By the time they compete they will have spent many hours thinking about how they intend to compete. Such mental rehearsals will toughen their minds just as training strengthens their muscles. An opponent's move will call forth precisely the response they have prepared for. Pain will produce the instruction not to slow down. Being overtaken will produce a counterburst of acceleration.

To strengthen such responses, some athletes have recently been experimenting with transcendental meditation, which first came to the attention of runners after some researchers claimed it improved cardio-vascular efficiency. Since then a number of other athletic benefits have been attributed to it. A doctor with whom I discussed the matter told me that in his opinion the principles outlined in *The Relaxation Response*, by Herbert Benson, achieve much the same result as transcendental meditation. A number of his patients, he said, have benefited from them. Another doctor told me, however, that his research shows transcendental meditation doesn't do any good at all.

Whatever technique you use, you'll race better, and have more fun doing it, if you give some thought to what you plan to do with your mind while you're running. Then you'll be ready to cope with such things as pain, fatigue and the efforts of your opponents.

Pain and fatigue are different in practice from what they are in theory. Before a race it's easy to tell yourself you'll continue to run hard even after you've started to hurt. In the race itself it's a hard resolution to keep; pain and fatigue erode the will. No matter how much you race you'll never entirely surmount this problem. You can, however, become cleverer at dealing with it.

The example of top runners is instructive. Dr William Morgan reported recently on a psychological comparison of world-class distance runners and ordinary ones. The two groups differed most in what he has called 'their perceptual processing of sensory information during running'. What caught Morgan's attention was the ability of the best runners to tolerate pain. Ordinary athletes, he found, characteristically try to escape the pain of running by thinking about other things. Before a marathon, for example, one man he interviewed customarily put an imaginary stack of Beethoven records on an imaginary turntable and played them as he ran. Another, a Ph.D. candidate, reviewed his schooling year by year. In contrast, the world-class runners thought only about the race. They monitored their bodies, urged themselves to relax, assessed the degree of pain they were experiencing, and asked themselves how much more they could tolerate. Try to follow their example. After all, it doesn't make much sense to enter a race and then try to forget you're in it.

Top runners have also come to grips with what it means to win or lose. Competition is a complicated matter. In *The Madness in Sports*

Arnold Beisser writes of a tennis champion who never had an easy match but always won by a narrow margin. By doing so, according to Beisser's analysis, he was implying that there were only slight differences between himself and his opponents, thereby protecting himself from the guilt—and the consequent punishment—that would result from defeating someone one-sidedly.

Such fear is not as far-fetched as it may seem. I had run four or five marathons, all badly, before I finally finished one fast enough to qualify for the Boston Marathon. In the final fifteen or twenty minutes, when I knew I had a good chance of success, I experienced distinct feelings of anxiety. When I passed other runners, I felt there was something unseemly about what I was doing; it seemed wrong to succeed when they were going to fail. Perhaps you'll never have such feelings, but before a race it's a good idea to acknowledge the possibility you might, so you won't be caught off guard by them if they appear.

Of course, there is more to getting ready for a race than psychological preparation. If the race is important to you, try to arrive early enough so that the carbon monoxide your system has absorbed while driving to it will have a chance to dissipate.

Also be careful about what you eat and drink before a race. Although it increases endurance, the common practice of carbohydrate loading (see Chapter 14) can be overdone, particularly if it results in your gaining a couple of unneeded pounds. And even a small amount of alcohol the night before a race will diminish your ability to run well. Above all, avoid gas-producing foods such as beans, cucumbers, and freshly baked bread, all of which can cause stomach discomfort. Try to develop the habit of eating and drinking wisely and sparingly; then before a race you need only stick to your routine.

Take along everything you need. Few distractions are more frustrating than getting to a race and discovering that you've forgotten something. Some runners make a check list of what to take—everything from extra shoelaces to rain gear. Although I'm not that organized, it's unquestionably a good idea.

If you can, study the course before a race, either by taking a slow run on it as a warm-up or else by driving over it. It's good to know where any hills or sharp bends come and, in the case of a cross-country race over difficult terrain, where the path is too narrow for passing. It's helpful, too, in the final stages of a race, to know exactly how far away the finishing line is. Few things are more discouraging than to expect a finishing line that never seems to arrive.

Finally, just before the start, tie your shoelaces in double knots, make a final visit to the lavatory—or, if there isn't one, to an out-of-the-way bush. Forgetting this rule can produce highly distracting thoughts during a race.

As you hear runners talking before a race you'll notice that few of them seem to be in good health. There is always much conversation about ailments and symptoms and to hear them talk, hardly one of the contestants has been able to take more than half a dozen halting steps during the past month. This is a tradition of long standing, a reflection of the runner's superstition that to admit you're feeling fine is to guarantee that you'll run poorly. Don't waste sympathy on your sickly rivals; starting guns have produced more miraculous cures than Our Lady of Lourdes.

Even if you yourself don't exactly imply that you've just risen from a sickbed, it's wise to understate your expectations. If, for example, you think that with luck you'll run five miles in 35 minutes, tell anyone who asks, 'I'm hoping to break 38'. Then if you do succeed in breaking 35 the accolades will be more enthusiastic. A runner named Gerry Miller is a master at this. 'I was at a party until four this morning,' he'll say, 'and I haven't run in the last six weeks because of leg trouble. I'm just going to run this one slowly, as a training session.' A moment later he's off, bright as a bird, matching the leaders step for step.

Another preparation before the race starts is the warm-up. If it's a hot day, keep it to a minimum in order to avoid raising your body temperature unnecessarily. Otherwise, run slowly for eight to ten minutes, do some stretches and finish with a couple of brief sprints to get your heart, lungs and muscles ready for hard work. As mentioned earlier, there's controversy about how much good a warm-up does. Åstrand has reported a 5% increase in oxygen-processing ability after warming up. Since oxygen use and running speed are closely related, the warm-up seems to be a tradition worth adhering to.

Now for the race itself. The strategy and tactics of racing are complex, unless, that is, you adhere to the practice of a British Olympic marathoner who told me his secret strategy: 'I start at a brisk pace and run at ever-increasing speeds.' They depend on such factors as distance, rain, weather, opponents, and your own

strengths and weaknesses. Millions of words have been written on
the subject. Your first decision is where in the pack to start. If you're
too far forward, the runners behind you may jostle you or even
knock you down as they pass. If you're too far back, you'll have to
snake your way forward through the crowd. When you're new at the
sport, you'll find it easiest to start towards the rear. You can always
pass other runners later on. As you gain experience, you'll be able to
pick the right spot by looking for runners of approximately your
own ability. (Should you be running in a relay road race, one in
which as many as six team members cover from two and a half to five
miles apiece, crowding is of course not a factor.)

Once underway, your most important task is to find the right pace and stick to it. Starting too fast is a common mistake. At the beginning you should feel as if you're going a bit too slowly. If your pace is too quick, fatigue will force you to slow down later. The body is parsimonious with its energy supply; there's only so much available.

I witnessed a good example of this in the 1978 Shaftesbury Ten Mile run, held every summer at the Copthall Stadium in Hendon. Early in the race another runner and I were running stride for stride. He looked fit and was running well, but if I got close to him I could hear that he was breathing somewhat harder than is desirable in the early stages of competition. Instead of trying to push on ahead I decided to stay with him, betting on my hunch that he was running too fast and would eventually tire. Just before the eight mile mark we came to a long hill. Sure enough, halfway up the hill, I heard his footsteps fading away behind me.

As you search for the right pace, also establish a comfortable rhythm. Most runners can settle into an efficient rhythm only by giving full attention to it; when their minds wander they run jerkily. So keep your mind on your running: remind yourself to relax, stay loose and run easily. Since excess motion consumes oxygen and energy, try not to flail your arms, bounce up and down, or let your head bob any more than it must.

If it's a hot day or a long race, drink a cup or so of water just before you start. At the water stations along the way, take fluids early and often. Even if you don't feel thirsty, you're already sweating. By the time thirst signals you that it's time to drink, it's too late to catch up.

To race well, you must acknowledge your strengths and weaknesses. Some runners do best downhill, some uphill and others on the flat. Put extra effort into your strength; the advantage you'll gain will discourage your opponents.

Running uphill is hardest, of course, and this is why many runners, looking forward to a respite, slow down as they approach the crest of a hill. Don't: that's the time to push harder. If you run powerfully over the crest on to the downhill part, and only then relax, you'll find you've gained a lot of yards over many of your opponents.

Downhill parts of a course also have their hazards, the chief being that you'll run too fast and tire yourself. Unless it's close to the finishing line, don't go all out in downhill running. Occasionally you'll be passed by a runner as he sprints downhill. Don't worry;

you'll probably catch him soon after you reach the bottom—a sure sign he was going too fast.

Physiologically, the most efficient way to run a race is at an even pace, with a fast finish. However, you'll find that for tactical reasons you'll sometimes want to vary your pace. For example, if you're approaching a narrow path or stile in a cross-country race, get ahead of as many opponents as you reasonably can. As soon as you hit the narrow place you'll get strung out, and afterwards it's better to be towards the front.

When an opponent threatens to pass you, a brief show of strength may discourage him. Don't simply let someone go by unchallenged, for you may discover that *his* show of strength was only bravado. Tom Talbott used this tactic on me with good effect in a five mile race not long ago. I have been trying to beat him for five or six years, and finally thought I had him. On a steep uphill part of the race I passed him. He struggled back, passing me. I passed him twice more, but each time he fought back. Finally, discouraged by his tenacity, I let him go. He beat me by several seconds.

In overtaking someone, surprise him if you can and pass with a show of authority. If he speeds up, don't be discouraged.

It also makes sense to vary your speed in order to take advantage of an opponent's wind shadow. About 7% of a runner's energy goes into moving air molecules out of the way. If, therefore, you can run in the lee of another runner, where the air has been broken or where you can escape the wind's full force, you'll save significant amounts of energy. You'll also put the runner you're following under psychological pressure. It's harder to lead than to follow, since the leader must constantly wonder whether the runner following him is going to make a move.

How can you tell how well you're doing in a race? One way is to wear a stopwatch and keep an eye out for mile markers. (In some races someone will call out your time at them.) The only problem, as mentioned in Chapter 12, is doing the maths in your head as you run, particularly as you tire, but it's not impossible. Assume that your time at the three-mile mark is 19:57. A seven-minute pace would give you exactly 21 minutes. You're 63 seconds under that. That's 21 seconds a mile. Your pace, therefore, is seven minutes minus 21 seconds, or 6:39 a mile. Some runners simplify things for themselves by writing down their projected timetable and carrying it with them.

There's also a way to tell whether you're gaining on a runner ahead of you. Start counting your footsteps when he passes a particular point, then count how many steps it takes you to reach that point. After a while do this again. If it takes you fewer steps, you're gaining on him; if more, you're losing ground.

Strategy in a race depends partly on conditions. On a hot day run more slowly than usual at the start, even if you feel you could go faster. Heat wears runners out, and towards the end you'll be glad you saved some energy. On hot, sunny days, run in shade whenever you can. If spectators are offering cold water, drink some and douse yourself with the rest.

In road races you won't vary your stride much except in going up and down hills. Cross-country races are different. Here it's important to adapt to varying terrain, to take short, choppy steps in mud and sand, or to lengthen your stride during flat stretches.

In races on tracks, if you're like me, your chief enemy will be boredom. As I've already said, I stay away from them as much as possible. On a track your main task is to concentrate on what you're doing; if you let your attention wander you're sure to slow down.

Because of the turns and cramped conditions, strategy is tricky in track running. You have to choose precisely the right place to pass, usually as you come out of a bend, though the element of surprise is greater if you pass unexpectedly as you enter one. It follows, too, that you should run hard while you're in a bend to avoid being passed as you come out of it. And you have to time your finishing kick, or final burst of speed, so it comes at just the right moment, neither so soon that you'll tire and slow down nor so late that you'll fail to catch your opponent.

Finishing is equally tricky in a road race. You need to know exactly what you're capable of. If you have a weak finish, you'll want to put plenty of distance between yourself and your nearest rivals. If you're strong at the end, you can afford to wait.

Finally, as you approach the finishing line, keep pushing. Resist the supplications of your aching muscles; run at top speed across the line. More than one race has been lost a foot from the finishing line.

There are more nuances to racing, of course, than this brief survey suggests. If you want to, you can look more deeply into the subject by subscribing to such magazines as *Athletics Weekly*, *Road and Country Enthusiast*, and *Veteris*. When I was in touch with the chairman of *R.A.C.E.*, E. W. Barrett, not long ago, he pointed out that this publication's monthly circulation at 27 000 makes it Britain's largest athletic journal. One recent issue covered everything from fell racing to orienteering and even included a deftly humorous piece called: 'My Dad Never Wanted Me to Be a Runner.' ('It's not normal hanging around with those thin, anaemic-looking blokes....') *Athletics Weekly*, with a circulation of some 20 000 copies, is perhaps even more widely consulted, partly because of its wealth of race announcements and its extensive coverage of competitive events. Mel Watman, the editor, told me, 'the magazine stands or falls on the results and news service it provides.' Reading about the achievements of the great runners is, needless to say, one of the most entertaining ways to find out how running at its best should be done.

In this chapter I've mentioned three distinct types of competition—road racing, track racing, and cross-country. Since each has its passionate adherents, now, perhaps, is the time for me to confess a prejudice. Of all three, cross-country is my particular favourite. Especially in Britain, with its varied scenery and terrain, its footpaths, parks, and open spaces, cross-country is as inspiring an activity as anyone could ask for. This is why thousands of runners participate in cross-country races every weekend from November to April and why so many local cross-country leagues have come into existence. Even if you don't race, the lure of running the British countryside should not be resisted. Consider, for example, covering part—or, if you're feeling particularly stalwart, all—of one of the country's long-distance footpaths. The most famous is the Pennine Way, 270-odd picturesque miles from the Peak District to just beyond the Scottish border.

There's only one disadvantage to such runs. They will irrevocably spoil you for anything less scenic.

PART THREE
The World of Running

I'd rather run. The truth is, I hate walking.
Bill Rodgers, marathon champion

18 · Off the beaten track

The fine art of not getting hopelessly lost

Britons have a way of doing things in their own fashion, and so it is, naturally enough, with running. In most parts of the world today, runners do their running largely on roads, with only an occasional foray into a wood or park. That is simply not the British way. In addition to leavening their running with track and cross-country, Britons spend many running hours on the brink of becoming irretrievably lost. Moreover, they do so deliberately. The instruments of this curious athletic persuasion are two distinctive branches of the running experience known as orienteering and fell racing.

Orienteering

Orienteering consists of running as quickly as possible through a series of designated checkpoints, or controls, while guiding oneself with a map and, usually, a compass. To say no more than that, however, is to ignore the special appeal of the sport. During my last visit to Britain I talked with Martin Hyman, the Wiltshire schoolmaster who is not only a former national six-mile champion but also serves as Chairman of the British Orienteering Squad. 'Many orienteers,' he said, 'are joggers who are looking for something more. They find orienteering enormously attractive. For one thing, it brings out your self-reliance; out there in the wilds no one can help you. Furthermore, you're in a rare kind of symbiotic relationship with nature. You see deer and other animals. You get to know the land and the effect of the seasons on it.'

Hyman spoke of going out one spring to study a course in preparation for an orienteering event a couple of months later. 'I completely wasted my time,' he said. 'In the intervening weeks impenetrable brambles had grown up, and where there had once been dry land there were now deep puddles. I had to change my strategy entirely.'

Orienteering, which got its start in Sweden in the early years of this century, finally began to take root in Britain in the 1960s. Its popularity grew rapidly—the number of orienteers had tripled in the past decade—and today orienteering events abound. Most are held on Sundays, but because a dozen or so permanent courses have recently been established in Forestry Commission preserves throughout Britain it is now possible to go orienteering at just about any time the fancy strikes.

More and more people of all kinds are doing just that. The British Orienteering Federation, the sports's governing body, is unprecedentedly busy. Orienteers range from top competitors who scramble through the roughest terrain at an improbable seven minutes a mile to so-called wayfarers (beginners) who amble along without much regard to the time. Whatever the speed, however, orienteering is excellent exercise. One reason is that the terrain is usually hilly; the sport is most interesting in topographically complex country.

Upon arrival at an orienteering site, a competitor pays a fee, typically fifty pence, registers and is told the time he is scheduled to start. (Were all competitors to start together, orienteering would consist of nothing more than following the best navigator.) He is given a control card and map. Competitors start at one minute intervals. At the appointed time, a whistle is blown and the orienteer sprints to a master map imprinted with the day's checkpoints and copies these on to his own map. Then he sets out, map and compass in hand, to get from point to point in the proper order. Upon reaching each control he stamps his card with a punch that hangs by the marker. Having visited all the check-points he runs to a finishing funnel where his time is recorded and his card verified.

Fledgling orienteers often wear old clothes or ordinary running gear. Experienced participants, however, like to wear special orienteering suits made of light, closely woven nylon that help to protect them against brambles, nettles and branches. Orienteering shoes, which are studded and waterproof, are a particular help because they keep you from slipping in wet terrain.

The best orienteers are invariably skilled map-readers. Orienteering maps are specially surveyed, and drawn on an extra large scale to show such important features as the degree of penetrability of woodland, from dark green for impenetrable through lighter shades of green, to white for mature forest without undergrowth. Studying

contour lines and other indicators, an orienteer must decide, for example, whether to take the most direct route—up a steep hillside, let us say—or go the long way round and enjoy gentler terrain.

There are also some tricks of the trade.

If a control is located on some continuous feature, such as a path, the shrewd orienteer moves on a compass bearing that will take him somewhat to the right or left of it. Upon arrival at the path, he thus knows immediately which way to turn. Had he headed directly for the control and missed it, he could only have guessed which way to turn.

If there is a choice between traversing a thick forest and reaching a control by taking a path, the experienced orienteer knows how much extra time to allow for negotiating forests of differing degrees of penetrability.

Approaching a control, the knowledgeable competitor decides in advance in what direction he will leave it. That way, he can cut to a few seconds the time spent there.

In their authoritative book on the sport, *This is Orienteering*, Jim

Rand and Tony Walker sum it all up neatly: 'Results every week defy age and the Harvard Step Test, for speed of thought is as important as speed of foot, and concentration as important as stamina.' That, perhaps, is why orienteering is so often the first choice of runners who enjoy not just running but thinking hard while they do it.

Fell racing

The fells of Britain are like mountains nowhere else in the world. Although not notably high as mountains go—the highest, Ben Nevis, above Fort William in Scotland, reaches a mere 4406 feet—they are so craggy and unruly that they are comparable in climbing difficulty to mountains two or three times their size. I remember my astonishment the first time I drove northward out of Windermere and, after only a brief ascent, found myself in country so steep, rocky, and bare of vegetation that I was reminded of the treeless wasteland that surrounds the peak of Mount Washington in New Hampshire. Mount Washington towers 6293 feet high, two or three times the height of the typical Lake District mountain.

The fells are best suited, one would think, for viewing from afar, or at the very most for stumbling awkwardly over if we are in an intrepid mood, the weather is excellent, and we have a good lunch packed away in our rucksack. They are emphatically, one would suppose, not the place to go when the wind howls, the mists roll in, and the rains turn the trails to watery mud.

It is, however, their unfathomable paradox that at precisely such times they attract their most passionate aficionados, an indomitable breed of athlete known—though not as widely as they deserve to be—as the fell racer. A fell racer is not like you or me. Poised to hurl himself down a 45 degree rocky slope, he never foresees the barked shins and broken bones that would spring to the minds of more earthbound sorts. No, he beholds pure challenge, and he revels in it.

Fell racing is a peculiarly British sport, one that flourishes in the North of England and in Scotland, with occasional manifestations in Wales, Ireland and the Isle of Man. Races range in distance from two or three miles to 100 miles. In difficulty they range from a gentle romp across a moor to the jarring, twisting, terrifying clamber through countryside, that no prudent mountain goat would willingly visit, of the celebrated Three Peaks race in Yorkshire.

Although fell racing can be dauntingly competitive, its adherents like to cite its friendly and democratic spirit. It is not uncommon for a fell racer, passing a check-point, to be offered a pint of bitter, and on at least one occasion a participant who was an automobile salesman offered a rival a good bargain in a used car. Some fell racers compete occasionally in track and cross-country, but only when they can find nothing better. Life, for them, is fully lived only in the harrowing, hard-breathing world of the fells.

Fell racing was flourishing in the Lake District as early as the 1850s. The annual Grasmere Guides race was first held in 1868. The Burnsall race dates back to some time before 1881. The Ben Nevis race was solidly established by the turn of the century. Despite the rigours involved in running such races, it is not difficult to see why they have been so long-lived. Bill Smith, a prolific writer on fell racing and currently its reigning historian, writes, 'The atmosphere of a fell race is very informal and down-to-earth. There is none of the pompous officialdom which is to be found in track running, and most of the runners are on friendly first-name terms with the organizers, helpers, check-point marshals and mountain-rescue team members. If there's a pub handy, there's usually a session after the race, where the top men drink and joke with the scrubbers.'

Almost all fell racers enjoy living close to the land. Says Smith: 'Everyone who is seriously involved in fell racing is a lover of mountains, fells and moors. Many are also fell walkers, rock

climbers and all-round mountaineers. There are no poseurs or out-
rageous extroverts. No one goes around blowing kisses to the
crowd.' Recently several notable fell runners have successfully
turned to marathoning. Dave Cannon has made the move and raced
for Britain in the 1978 European Games. So has Jeff Norman, who
competed in the 1976 Olympics.

A few years ago the then secretary of the Fell Runners' Association, Eddie Leal, was speculating about why his sport remains so
undeservedly obscure. Leal mused, 'One point which may well be
contributory to a lack of information on the fell running scene is the
utter modesty which prevails throughout the whole fraternity.
Perhaps it has something to do with the vast majesty of the high and
lonely places in which the fell runner performs.'

All sorts of people seek out that vast majesty. One of the most
admired, Jos Naylor, is a sheep farmer. Others are stone-masons,
plasterers, schoolteachers, clerks. Another is an Outward Bound
instructor and tester of mountaineering equipment. In 1977 women
were at last permitted to participate in this most hazardous of all
running sports. Thus far, happily, they have failed to confirm the
fears of the fainthearted that, confronted with the mist-shrouded
perils of the fells, they would simply collapse into helpless exhaustion; and indeed, in many races they are beating half the men. In the
1978 Ben Nevis Race, the first woman to finish, Ros Coats, recorded
an astonishing one hour 55 minutes, finishing in the first third of the
field of more than 400.

Entering a fell race is simplicity itself. The Fell Runners' Association (see Appendix A) publishes an annual fixture calendar that lists
seventy or so races and includes descriptions of each. Some are so
simple that a child would be unlikely to stumble or get lost. Others
require advanced navigational skills unless you want to spend half
the day scratching your head on some desolate moor.

Training for the fells, on the other hand, is not so simple. More
than once, runners who are acclaimed on the track have swaggered to
their first fell race, only to be publicly humbled as their muscles
turned to tapioca under the relentless punishment of the high places.
Like runners everywhere, the best fell runners have their training
secrets and superstitions. But there is at least one incontrovertible
principle: To race well on fells you've got to do lots of training on
them. (Some fell runners obey the spirit if not the letter of this law by
training down below but racing every week on the fells.) Mike

Short, who won the Fell Runner of the Year award in 1975, takes a two and a half hour moor run every Sunday, even during the off season. Other top runners spend as many of their spare hours as they can in the fells.

Curiously, not all fell runners feel a need for formal coaching, an aid considered indispensable by many athletes. Rather, they prefer to let their bodies tell them how they're doing. 'I have very much got a mind of my own,' says Martin Weeks, a Bradford engineer who won the Fell Runner of the Year title in 1976. 'I don't think I would ever let a coach organise me. We pool our ideas among all ranks of athletes and do the best we can from that. We all discuss our ideas and theories, usually in a pub after a training session.' (The topic of pubs, one quickly notices, comes up often in the free-and-easy world of the fell runner.)

During such discussions one name is sure to be prominent—that of the incomparable Jos Naylor, who in his early forties still runs the fells with such speed, precision and navigational cunning that more than one athlete half his age has had to look twice to be sure his eyes were not deceiving him as this ageless wonder plunged by, arms and legs flailing. During the past decade Naylor has set a dozen or more fell records. His most celebrated achievement was visiting no fewer than seventy-two Lake District peaks in twenty-four hours, an achievement made doubly remarkable by the fact that it was accomplished during a heat wave. While standing around with his fellow competitors before a race, Naylor hardly looks the part of history's most preternaturally gifted fell runner. Lean and compact, with the high cheekbones and deep-set eyes common to well-trained runners everywhere, he has been described as 'an unspoiled, down-to-earth man of the hills.' It is only when the race starts and one sees Naylor's crisply efficient style that it becomes clear why he is so much at home in the rocky highlands. It is a style that has frequently left the most sober of observers, the knowledgeable Chris Brasher among them, in open-mouthed wonder. Some time ago, when Naylor covered the $271\frac{1}{2}$ miles of the Pennine Way in an astonishing three days, four hours and 36 minutes, Brasher summed it up in one phrase: 'The greatest long-distance performance ever seen in these islands.'

The most popular fell race in Britain is not, however, an improbable test like the Pennine Way run but a more manageable course that starts in Horton-in-Ribblesdale and snakes its twenty-three-mile way over three Yorkshire summits. Held every April and known as the Three Peaks race, the event attracts 400 or so entries. It is, however, by no means as easy as its popularity might suggest. In one recent year some ten percent of the field, dazed into submission by the hardships of the fells, simply gave up and hobbled dejectedly back home. Clearly, fell racing isn't for everyone. But if you enjoy the idea of testing your limits it's one of the best ways to do it. Especially if you can persuade yourself to be philosophical about scraped shins and bruised elbows.

19 · Boston and/or bust

How to get there blisterless
and beatified

Each Patriots' Day, a Monday in mid-April, several thousand lithe, hollow-cheeked men and women in running shoes gather near an undistinguished side road called Hayden Rowe Street in the hamlet of Hopkinton, Massachusetts, some 26·21875 tortuous miles west of downtown Boston. There they take a last drink of water, smear a final gob of Vaseline wherever their clothing can rub, tie their shoelaces into double knots and empty their bladders on the vegetable gardens and flowerbeds of the imperturbable residents of Hopkinton's big old frame houses. Overhead, helicopters from the Boston television stations prowl the heavens, waiting, and children perch in the leafless trees. Friends and families say goodbye as if their loved ones were bound for the moon. At precisely noon, when an official points a pistol towards the skies and fires a shot, a bobbing mass of lean, gristled humanity heads past Hayden Rowe and the First Congregational Church and begins a purposeful jog down Route 135 towards the towers of Boston far to the east.

Just over two hours later one of the participants, having traversed the hilly, winding road at some five minutes a mile, and in the process suffered the agonies of the damned, crosses the finishing line. Thereafter his slower fellows arrive. The first comes into view swiftly, with determination; the last run haltingly and wear gaunt and haggard expressions. Some limp or are bleeding where their skin has worn raw or, because they are past caring what anyone thinks, are crying and clutching each other like soldiers after a dreadful retreat. Hal Higdon summed up the mystique of the race when he wrote, 'The difference between the mile and the marathon is the difference between burning your fingers with a match and being slowly roasted over hot coals.' Later, however, as the tortures of the race subside, something like a miracle occurs. A mood of beatific calm settles in, a certitude that no matter what terrible tortures were endured out there on that lonely road, running the Boston Marathon was worth every ache, cramp and anguished moan.

Curiously, Boston is not the world's most prestigious race at that distance (the quadrennial Olympic marathon is), nor its most difficult (the course is more downhill than up), nor even its most scenic (unless you have a liking for railway yards, tram lines and urban sprawl). Nevertheless, it is the single race that captures and summarizes most of what is excellent in marathoning. Despite brisk competition from other important marathons, Boston is still the one that counts. Sooner or later all the great runners come here—England's Ron Hill, America's Frank Shorter and Bill Rodgers, scores of runners from Germany, Japan, Scandinavia—with the result that the race has a wondrously international flavour. To know Boston is to know the essence of marathoning.

This has been particularly true since 1972, when for the first time women were permitted to compete officially. Until then they ran by various ruses (false names, disguises and other subterfuges) because officials were convinced that they couldn't bear up under the punishment. In 1976, when a 20-year-old university student named Kim Merritt won the women's division in 2:47.10, faster than all but 145 of the male entrants, her record pace laid such anxieties to rest forever.

Boston's mystique persists despite the fact that in recent years it has, perhaps unavoidably, turned élitist. Until only a few years ago it was open to anyone; then, as entries became so numerous as to be unmanageable, officials reluctantly instituted a qualifying standard: three hours or better in a previous marathon, unless you're woman or over 40, in which case three and a half hours qualifies you.

Part of the marathon's appeal is attributable to its origin, in the year 490 B.C. In that year, according to legend, a messenger, one Phidippides, ran from Marathon to Athens to carry word of a Greek victory over 30 000 Persians. ('Rejoice,' he declared. 'We conquer.' Whereat, the story goes, he died.) It was another two and a half millennia before the marathon took root in America. Inspired by the 1896 Olympics in Athens, a group of Bostonians decided to stage one in 1897. The course, just under 25 miles long, was laid out mainly on dirt roads, and the contestants were mostly local men, machinists, milkmen, farmers, who made their own running shoes, trained

without coaching and ran largely on will power. First across the line
that year was John McDermott of New York City, with a time of
2:55.10, which is more than 45 minutes slower than today's record
over a longer distance.

Marathon courses varied greatly in length in the early days, but the
standard distance finally emerged at the 1908 Olympics in England,
when officials added a few yards in order to stretch the starting line to
the walls of Windsor Castle, to afford the Royal family a better view.
Slow to tamper with tradition, Boston finally adopted the official
distance in 1927. (The longer course didn't bother the tireless
Clarence DeMar who won that year for the fifth time in 2:40.22.)
Even as the marathon came to maturity, however, it remained a race
for the dark horse, many of the winners apparently coming from
nowhere. In 1926, for example, it was thought to be a toss-up
between DeMar and Finland's Albin Stenroos, the 1924 Olympic
winner. No one paid much attention to a nineteen-year-old delivery
boy from Sydney Mines, Nova Scotia, named John Miles, who wore
swimming trunks and white sneakers and had never run more than
ten miles. But it was Miles who, running with Stenroos and DeMar
until they weakened, finally slipped both and won in 2:25.40. A
decade later an equally improbable winner was a Narragansett Indian
named Ellison M. 'Tarzan' Brown, one of history's great marathoners. Brown lived in Alton, Rhode Island, where he trained by chop-
ping wood. He once ran a 4:24 mile on a cinder track in bare feet, and
on another occasion ran two marathons in one 24 hour period,
winning both despite a double hernia. In our own time, one thinks of
Bill Rodgers, as unheralded an athlete as ever took the lead, and a
runner who, despite having stopped several times to drink water and
tie his shoe, currently holds the course record.

Part of Boston's appeal also is due to the fact that its spectators are
like no others. A Bostonian will get a faraway look in his eyes as he
tells you of perching on his grandfather's shoulder to watch the race.
As you run along roads lined with these wonderfully appreciative
onlookers, you know that they really understand what you're going
through. There are perhaps half a million of them each year, yet no
one taunts you or jeers at your knobbly knees. Where else would a
policeman stationed on Heartbreak Hill address a runner through his
public-address system with these words: 'When you reach the crest
of the hill you have six miles to go, and it's all downhill. Your
achievement has been superb, and you have my fullest admiration'?

Where else would children line the course with outstretched hands in the hope of touching an athlete, even if it is only you or me? If you're going to feel terrible, what better place to do it than in plain view of people capable of understanding the scope and meaning of your suffering?

The Boston Marathon begins weeks before the event itself, with long runs on winter's icy roads. By New Year's Day the race begins to tug at your mind. You may be out on a wind-blasted plain, the snow howling in your ears, yet in your imagination you are bobbing past the cheering crowds of Boston. One day in New York City's Central Park, as I was circling the 1.6-mile path around the reservoir, a runner confided that during the rigours of training he kept his spirits up by imagining that he had reached various points along the Boston course. For such people the race has an almost mystical power.

Two or three years ago, arriving in Boston a day early, I took a detour off the Massachusetts Turnpike to see what Hopkinton looked like without the crowds. The town was quiet, a New England village with a silent, tree-filled square, and for the first time I saw that it was really quite an ordinary place. Number 4 Hayden Rowe, the last house of the left, was trimmed with old-fashioned fish-scale shingles and an incongruously decorative turret. The First Congregational Church at the end of the street had a gold weather-vane and a tower capped with copper long since turned green with oxidation. It was much like any of a hundred towns you've seen except for one detail; in a stretch near the square were painted two broad white lines, between which the best runners, and for some reason the women, start in a sort of seeding system. Near those lines, to my surprise, stood half-a-dozen people, obviously runners, who like me had come for no other reason than to pay sentimental homage.

There is a curious uneasiness when you finally arrive in Boston. Your preparations are finished; whatever training you have failed to do will never be done now. Furthermore, the night before the race you will sleep badly, have restless dreams and awake too early. One runner I know, sharing a hotel room with a friend, awoke at three a.m. on the day of the race to discover his room-mate working off nervous energy by doing push-ups. Another participant, half crazed with nerves before 1976's Bicentennial Marathon, went out on Boston Common and by the early light of dawn ran six miles.

Eventually, however, morning finally comes, and then Boston restaurants do a roaring trade serving pancakes to runners who hope to pack in one last morsel of carbohydrate. At 8.30 the buses leave for Hopkinton. There, in the old days, you used to undergo the world's most perfunctory physical examination, a practice abandoned in 1976. Now you merely report to the high school gym where you are handed your number, along with four safety pins to fasten it to your vest, and a perforated tag, one end of which reads 'Retain this Check', to affix to whatever clothes you want to have waiting for you at the finishing line. The gym is noisy and smells of disinfectant. Runners, who train much of the time in old grey tatters, are wearing their finery—shorts imprinted with stars and stripes, bright headbands and crisp nylon jerseys bearing the names of their running clubs (the Kettering, Ohio, Striders, the Enfield, England, Harriers, The Sugarloaf Mountain Athletic Club, and the Ondekoza, Japan, Drummers, the last an impressively indefatigable percussion orchestra that first participates in the race, and then, hardly pausing for breath, starts entertaining the crowd with its huge drums).

Towards noon, feigning calmness, you wander towards the growing crowd at the starting line on Route 135. Now is the moment to take one last drink and to head one last time into those backyard gardens. The helicopters are in place overhead, their rotors flailing the April skies. At the foot of Hayden Rowe Street the press photographers' van waits, its tiers of wooden seats bristling with long lenses. Near the starting line stand the best runners—the likes of Rodgers, New Jersey's two-time runner-up, Tom Fleming and Connecticut's dark horse John Vitale. Farther back is the vast mass of ordinary mortals, and behind them the former cardiac patients seeking unassailable confirmation of their cures, the unofficial participants bent on a lark, and those who simply like to start slowly and work their way up through the crowd, picking off their rivals one by one.

The starting gun sounds. Unless you're up front with the top athletes, in the beginning you have trouble finding room to run until the crowd thins, so you bounce in place or simply walk until you can finally break into a run. At last you're on your way in earnest, feeling good and moving with an easy, relaxed gait. This feeling is deceptive; it will not last more than an hour or so, and that will leave another ninety minutes or more during which the race will be, to one degree or another, a struggle. How much of a struggle depends upon 1) what kind of shape you're in 2) what the weather is like 3) what kind of day you're having, and 4) how intelligently you pace yourself.

At least some of these factors are controllable, so if you know what to expect at each stage of the race, your chances of running well are considerably improved. To that end, here is a mile-by-mile gazetteer of the Boston course.

0 to ·8 miles: getting started. The first part of the Boston Marathon is entirely downhill, but now is no time to press hard and tire yourself. Anyway, at this point the course is so clogged that passing requires an inefficient, weaving path. Simply hold your position and try to stay out of harm's way in the crush. More than one runner has been knocked down in the first few hundred yards.

·8 to 3 miles: A time for caution. The hills flatten out at exactly ·8 mile, where there's a house on the right with a swimming-pool in the yard, and soon a gentle uphill begins. At the 1-mile mark you'll see a Christmas-tree nursery and a sign reading 'Liberty Mutual Research Center'. The next half-mile takes you past rocky pastureland on the right. At 2·1 miles a sign announces 'Entering Ashland', and at 2·7 miles another sign indicates 'Laborers' Training Center'. At 3 miles a gentle downhill tendency has begun to level off. (It ends at about 4 miles.)

Thus far, the course, though gently rolling, has been mainly downhill. The chief danger, therefore, is that you'll run this segment too fast. Jerry Nason, who has covered more than forty of the annual marathons for the *Boston Globe*, believes that the most common error is a failure to realize how fast you're going in the first part of the race. 'Too many people,' he says, 'run a fast first half, then have to slow down. An even pace almost always works best.'

3 to 6·7 miles: Ashland to Framingham. You're settling in now. You've calmed down and started to sweat. You're breathing more easily and your legs are loose. If you're the sort of runner who likes conversation now is the time, while your body still feels right. At 3·5 miles you swing sharply right past Romeo's Supermarket, and ·3 mile later you cross Main Street in Ashland. This is a good place to start drinking fluids, whether you're thirsty or not. In

another half-mile you pass Brackett Reservoir and start climbing a gentle hill. The numeral 5 on a pole to the right indicates the 5-mile mark. At 5·7 miles you pass La Cantina Pizza and the Werby Industries building on the left, and at 6·7 miles are running past the Framingham railway station. (For marathoners, probably the fittest group of people in the world, an incidental point of interest about Framingham is that it was the scene of the famous Framingham heart-disease study.)

6·7 to 10·5 miles: Framingham to Natick. Moving out of Framingham you reach a restful level stretch. Should you want to check your running style, you can catch a glimpse of your reflection at 7·8 miles in the long front window of the Hansen Electrical Supply Company. A tenth of a mile later the road begins to slope uphill again. A mile farther on, Lake Cochituate comes into view on your left and Fisk Pond on your right. You pass a dense stand of pines and finally you're in the pleasant town of Natick with its big nineteenth-century houses, each one on a rectangle of green lawn and with great

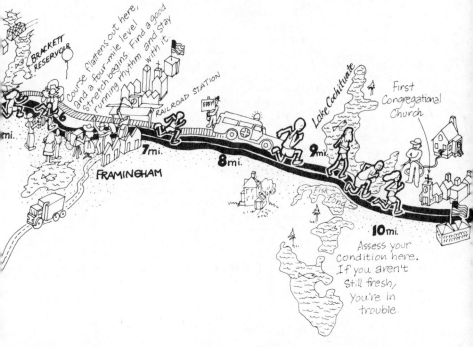

shady trees to shield you momentarily from sunshine. When you reach the intersection of Main Street and West Central Street you've run just about 10·5 miles, and the clock on the tower of the First Congregational Church gives you a chance to check your pace.

At this point you should still feel fresh and springy. A marathoner who is tiring at ten miles is in trouble.

10·5 to 13·1 miles: Natick to Wellesley. Moving eastwards out of Natick you pass St. Patrick's Hall and, a bit farther along, the 726th Maintenance Battalion armory. At 11·3 miles a long, gentle downhill stretch begins, and at 11·9 miles you pass a sign: 'Entering Wellesley'. Four-tenths of a mile farther along you pass the courts of the Wellesley Tennis Association, and in another ·3 miles, the modern world's most appreciative marathon fans, the girls of Wellesley College. In another half-mile you're in the town. The halfway point is here, not far from the Marco Polo Gift and Garden Center and the Idiot's Delight Clothing Store.

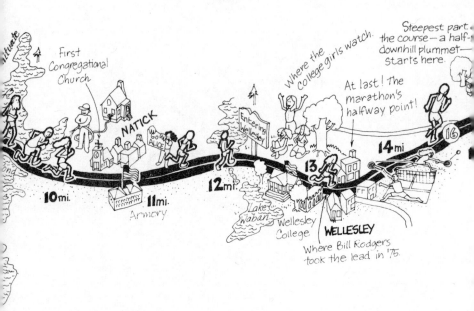

13·1 to 16·2 miles: Wellesley to the Charles. Now, before fatigue and hills wear you down, assess your running style. Concentrate on staying relaxed and minimizing bounce and needless arm movements. From this point on, you'll be grateful for whatever energy you can find.

Half a mile past the marathon's halfway mark you leave Route 135 and swing on to Route 16, headed for Wellesley Hills. At 14·2 miles you pass some grassy playing-fields, seven tennis courts, and soon, in Wellesley Hills itself, the yellow canopy of the Berkeley Restaurant (14·8 miles). A long flat stretch carries you across Route 9 and, at 15·6 miles, to the brink of the steepest section of the course, a long downhill that is a harbinger of the torture to come. The hills are always the race's big test. Two runners can be matching each other stride for stride when the hills begin, but when they end, one runner has almost always established a decisive lead.

The downhill stretch ends at the Continentale Barber Shop in Newton Lower Falls. At 16·1 miles you cross the Charles River, and

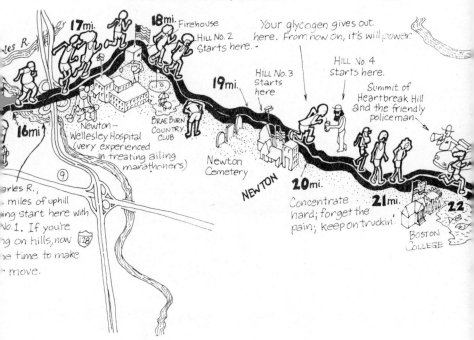

now, exactly when your body least craves uphill running, you start climbing.

16·2 to 21·4 miles: The hills.   There's no question about it: this is the toughest part of the course. You can reach the 16·2-mile mark feeling fit and optimistic, and five miles later you may be a ruin. This is the beginning of what is known collectively as Heartbreak Hill, a series of either three or four hills (depending on how you count them) that wear down the toughest athlete. No single hill is particularly steep or long; it is simply that they come at the wrong part of the race and as a combination are more than anyone but a masochist would wish for.

The first hill starts at precisely 16·3 miles, the second at 17·7, the third at 19·4 and the fourth at 20·4. While you're climbing them you cross Route 128, pass the Newton-Wellesley Hospital, make a ninety-degree right turn at the Newton fire-station, and in the process pass the race's most drama-conscious spectators—an attentive throng with a finely-honed taste for the sight of suffering.

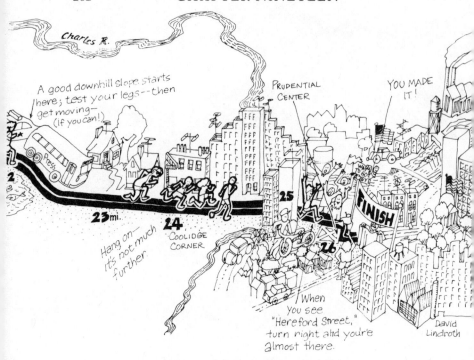

Why else would they choose to do their watching on Heartbreak Hill?

There are many theories about how to handle hills. Whatever yours is, this section of the race will put it to the test. What seems to work best for me is to take the first couple of hills fairly slowly, remembering that there are more to come. It also helps if you keep your mind off the distance still to be travelled.

21·2 to 26·2 miles: Heartbreak Hill to the Pru.   When you reach the top of Heartbreak Hill you'll know it, for the crowds will tell you. They'll also shout that from here on it's all downhill, a statement so palpably false that it could only come from someone who has never run the race. It's true that there are many downhill portions; in particular as you run past the Boston College Alumni

Hall and the Baptist Home of Massachusetts, but the course quickly flattens out at 21·7 miles as you start running alongside tram lines. Finally, however, starting at 22·3 miles, you reach a good downhill stretch. The crowds here are denser. People jam the course and hang from windows, so if you're not dazed with fatigue you feel like a hero. Suddenly, at 25·2 miles, you catch a glimpse of the Prudential Center, looking reachable for the first time. You pass the Korean Karate School (25·6 miles), the Bull Restaurant (25·7 miles) and the Harvard Club of Boston (25·8 miles). Finally you turn right on to Hereford Street, negotiate a long, shallow hill, swing left at the Prudential Center and coast down a ramp bearing a yellow banner that reads FINISH. There is no experience quite like reaching that banner. In the 1976 Boston Marathon I arrived only a step ahead of a runner from Japan. We threw our arms around each other in a sweaty embrace. Neither of us spoke the other's language but it didn't matter; there was nothing that needed saying.

To the right of the finishing line, towards the Pru Center, is a fountain. It's a good place to cool your feet. Wait for me. With luck I'll be along in a while.

For all its fame, the Boston Marathon course is not an unusually gruelling one. Using Geodetic Survey maps and a precision altimeter, a group of Boston runners discovered that the descent from start to finish is 465 feet, not 225 as had generally been thought. As you run it, however, you'd never guess it.

20 · A run with a champion

An Olympic marathoner with a thought or two about his craft

I am on a road a few miles north of Boston, running with Bill Rodgers, an Olympic marathoner and one of the world's fastest runners of 26·2 miles. My feet make their customary *slapslapslap* sound on the pavement. Rodgers moves without a sound, gliding smooth as a cat along the left-hand edge of the road. In the past three weeks he has won two marathons, first defeating 2001 other runners (Frank Shorter among them) in New York City and then, ten days later, flying to Japan to leave a five-man Japanese relay team in ruins. He is still feeling the jet lag, he tells me, and his stomach is upset.

His problems don't show. He bobs along rhythmically, and is cheerful and talkative. He is wearing a green and orange warm-up suit that flops loosely on his thin, bony body. It is late afternoon and it is turning cold, the way he likes it. It was on a day like this in April 1975 that he covered the Boston Marathon course so decisively that he not only won the race, a handsome achievement in itself, but set a course record of 2:09.55. ('It can't be true,' he said afterwards. 'I can't run that fast.')

Rodgers is in his early thirties, just the age when marathoners ripen, but he could easily be taken for five or six years younger. He is five feet eight and a half inches tall and weighs 125 lbs, exactly what he weighed in the junior high school. His hair is sandy blond, his teeth are small and startlingly regular. As he runs, he suggests an extraordinary mechanical harmony, every part working in diligent concert with every other. His arms rock like pendulums. His feet strike the ground softly, at the heel, then roll forwards until only his toes link his body to the earth. Then he floats through the air for an unbelievably long time until another heel finally sinks gently to the pavement. As he moves, his head neither rises nor falls but acts as is it were gyroscopically stabilized.

'If I ever stopped running I'd feel terrible,' he says, 'as if I were slowly decomposing. I enjoy being fit. There's a feeling of independence about it. If I get a flat tyre and am ten miles from a garage I can just run there, instead of sitting for three hours and freezing.'

I am running with Rodgers because I hope to find out how a world-class runner looks on his craft and what he thinks about during a race. But I am also interested in Rodgers as a phenomenon. He is, I believe, a particularly interesting runner—one with an unusual ability to push himself when no rivals are around. (His best marathons have been his loneliest.) Most runners run hardest when they can see the tormented faces of their opponents and hear their laboured breathing. What is it, I wonder, that makes Rodgers different?

We had started our run accompanied by Rodgers's wife, Ellen. It was she who, before they were married, encouraged him to train hard for the 1975 Boston Marathon. (Recalling that he looked droopy at the halfway mark, she remarked later, 'I was ready to kill him.') Ellen has wavy brown hair, a nice smile and a gentle manner. For a mile or so she chatted with us; then, explaining that two miles is her limit, she turned back. Rodgers said goodbye, and picked up the pace.

We are running beside a small muddy pasture. The trees are bare, and a horse stares at us as we pass. 'There's not much room for the poor horses around here any more,' Rodgers says.

I ask him how he felt when he won the Boston Marathon.

'I was very nervous before it started,' he replies. 'The year before, I was in fourth place for eighteen or 20 miles. Then I faded and came in fourteenth. I knew I could be up there even farther so I was psyched up. I knew the top runners were there, but I felt very strong mentally. When the gun went off we took off fairly quickly. I was a little bit back at first, but after a mile or two I caught up with the leaders. The pace was pretty even. Then after about eight miles Mario Quevas, a Mexican runner, went out ahead. Jerome Drayton went with him and I decided what the heck, I'd go after them. Drayton and I ran together for about three miles. Then he moved out.'

I ask Rodgers whether he had known who Drayton was. Rodgers gives a quick, nervous laugh and says, 'Oh, I knew who he was, and I knew he had run a 2:11. What happened was that people were cheering for him, and it irritated me. Why would they cheer for him, from Canada, more than for me, from Boston? I got furious. I ran really hard for a while, and he fell back. That was the race right there.'

Bill Rodgers stops during the 1975 Boston Marathon

Rodgers set his record in that marathon despite the fact that he stopped once to tie his shoe and four times to gulp some water. 'I can't run and drink at the same time,' he maintains. He laughs again and then goes on: 'I guess tying my shoe freaked a lot of people out. The lace was loose, and I remember thinking, *Maybe I'll trip on it*. It was a good chance to stop and relax. So I stopped, tied it, took a deep breath and started in again. It was really no big deal, but it freaked out a lot of people. Some of the runners, too, I guess.'

Rodgers and I are running along a route just west of where he lives. Two runners, a boy of ten or so and a man, approach us. We all wave. The boy looks up at Rodgers, recognizes him and says, 'Hi, Bill.' Rodgers says, 'Hi, son.' For a few seconds we can hear the sound of running shoes on the pavement behind us. Then it is quiet again.

Rodgers talks about his childhood. 'I was okay at most sports,' he tells me, 'but not at baseball. I was pretty inefficient at that. In the first place, I have poor eyesight. I remember I was trying for the Little League, and a guy hit a fly ball. I had glasses on and was staring up at the sun. The ball went right through my hands and hit the ground. *Gloom!* But even in elementary school I was faster than most kids. I always loved to run. They would time me around a baseball diamond and I was fast. I forget what my time was, but it was good. When I was sixteen I ran my first race, a mile, a super distance to me then. My time was good but not earth-shattering. During sophomore year in high school I used to go out on the track and try to run a mile as fast as I could. I was trying to break five minutes, but I never could do it.'

It was during this year that Rodgers began to suspect that he had some unusual abilities. 'They had a distance run,' he tells me, 'and all the gym classes at High School ran it. It was a mile and a tenth, I think. I was the fastest in the school. During my last two years we had a coach who was pretty good. He had about the loudest voice in all of Connecticut. I improved quite a bit.'

Rodgers is feeling better now and running harder. I have to work to keep up. He makes a left turn into an underpass. My footsteps echo noisily off the walls, but Rodgers' are silent, as if he were moving through cotton wool. In a few minutes we reach a reservoir. The late-afternoon sun has turned the water to gold. 'If we go around the reservoir,' Rodgers says, 'it will be exactly nine miles.'

As we run along the water's edge, Rodgers says, 'Four years ago I had never thought of entering a marathon. After I graduated from university I worked for the post office for a few months. Then I got my conscientious objector's classification and found a job at Peter Bent Brigham Hospital in Boston. For two or three years I watched the Boston Marathon. I was smoking a packet of cigarettes a day at the time—*bad news!* Then I joined a Y.M.C.A. and started running again. I ran indoors on this dingy little track. I couldn't even remember what it was like to run out of doors. Finally, one day I went out to a park. I started feeling strength coming back, and I remember saying: *This is great. I've got to do more of this.* So in '74 I ran in the Boston Marathon. I bombed out. It was hot and I had a cold and I remember cramping and having to stop. I quit running for two months. I thought, *I will never be a really top-level runner.* I was sure I could never force myself to run hard in the heat.'

Although Rodgers has been talking steadily ever since we started, he has showed no signs of breathlessness, not even on the hills. Furthermore, he has demonstrated a continual concern for my safety. 'This is a bad part,' he'll say. 'We'd better go single file here . . . Don't cross now, wait for these cars . . . We've got a nice pavement to run on just ahead . . . Watch out for those rocks.'

He starts talking about racing tactics. 'In the '76 New York Marathon,' he says, 'Chris Stewart, an English runner from Bournemouth, caught up with me. I had been in the lead for a while and suddenly there he was. So I said to myself, Okay, I'm not going to try to break away from him immediately. I'll run with him for a while and see what he's like. I try to assess each runner. Are they really strong? I look at their running style; I listen to them breathe. Maybe I even talk to them to see what they have to say. That's what I did with Stewart. I didn't know who he was, so I asked him his name and he told me. Then I knew who he was, and that he had a fast marathon time. So after a while, I said to myself, *Okay, now I'm going to run a little bit harder and see what happens.* Fortunately he began to have some difficulty and fell back.'

We are nearly around the reservoir now. It is dusk, and in the west the sky is streaked with red. Rodgers looks at it and says, 'Wow! Look at that!' He is still running without a sound. I am feeling ragged.

An athletics writer once told me that Rodgers had been slow to reach his potential because he isn't tough enough mentally. The writer claimed that Rodgers is intimidated when he looks around before a race and sees all those world-class runners. I ask Rodgers what he thinks of the criticism. 'I've heard that,' he replies thoughtfully. 'I know I have that reputation, but I don't think I'm that way any more. If I'm psyched up for a race I'm ready to run with anybody. The top runners in the world can be there, but I'm not intimidated at all; I'm looking forward to it. It's only if it's humid that I worry. At the Montreal Olympics I had this feeling of doom because it was so humid. As a result I over-reacted. Whenever anyone made a push, I went with him. I wanted a world record pace. Then I felt this weakness coming on, and I knew there was nothing I could do. It was'—he uses the word again, with feeling—'*doom*.' Rodgers finished well down in the field.

Ordinarily, he continues, he feels fine during a marathon. 'If I don't lose a lot through perspiration,' he tells me, 'I won't cramp and it won't be too strenuous. I try to run efficiently. I have certain ways of holding my arms. I'll try not to bounce up and down too much, to concentrate on running forwards. If my legs are cramping a little I'll position my feet in different ways, maybe land a little differently. Or maybe lean forwards a little, or stretch my back if it's tight. A marathon is a forcing—trying to maintain equilibrium, smoothness, and efficiency all the way to the end. It's especially tough towards the end—that's what makes the marathon unique. If you're well trained, then you can hold up in those last miles. If you're not. . . .'

During our run Rodgers has mentioned the mental aspects of running several times. He returns to it again now. 'In a marathon,' he says, 'I never let myself think, *I've got 26 miles ahead of me*. You have to think of your race as it is right then and there. At the same time you keep in mind the prospects for the future. For example, if someone is three hundred yards ahead, it's nice to know who he is and how he's running. If he's running at the same pace you are, you can sit back, nice and cool, and say, *I'll catch him later*. But you don't say to yourself, *I've got fifteen miles left to go*. Never! I just take it in little segments at a time. In a marathon I like to start easy, run hard for a while in the middle to try to shake the others, and then coast home. I'm able to do some pretty hard running in the middle because I don't worry too much about the next part.'

Now, suddenly, I understand how Rodgers races. He does his best running not when he is alone, but when he is pressed. But his best is so good that very often there is simply no one left for him to run with. Running alone in the later part of a race is his reward for running so well earlier.

Rodgers begins to talk about his future. 'I'd like to get myself ready for some marathon where there might be ideal conditions,' he says, 'and maybe get under 2·09.* Then, someday, I'd like to knock off a 2·07. I'd like to push things down a little bit.'

We are running along a country road not far from Rodgers's house. It is nearly dark, and on impulse I ask him if he'll show me the way he runs in a marathon. I want to know what a world-record pace feels like. 'Okay,' he says. 'We'll go a little faster when we get to that next telephone pole.' When we reach the pole Rodgers rises on to his toes and accelerates with sinuous smoothness until he is floating along at just under five minutes a mile. It is a pace he knows well. With considerable ungainly effort I manage to stay with him. The road is smooth, and I am able to turn my head and watch him as he runs. His arms rock back and forth effortlessly, his gloved hands as loose as laundry on a clothesline. With each step his legs cover so much road that I take three steps for every two of his. Now, for the first time, his shoes make a faint sound, a feathery *whooshwhoosh*. 'I guess I'd be running about like this in a race,' he says. 'It's hard to tell exactly.' I feel a stitch forming an ugly knot in my rib cage.

'Maybe I'd be going a little bit slower,' he says. 'It could be faster, though. It would depend on who was there.' I notice that he is not breathing hard, and it occurs to me that I am running a foot or so from one of the most perfect cardio-vascular systems on earth.

Mercifully, Rodgers slows down, and once again we move at a bearable pace until we reach Rockland Street, where he lives.

Rodgers and his wife rent the top floor of an old house at the far end of a horseshoe-shaped street. To get to their flat, you climb an outside flight of wooden steps. Their living quarters consist of four or five small rooms. It is a pleasant place. Bright green plants hang in the windows, and in the kitchen Ellen is cooking macaroni cheese and baking chocolate biscuits. Rodgers opens the refrigerator and, ignoring three bottles of beer, gets out a quart of ginger ale. He pours some of it into a glass and drinks it. On the kitchen table are bottles of Vitamin C, Thermotabs and something called Body Ammo 2.

I have a shower. Later, while Rodgers showers, I talk with Ellen and look around. On a table next to a medium-size television set is a silver platter, his first place trophy from the 1976 New York Marathon. On the wall of one room mementos are hung: a 'Bill Rodgers Day' proclamation from the mayor of his home town,

* The record is 2·08·34, set by Derek Clayton of Australia in 1969.

awarded after he won the Boston Marathon; a photograph of Rodgers and Shorter finishing a race together; an enormous plaque won at a marathon in Japan; a poster advertising the Montreal Olympics.

Rodgers returns, and I ask him whether any of his training techniques are applicable to beginners. 'Sure,' he says. 'Run whenever you feel like it. If you want to run, just take off and go. I do that all the time. I'm uncomfortable when I walk. I have a very awkward kind of walk, so I don't feel very good doing it. One of my legs is an inch longer than the other; a doctor told me that. So I'd rather run. The truth is, I hate walking.'

21 · The world's sickest running club

Dr Terence Kavanagh, right, with heart patients

Sometimes a heart attack is the best thing that ever happened

One day in 1965 Mort Hirschfield, a tall, athletic-looking insurance salesman, was sitting in his living-room watching television when suddenly his chest began to feel peculiar. At first, he said later, it was as if someone were tightening a steel band with a thumbscrew. It was a heart attack, a bad one, but Hirschfield was lucky. He did not die, though one out of every two heart attack victims do within the first month.

Hirschfield had always worked and played hard, skied in the winter, and done whatever he wanted to do. Now, suddenly he was an invalid, so when, a few weeks later, his doctor prescribed exercises, Hirschfield was startled. 'How can I exercise?' he said. 'I've had a heart attack.'

'That's right,' said the doctor, 'but that's in the past.'

Following instructions, Hirschfield reported to a gymnasium, and under his doctor's vigilant eye began exercising, something he thought he would never do again. 'He'd make me try a little of this and a little of that, very moderate stuff,' Hirschfield remembers. 'I'd run around the track once or twice and he'd take my pulse. I'd exercise for maybe fifteen minutes, then have to stop and take a shower.' Still, he stuck at it, and in time began to notice some improvement. To his astonishment, before long he felt as good as he ever had. 'Now I can train for 45 minutes easily and feel great,' he says. 'I don't know where I'd be without running.'

By studying the electrical signature of Hirschfield's heart on a cardiogram, a specialist can see that he once had a heart attack, but that his heart is now functioning efficiently. Hirschfield, who is in his late sixties, works a full schedule, does whatever he wants to in his leisure time, and three nights a week goes to the Y.M.C.A. for exercise classes designed especially for heart patients.

I visited one of these classes recently, and if I hadn't been told that the participants had once been seriously ill, I would never have guessed it. Two or three were only in their thirties; the rest were men in their forties, fifties and sixties. (Most heart attack victims are men, although, as noted in Chapter 8, women after menopause begin to catch up as they lose their mysterious natural immunity.) Everyone in the class was running, chatting and laughing, and there was a lot of good-natured joking, much of it directed at the imperturbable instructor.

A generation ago people like Hirschfield and his associates would have been told to avoid exercise, relax and make the best of a bad situation. Within a few years many of them would have been dead. My father had a heart attack when he was 35, and until he died eight years later he lived the life of an invalid. Once, just once, in those eight years I remember seeing him toss a football. The rest of the time he sat quietly, read, listened to music and (as I came to realize much later) put his affairs in order.

In the years since then, cardiologists have learned that it isn't necessary for their patients to go gently into that good night. They've learned how to help them fight back and in that battle one of their most effective weapons has been running. Even the scarred heart has remarkable adaptive abilities. Under the rigours of exercise it does not weaken but becomes significantly stronger, strong enough, in many cases, to withstand easily the strain of running a marathon (described by Dr Loring Rowell as 'one of the major insults a person can voluntarily give his cardio-vascular system'). The psychological benefits of such a return to physical fitness are enormous. People feel less fear, more confidence and less depression (a well-known post-cardiac symptom.) Furthermore in practically every case their sex lives improve.

All this would be of little general interest if only the occasional person fell victim to a heart attack, but currently we are experiencing an epidemic. Of the heart patients who survive an initial attack, 4–6% die each year. If they start a medically supervised programme of running and other exercise, the rate drops to well under 2%. Although a degree of self-selection may be involved (some patients simply will not exercise, even to save their lives), the decline is none the less impressive. Furthermore, says Dr Terence Kavanagh, the director of one of the most highly regarded cardiac rehabilitation programmes, 'In terms of the quality of life there are even more grounds for optimism. One study showed that one-third of a sample of our patients had neurotic-type personality and developed excessive depression after a heart attack. In most cases, patients became less depressed as they became more fit.'

As noted in Chapter 4, doctors are cautious about asserting that running guarantees a longer and better life. Kavanagh, a long-time champion of exercise and the author of a provocative book entitled *Heart Attack? Counterattack!*, reports that even though this programme is a decade old, it has not yet been in operation long enough to permit proper statistical evaluation. He says, 'A more thorough analysis of our figures is needed before these results can be accepted as anything more than encouraging.' Some doctors are even more wary. Dr Herman Hellerstein, an authority on the rehabilitation of heart patients, told a group of colleagues at a recent conference that distance running is potentially hazardous and has aroused unrealistic expectations. He said that even when it undeniably benefits a patient, it doesn't necessarily benefit him in the best possible way.

It is no surprise that medical authorities disagree with one another. Running is such a new therapeutic technique that its effects have not yet been fully measured. Still, whatever any interim evidence has emerged, it has tended to support the probability that running is beneficial. This is why Kavanagh insists, even in the face of his incomplete statistics, 'You've got to play the odds.'

An explanation of what a heart attack is will help us understand how exercise helps a heart patient. When it occurs, it seems like a sudden event, but it is not. The conditions that predispose one to a heart attack have usually begun decades earlier with the build-up of cholesterol and other materials that have narrowed the heart's arteries and thus limited its blood supply. In civilized countries atherosclerosis, as this narrowing is called, is common. It was found in a significant number of Americans killed in the Korean War (their average age was 22), and is frequently detected in schoolchildren. Sometimes an early warning comes in the form of angina pectoris (commonly referred to simply as angina). This is a chest pain, usually short-lived, indicating that the heart isn't receiving enough oxygen. Ordinarily this occurs during exertion and disappears when the activity stops. Some angina patients live for years without having a heart attack, but if the narrowing of the arteries continues the likelihood increases that a clump of debris will one day produce a blockage. When this happens, the supply of blood to part of the heart muscle is cut off. For a while the muscle aches, and it is this that a victim feels. Finally, the pain subsides and the attack ends, leaving in its wake a partially dead heart. The severity of an attack is determined by how much of the heart dies.

If the victim lives, no matter how much of the heart's blood supply has been affected by the attack (myocardial infarction is the medical term) the heart promptly begins to heal. In the recovery process, white blood cells arrive to remove the heart's spent muscle fibres, and new blood vessels, replacements for those damaged by the attack, begin to snake their way through the muscle. Finally, within a month or two, scar tissue forms. At this point, if the damage has not been too severe, exercise can begin to help the victim's recovery.

It has already been noted that aerobic exercise has a number of beneficial effects on a normal heart. Among other things, it slows the heartbeat, increases the amount of blood pumped with each contraction, lowers blood pressure and blood fats, and increases the ability of working muscles to remove oxygen from the blood. Exactly the same processes take place in the heart of a person who has had a myocardial infarction.

It is these changes that lie behind today's proliferation of post-cardiac exercise classes. A few years ago, a group of medical specialists, assembled at the American National Workshop on Exercise, wrote: 'Epidemiological and other studies have demonstrated that regular physical activity is associated with a better state of well being, enhanced quality of living, and apparently reduced morbidity and mortality from ischaemic heart disease i.e., disease caused by an inadequate blood supply. For these reasons, comprehensive patient care should include enhancement of physical fitness.'

Many doctors have rallied around this and similar endorsements of exercise for heart patients. In St Louis, for example, Dr Jon Cooksey, a cardiologist, has organized a running programme for cardiac patients. 'We've measured a 35% improvement,' he says. 'Heart rate is lower by an average of seventeen beats, and the blood pressure is lower.' The case of Howard Pattiz, a patient in his early fifties, is typical. When he began the programme not long after his heart attack, he could shuffle through only seven short laps around the track, but within six weeks he was doing 34.

In Greenwich, Connecticut, the hospital and the Health Association sponsor a medically supervised programme for heart patients. They recently reported on one patient who could hardly walk at all when he joined the programme, and who eventually ran a mile non-stop in eleven minutes.

In La Crosse, Wisconsin, a cardiac rehabilitation programme has been in operation since 1971. When I talked recently with its executive director, Philip Wilson, he said that several hundred patients had participated since classes started and that their results had matched those achieved elsewhere. The La Crosse programme is one of the few that puts out its own newspaper, the *Cardio-Gram*, a publication that includes articles on everything from foot trouble to heat stroke to sex after a heart attack.

One of the most ambitious and successful post-cardiac programmes is found in Hawaii. There Dr Jack Scaff, a cardiologist in his early forties, has long conducted a thrice-weekly programme for heart patients. In 1974 Scaff and a cardiologist colleague, Dr John Wagner, got the idea of expanding the programme to include people who had not had attacks but who, because of sedentary lives, are in danger. Accordingly, they started a Sunday morning clinic to teach non-runners how to complete a marathon. 'The Honolulu Marathon Clinic,' Wagner says, 'has made it possible for middle-aged, sedentary non-running people to learn how to compete in a marathon without being intimidated by the élite, young, skinny runners they see around all the time.' The Honolulu programme has spawned similar clinics in other cities.

Dr Kavanagh's Rehabilitation Centre in Toronto conducts a programme that has attracted interest and envy the world over. More than a decade ago, Kavanagh's background as doctor/athlete and athletic official (he is much involved in Canadian amateur sport) prompted him to start looking into endurance exercise as a rehabilitative measure for heart patients. Within five years seven of his patients, three of whom had had not just one attack but two, were able to run in and complete the Boston Marathon. Interestingly, the idea for attempting the 26·2-mile run didn't come from Kavanagh himself, but from one of his patients. In his book the doctor describes how it developed:

One day, while we were changing after a five-mile run, someone half jokingly remarked how great an achievement it would be to finish a marathon. For a second or two there was complete silence, a few questioning glances, an uneasy grin, and finally one or two doubtful laughs. Then the moment was gone. Gradually, week by week, the idea grew in our minds. What at first seemed to be a preposterous joke became a serious consideration and then a firm resolve. For me it was, in a way, the moment of truth. I had motivated these men to run; as far as I was concerned they were rehabilitated, and I had made no bones in telling them so. They had trusted me. To put it succinctly, the time had come to put up or shut up! I decided that we would make the attempt.

Kavanagh was criticized by colleagues. None the less, all seven patients finished the marathon in good condition. It is hardly surprising that they presented him with his own special trophy inscribed to 'Dr T. Kavanagh. Supercoach, the World's Sickest Track Club.'

Kavanagh's rehabilitation programme is not as dangerous or as foolhardy as it might seem. For one thing, it is based on a careful assessment of each patient's condition; for another, it consists of a carefully graduated programme, beginning in some cases with as little as a 30-minute one-mile walk. Finally, even after a patient has graduated to running, Kavanagh does not recommend a pace faster than a ten-minute mile. (His programme is outlined in detail in his book.)

Though cardiologists shudder at the thought, some heart patients, simply prescribed their own programmes. Tex Maule, author of *Running Scarred*, was a *Sports Illustrated* writer when he had a heart attack a few years ago. Maule not only spent much of his time with athletes, but had always been energetic himself; hence it seemed natural to start running as soon as he was able to. Training every morning at a track not far from his office, he finally developed enough endurance to run the first several miles of the Boston Marathon without mishap.

Al Martin, a physical therapist interested in cardio-vascular rehabilitation, also prescribed his own programme against medical advice. He was 31 when he had his heart attack. He followed standard medical textbooks and started alternately running and walking specific distances with a stopwatch. Whenever he felt pains in his chest he slowed down. Martin says, 'I emphasized long periods of low intensity rather than intense short runs. I worked up to 40 five-minute sessions, starting slowly and gradually picking up the pace. Today I can go five miles a day in under 40 minutes. I no longer get angina with heavy exertion, that is, heart rates as high as 190. I used nitroglycerin at first, but don't need it any more.'

In the end it may be that running's most important changes in this field are in styles of living. It has been established that the most likely victim of heart disease is a person with a so-called Type A personality—hard-driving, competitive, irritable and impatient. As mentioned in Chapter 2, the tranquillity gained by running has a radiating power that irresistibly affects other parts of our lives. If this tranquillity transforms a Type A person into a less competitive Type B, the chances of avoiding a heart attack and of leading a happier life are substantially increased.

Rate your heart attack risk

This chart, based on the factors that are most decisive in determining a person's risk of heart attack, will give you a reliable estimate of the danger you face. Although it is not an infallible predictor of health, it is based on current scientific research and is therefore a useful guide. Some factors, such as heredity, are beyond an individual's control, while others, such as exercise, weight and smoking, are in most cases within our power to change. The important point is not to worry about factors you can't affect, but to work on those you can. To score yourself, mark the appropriate description for each risk factor; then, using the indicator numbers at the left of each row, add up your total number of points. Ten to 20 points indicates low risk; 21 to 40 moderate risk; 41 to 60 high risk.

	Heredity	Blood Pressure	Diabetes	Smoking	Weight	Cholesterol	Exercise	Emotional Stress	Age	Sex and Build
6	Three or more relatives who had heart attacks before age 60 (parents & siblings only)	High blood pressure not controlled by medication	Diabetic with complications (circulation, kidneys, eyes)	More than 40 cigarettes daily	More than 50 lbs overweight	Over 281	Complete lack of exercise	Intense problems, can't cope, see a psychiatrist	Over 60	Male, very stocky
5	Two relatives who had heart attacks before age 60	High blood pressure partly controlled by medication	Diabetic on insulin – no complications	21–39 cigarettes daily	36–50 lbs overweight	256–280	Sedentary job, light recreational exercise	Constantly need pills or drink for stress	51–60	Male, fairly stocky
4	One relative who had a heart attack before age 60	Persistent mild high blood pressure, untreated	High sugar controlled by tablets	6–20 cigarettes daily	21–35 lbs overweight	231–255	Sedentary job, moderately active recreation	Take pills or drink for stress on occasion	41–50	Male, average build
3	Two or more relatives who had heart attacks after age 60	High blood pressure only when upset	High sugar controlled by diet	Fewer than 5 cigarettes daily	6–20 lbs overweight	206–230 (or don't know)	Sedentary job, very active in recreation	Moderate business or personal pressures	31–40	Female after menopause
2	One relative who had a heart attack after age 60	Normal blood pressure (or don't know)	Normal blood sugar (or don't know)	Cigars or pipe only	Up to 5 lbs overweight	181–205	Moderately active in job and recreation	Rare business or personal pressure	21–30	Male, thin build
1	No heart disease in family	Low blood pressure	Low blood sugar	Nonuser or stopped permanently	More than 5 lbs underweight	180 or below	Very active physically in job and recreation	No real business or personal pressures	10–20	Female still menstruating

22 · The scientists of sport

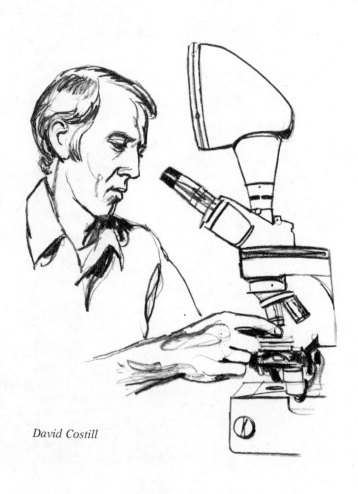

David Costill

Laboratories that search out
the secrets of running

At a laboratory in Dallas, Texas, a research scientist swabs Frank Shorter's slim, grisly calf with an antiseptic. As Shorter makes a face the researcher injects an anaesthetic into the calf and, once it has taken effect, makes a deft quarter-of-an-inch incision with a scalpel. An assistant hands him a stainless-steel instrument, a hollow, needle-like apparatus six inches long and half as big around as a pencil. The scientist inserts its rounded end into the incision and presses until it is embedded in the fibres of Shorter's gastrocnemius muscle. Into the needle's hollow centre he now slides a small cylinder with a sharpened end that is not unlike a miniature round biscuit cutter. Within Shorter's calf the cylinder lops off a piece of tissue the size of an orange seed. Now both needles are withdrawn, the incision in Shorter's calf is closed with elastoplast and the tiny sample of tissue from deep within his leg is frozen in liquid nitrogen.

The scientists of sport are at work again. Not too many years ago runners were largely on their own in planning their training. Even if one of them was lucky enough to have a knowledgeable coach, so little was known about the ultimate sources of speed and endurance that any training method that worked was bound to be mostly the result of luck. All that, or much of it, anyway, has changed. In the past few years so much has been learned about the physiology of running, about nutrition, and even about that most elusive of all factors, motivation, that any athlete who wants to take the trouble can quickly soak up a whole lifetime of vicarious experience simply by reading. And not just top athletes; you and I can do it too. Take, as an example, just one nutritional point. Until recently, many athletes, and even many coaches, assumed that if you wanted energy you had to eat protein. Eventually, however, researchers discovered to their astonishment that carbohydrates rather than protein are the main source of energy during hard exercise. For some football teams, the pre-game meal is still steak: but it is only because common sense is too often no match for tradition.

The carbohydrate secret, along with many others, emerged from a phenomenon that began in the early years of this century; the exercise physiology laboratory. The first such laboratories were established in England and Germany. By the 1920s the idea had caught on in America, and the Harvard Fatigue Laboratory—which owned, among other equipment, one of the first treadmills built for exercise—was in full cry. But the big growth period didn't come until the 1960s, when physiological curiosity spawned laboratories all over the world.

In England alone, work relevant to the needs of runners is being done at Salford, Loughborough, Birmingham, Exeter and Eastbourne. Because there are now so many of them, these laboratories do diverse kinds of research. At the University of Illinois, Dr Lawrence Oscai is trying to find out how exercise affects the size and quantity of fat cells; his study may one day be seen as a significant milestone in the fight against overweight. At the Noll Laboratory, Elsworth Buskirk has been investigating the effectiveness of portable defibrillators, devices designed to start a heart beating again after it has slipped into ineffectual spasms. And at Ball State University researchers have been looking into such subjects as the rehabilitation of patients after knee surgery and the role of exercise in helping diabetics lead more normal lives. Yet sooner or later most of the laboratories return to the first love of practically all exercise physiologists: running. The reason is that in running the human body is under such heavy stress that changes occur quickly and in easily measurable amounts. In the course of a year the body of a person who bowls one night a week may be slighly altered, but who could devise a way to measure the alteration? On the other hand, the change in the body of a person who runs five miles a day leaves no doubt that something significant is happening.

The work of the exercise physiology laboratories has had some impressive practical effects. As I write this, John Walker of New Zealand is the world's fastest miler. He also receives more medical attention than perhaps any other runner in history. His doctor, Lloyd Drake, keeps close watch on his pulse rate, his blood count, his aerobic capacity. If his haemoglobin level falls—and with it his blood's oxygen-carrying ability—Drake gives it a boost with an injection of Vitamin B_{12}, intended to stimulate the bone marrow to produce more haemoglobin. If Walker suffers a slight injury, Drake takes care of it before it can turn into a serious one. He even specifies how fast Walker should run when he's training. (It's often at a five-minute pace.)

Not everyone applauds this trend. At a symposium on exercise and heart disease, Sir Roger Bannister said he thought scientific research hadn't helped athletes much because each athlete is different from all others. 'He has to try running fast and slow,' said Sir Roger, 'learn from his own mistakes and then work out his own magic training formula.' Furthermore, he said, physical factors are only part of what makes a successful runner: 'I think the final quality that makes a runner better is his own drive and mental toughness. That's as important as any physical quality.' Some critics also fear that we will end up creating a breed of robot superstars, athletically perfected bodies manipulated by squads of researchers and technicians.

This seems unlikely. For one thing, as Sir Roger points out, mental qualities are important in running. For another, so many variables contribute to athletic success that it would be all but impossible to have each of them precisely tuned at any given moment. But who knows? After all, there *is* the example of East Germany, whose ability to win Olympic medals has climbed markedly since its doctors began exploiting the latest research from around the world.

To find out exactly what an exercise physiology laboratory does, I paid a visit to one of the best-known and most highly regarded: The Human Performance Laboratory at Ball State University in Indiana, presided over by an articulate, quick-thinking physiologist named David Costill.

Established in the mid-sixties with nothing but a bicycle, a step bench and a drawer filled with old stethoscopes, it began to attract attention only after Costill's arrival in 1966. Costill is a lean, greying man in his mid-forties who, practising what he preaches, runs five miles a day. Although he had been interested in athletics since childhood, exercise physiology didn't occur to him as a career until fairly late. 'After I left university,' he told me, 'I was a high school swimming coach for a while. I quickly realized I didn't want to be a coach for the rest of my life—there wasn't much satisfaction beyond my enjoyment of the kids. What I did like was doing studies on athletes. I'd spend hundreds of my free hours on those studies, just because they were fun. Finally I went to Ohio for a doctorate, but even then I didn't know what I wanted to do. Then I started hanging around the research lab. I'd go in and stay all day and just play. I suddenly realized that this was what I enjoyed most.' With a Ph.D. in physiology, Costill started looking for work. Chance came to the rescue when someone sent him an advertisement from Ball State, which was looking for a director for its lab. Costill answered it and got the job.

Along his laboratory's north wall are five or six ordinary-looking offices, crammed with up-to-the-minute scientific equipment—a computer; a centrifuge; devices for measuring oxygen, carbon dioxide and other gases as they go into and out of runners on treadmills; a ten-by-ten-foot heat chamber that is used to find out how people react to extreme temperatures; and, in a central place of honour, the treadmill on which some of the nation's best runners have given their all for science.

Out of these rooms have come a number of significant discoveries, some of which have changed the sport of running forever. A few years ago, for example, while doing research with Bengt Saltin, a doctor at the University of Copenhagen, Costill noticed that the muscles of world-class runners seemed to be different from those of less accomplished athletes. Pursuing elusive clues, the researchers were led finally to the muscle fibres themselves. When they looked closely at these hair-like filaments, they noticed something interesting. After staining, two distinct types could be identified. Furthermore, the top runners all had a preponderance of the same type of fibre. What did this mean? Using complex analytical techniques, they began to examine muscle fibres for such factors as enzyme activity and contractile characteristics. A discovery of considerable significance eventually emerged out of this research: some muscle fibres, designated S.T., contract slowly; others, designated F.T., contract quickly. Virtually every top distance runner, they found, has more S.T. than F.T. fibres. When, for example, fourteen of them, including Frank Shorter and the late Steve Prefontaine, were examined, it was found that the average percentage of slow-twitch fibres was 79. In a random sample of people, the average was only 57. Since middle-distance runners (half-milers to two-milers) were found to have only 62% slow-twitch fibres, there was clearly a difference between the two groups. But was it the crucial difference, the one that makes one runner an excellent marathoner and another a top half-miler? Further research has indicated that it probably is.

To some this might seem to suggest that top runners are born, not made. To Costill it implies nothing of the kind. What it does suggest is that some day athletes may be able to stay out of fruitless dead ends where the possibility for improvement is markedly limited, and to concentrate instead on what they're best at. That won't guarantee that a particular athlete will become a champion, but it will at least spare him or her a pre-ordained mediocrity. 'We've shown that you're never going to be a long-distance champion unless you've got a lot of slow-twitch muscle fibres,' Costill says.

Costill has also made some important discoveries about what happens to the body's fluids during intense exercise like marathon running. In the process he has probably saved a number of lives. A few years ago he grew curious about whether the hoary old prohibition against taking fluids during exercise made sense. Investigation, both by him and by other researchers, showed that it did not, and that in fact a failure to ingest fluids, especially in hot, humid weather, could contribute to heat stroke. Further experiments revealed that far from reducing efficiency, drinking during exercise increases it. One results was a change in I.A.A.F. rules to allow more drinking stations in long races.

Another practice Costill is currently changing involves mileage. Runners traditionally add up their mileage a week at a time. When I talked with Bill Rodgers, for example, he said, 'I've put in a hundred and forty miles a week for the past three years.' Weekly rather than daily mileage has become the accepted measure because that way a runner can more easily compensate for day-to-day fluctuations. Costill argues that even this isn't going far enough. He has the figures to back up his argument, derived from an experimental subject he knows better than any other: himself. The energy for running comes from a sugar-like substance called glycogen. Glycogen is stored in muscle tissue, and during exercise the supply is gradually used up. When it is gone, no matter how much will power you have, work must stop. Checking his own glycogen level in the days following three consecutive ten-mile runs, Costill found that it took as much as two weeks for the supply to return to normal. Plainly he could not possibly put in a full-scale training week and have enough muscle glycogen to get him through an important race. 'My glycogen is very slow in coming back,' he told me. 'It's an individual thing. There's nothing I can do about it except eat lots of carbohydrates.' (One doctor I talked with said, however, that he thought the resynthesization of glycogen has more to do with fitness than genetics.)

Costill's recommendation is that runners start keeping track of monthly rather than weekly mileage, thereby making it easier to permit themselves an occasional light week. He has included this recommendation, along with many others, in a remarkable unpublished manuscript which he calls *A Scientific Approach to Distance Running*. This is probably the most comprehensive collection of

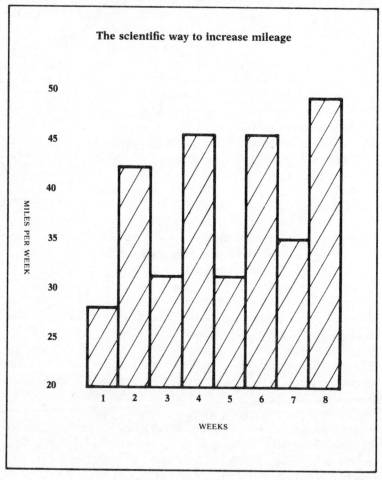

Adapted from A Scientific Approach to Distance Running.

training information ever assembled. On the week-vs.-month question he writes:

The purpose of training is to tax and often tear down the biological systems essential for prolonged high rates of energy production in the runner. Such training is of no value unless the organism is permitted sufficient rest to rebuild and super-compensate for the stress of training.... Thus, rest is an equally important part of the training programme, for without it the system will certainly fail.... In the light of the fact that most physiological systems (*i.e.*, muscle enzymes) require three to four weeks to respond to a given training stress, it seems the runner's training stress should be judged on the basis of total distance covered in a four-week period. This system offers the advantage of varying the weekly running effort, while permitting longer periods of light training to allow full recovery.

Costill's discovery that he has a sluggish glycogen system has led him to yet another conclusion: that no matter how scientifically valid a training principle is, it may have little application to some runners. 'Each of us is different,' he says. 'If you want to find out what you're capable of, try different things, even things that seem extreme and totally unreasonable.'

Among Costill's other findings:

1. Even distance runners need speed work. Some coaches deny this, but Costill's research shows that only during fast running are all the muscle fibres used in competition brought into play. Running fast also enhances biomechanical efficiency.

2. Heavy training depletes the glycogen supply for about three days. Thus more than just a single day of light training should precede a race. Costill recommends three light days. He has found, incidentally, that it is not necessary to avoid running on the day before a race, so long as the training session is not more than four to six miles and is done at a slow pace.

The week I visited Costill was a busy one. As we talked, just outside his window a bulldozer started digging the foundation for an extension to the laboratory. A salesman for a scientific instrument manufacturer arrived to give a demonstration. In the laboratory itself technicians peered through microscopes and with needle-like instruments sorted individual muscle fibres for chemical analysis later on. Before I left I asked Costill a question. What did he see as the next frontier in human physiology?

'Things are happening fast in this kind of work,' he replied. 'Only a few years ago we were using rats. The problem was you can't make a rat run hard, no matter how much you shock him. He'll just sit on his backside. Then we learned how to do muscle studies on living people, and that was a break-through. Now biochemistry is the frontier. We have to find out what happens in the muscle. I'm convinced that's where the action is. The work we've been doing up until now is like opening a door and peeping in. We know there's a lot in there. Now we've got to get busy, open the door wide, and find out what it is.'

23 · And something more

The rewards of the Mount Washington climb

Just in case 26·2 miles isn't enough

What does it feel like to run not just 26 but 50 miles? Bob Glover had just finished doing this when I interviewed him. What he had done was to run 200 times around a quarter-mile track, for the simple reason that he is one of those runners for whom ordinary races are not enough. Now he sat in his office reflecting on the experience. As we talked he used a penknife to cut slits into the toes of a pair of blue running shoes in an attempt to relieve pressure on his toenails which hurt because of blood blisters.

Glover is tall, hollow-cheeked and fit. The day after his 50 mile race he ran five miles. Now, two days later, he planned to run 20. He did not look tired.

'If you have a good base of cardio-vascular fitness and your legs are strong from a lot of running,' he said, 'the main problems in a fifty-mile race are only in your head. Between about thirty and thirty-eight miles was where the struggle was for me. After forty miles, it almost seemed as if I was surging on a new source of energy. First of all there's an emotional high. I'd decided before the race that if I got to 40 I was going to finish one way or another.'

Glover's plans were changed a little by the August weather. 'The temperature out there was 90°F,' he said, 'so my goal became not so much to race as simply to survive. How can I explain what I felt like between 30 and 38 miles? My bad knee was hurting. I'm not supposed to run at all. I was feeling tired, as if I just wanted to lie down and go to sleep. And my back ached. But the race was starting to affect me more psychologically than physically. I had to start playing games in my head to keep going.'

As he ran, Glover munched chocolate, drank tomato juice and water, and tried eating baby food—carrots, custard and a mixture of beef and vegetables. 'I thought it would be good because it digests easily,' he said. 'The trouble was, it had been out in the sun and was miserably hot. I had to force it down. I almost threw up.'

Glover finished in fifth place, in seven hours and 45 minutes. 'The first thing I did,' he said, 'was to have a beer. It tasted good. Then I went home, sat in the bath for half an hour, and finally had a shower. I stretched for about fifteen or 20 minutes, then ate. Then I had another bath and stretched again. Then I put my feet up and watched television for a while. When I started to doze off, I went to bed.'

What is it that prompts a person like Glover, a sane, industrious and productive citizen of the workaday world, to undertake such an ordeal? Not fitness. He is already superbly fit. Perhaps all that can be said is that Glover ran the 50 miles because they were there. He had already entered a number of marathons and one 50 kilometre race—a trifle more than 31 miles—so this, in some curious way, was the next logical step.

Whatever the reason, such a race demonstrates that in running there is always something else to do. If you are content with your customary pace or races, you can spend a lifetime running in a park or entering races of five or ten miles, perhaps occasionally trying a marathon to test yourself. But if you want more, there are endless possibilities.

There's no reason, in fact, to stop at 50 miles. Ted Corbitt likes 100 mile races. 'To race 100 miles was a natural extension of having run for as many years as I have,' he said. 'It's exactly the same impetus that causes you to run a marathon. Many marathoners finish a race and have too much left, so they speculate about how much farther they could have run.'

Corbitt knows as much about long races—ultramarathons as runners call them—as anyone alive, and he discussed their subtleties like a gardener describing prize roses. 'When you go up to 100 miles,' he said, 'you're in a different category. There are fatigue zones. At eighteen miles or so you hit the first one. You've got to run through it and come out on the other side. If you go farther, there are other zones waiting for you. You never know about these until you run a race of 50 or 100 miles. For instance, it's very hard to get past 85 miles. You have to be determined; otherwise you just won't make it. It seems it takes forever to push through it and get to 90 miles. It's different from the marathon fatigue zone because your energy level has changed several times.'

I asked Corbitt whether he had ever lost his will to continue. 'Oh, yes,' he replied. 'You think, *Why didn't I stay at home? What am I doing here?*'

None the less, for people like Corbitt and Glover there remains something magnetically appealing about exploring the limits of endurance. Nor are they the only people who relish the idea of looking into the more remote—and in some cases more bizarre—byways of running.

Every year in London, runners gather in the shadow of Big Ben for the start of the 52½ mile London-to-Brighton race. Rod MacNicholl, one recent contestant, described his experiences. 'At the end of the race I was bleeding from my nipples, feet, crotch, and a few other places. My legs were extremely painful, especially my thighs. Other than that, I felt terrific.' At least two women have also run the London-to-Brighton course.

In South Africa every spring, runners assemble in Pietermaritzburg and then spend the better part of the day running to Durban, 56 miles distant. The race, known as the Comrades Marathon, is so popular that in 1978 no fewer than 3000 competitors, masochists to a man, turned out for it.

Tony Rafferty of Belfast, Ireland, once ran for 50 hours, just to prove it could be done.

A runner named Park Barner ran a 50-mile race one day in 1976, then the next day ran a full 26-mile marathon.

Richard Inamorato, a 27-year-old auditor, set out in 1976 on a 2400 mile run from Fort Kent, Maine to Key West, Florida. 'Anyone who would attempt such a stunt,' he declared with unassailable logic, 'has to enjoy it or is an eccentric moron.'

Dick Traum, a personnel consultant, runs races—including marathons—despite the loss of his right leg in an automobile accident. (He wears an artificial one.)

Joe Pardo is regularly seen at races in New York and Connecticut. He is blind. So is Harry Cordellos of San Francisco, a 2:59 marathoner.

In Death Valley—a surprisingly popular place for running—two runners named Pax Beale and Ken Crutchlow, accompanied by a doctor who was curious about what would happen to them, ran 145 miles in two days, finishing on Mt Whitney, 14 495 feet above sea level. In Death Valley the temperature hit 135°F. Beale lost 55 lbs in the two days but replaced all but 11 lbs of it by drinking a special fluid.

In 1969 Bruce Tulloh forsook his job as an English schoolteacher to run the 3200 miles from Los Angeles to New York in 65 days. (He

gives a lively account of his experiences in his book *Four Million Footsteps*.)

Scores of British runners, members of teams seeking to immortalize themselves by setting records, have run the traditional course from Land's End to John O' Groats.

A New Zealander named Don Cameron ran nearly 60 miles a day to cover the length of his country, from Stirling Point on the Southern Coast to Cape Reinga lighthouse on the northernmost tip. It took him 23 days, and he celebrated by having a beer with the lighthouse keeper.

A group called the Liberty Torch, which combines religion and running, recently ran 8800 miles in all 50 states to demonstrate 'faith in America.'

Each year an uphill race is held in New Hampshire. It starts at the base of Mount Washington, snakes its way up an eight-mile road, and ends at the 6293-foot summit. A friend of mine named Al Meehan has run in it several times, coming well up in the pack each time. Meehan says: 'You hurt all the way. A marathon is nothing compared to that race. People think that because they've done a little mountain climbing they can handle it. They're in for a surprise.'

My own idea of fun is none of the above. I'm happiest taking a pleasant ten-mile run on a cool autumn day when the leaves are bright and the air is crisp. Only occasionally do I go in search of agony. But who is to say that I'm right and the people I've just described are wrong? Endless possibilities await you.

Afterword

The miracle of running

Throughout these pages we have explored the question of why running is such an extraordinarily satisfying avocation. Once you have been running for a few months, you invariably notice some remarkable psychological dividends, a feeling of calmness and power, of being in control of your life. Runners also speak of having an 'addiction', and in a sense they do. It is rare to meet a runner, no matter how busy, who considers giving up his sport. More often, the contrary is true; someone who runs three or four miles a day—quite enough for fitness alone—will in time inexplicably double or even triple his mileage.

Hence the search for health hardly explains the phenomenon. Mere good health can easily be earned without major dislocation of one's life; twenty or thirty minutes a day will do it. So why do people run eight, ten or more miles every day, summer and winter, particularly when the know that they will never become especially distinguished at it?

Many theories have been suggested. Sir Roger Bannister has compared running with music. Both stimulate our nervous systems in ways the human organism finds pleasurable. An hour's run massages the nerves with infinitesimal electrical impulses much as Handel's *Messiah* does.

Closely related to this theory is one recently offered by Thaddeus Kostrubala. Addressing a conference of doctors and researchers, Kostrubala wondered aloud whether a runner might, after 40 minutes or so of running, somehow 'obliterate' the influence of the left cortex (the logical part of the brain), allowing the right cortex (the intuitive, artistic part) to gain temporary dominance. It has also been suggested that the pleasurable feelings that accompany running may result from the production of natural protein substances called endorphins that reduce pain. (They have been called 'the poppies of the head'.)

In his perceptive book *Gods and Games*, David Miller offers a different explanation. As young children, he writes, we play games in innocent purity, for the pleasure they afford rather than with any thought of winning. In infancy we make no such artificial distinctions. A child tosses a toy, laughingly searches for it, exults in finding it, and then joyously does it all over again. Our adult games, Miller holds, are an attempt to recapture the innocent play of youth. What we want is not to play games at all but to play *play*. Because competitiveness in running is so infinitely variable and so controllable, we are able to do exactly that in our sport.

Perhaps there is something in all these theories. For my part, I have a different one. Most people who have considered the matter have, I believe, posed the wrong question. They have asked why running produces such extraordinary effects. Putting the question that way elicits a certain kind of answer, and I think it is the wrong one. My suspicion is that the effects of running are not extraordinary at all, but quite ordinary. It is the *other* states, all *other* feelings, that are peculiar, for they are an abnegation of the way you and I are intended to feel. As runners, I think we reach directly back along the endless chain of history. We experience what we would have felt had we lived ten thousand years ago, eating fruits, nuts and vegetables and keeping our hearts and lungs and muscles fit by constant movement. We are reasserting, as modern man seldom does, our kinship with ancient man, and even with the wild beasts that preceded him. This, I think, is our remarkable secret, one we share every time we go running.

APPENDIX A
The runner's address book

MAIL ORDER RUNNING GEAR

Catalogues are available from all these suppliers and will be sent if a stamped addressed envelope, at least 9"×4", is supplied.

Bourne Sports, 5 Glebe Street, Stoke-on-Trent, Staffs ST4 1HP. Tel: 0782 47138
The Four Seasons, 115–117 Northumberland Street, Newcastle-upon-Tyne. Tel: 0632 26452
K. G. Sports, 28/29 Winslade Way, Catford, London SE6 4JU. Tel: 01 690 7324
Ron Hill Sports, 148/150 Market Street, Hyde, Cheshire. Tel: 061 366 9191
The Runner's Shop, 140/142 Bolton Road, Bury, Greater Manchester BL8 2NP
The Sports Market, PO Box 247, Croydon, Surrey CR9 8AQ. Tel: 01 656 6471
The Sweat Shop, 10 The Causeway, Teddington, Middlesex. Tel: 01 943 0239
Tobi Sports, 242 Cowdray Avenue, Colchester, Essex. Tel: 0206 64350

ORGANIZATIONS THAT ENCOURAGE RUNNING

Amateur Athletics Association, 70 Brompton Road, London SW3 1EE. The governing body for the sport of amateur athletics in England and Wales. All athletic clubs are affiliated to the AAA. It offers a wide range of instructional publications on all aspects of track and field athletics, marathon, race walking, and event organization. Annual publications include *The AAA Handbook*, which contains the Rules of Competition and a complete list of clubs, and *British Athletics*, a yearbook giving details of performances over the previous twelve months. The principal regional addresses are:

Southern Counties AAA, 70 Brompton Road, London SW3 1EE
Midland Counties AAA, Devonshire House, High Street, Deritend, Birmingham B12 0LP
Northern Counties AA, Studio 44, Bluecoat Chambers, School Lane, Liverpool L13 BX
Welsh AAA, Dr W. A. L. Evans, 'Winterbourne', Greenway Close, Llandough, Penarth, South Glamorgan CF6 1LZ
Scottish AAA, E. S. Murray, 25 Bearsden Road, Glasgow G21 17L

British Veterans Athletic Federation, Hon. Secretary: Jack Fitzgerald, 6 Tyers House, Aldrington Road, London sw16. Co-ordinating body for veteran (men over 40, women over 35) athletic events in Britain. Publishes monthly magazine, *Veteris* (see 'Periodicals'). Addresses of area organizers can be obtained from the Secretary.

British Orienteering Federation, Lea Green Sports Centre, Matlock, Derbyshire DE4 5GJ (Tel: Dethick 628). The Federation incorporates twelve autonomous regional associations and is responsible for the conduct of orienteering in Great Britain and Northern Ireland.

English Cross Country Union, Hon. Secretary: Barry Wallman, 7 Wolsey Way, Cherry Hinton, Cambridge CB1 3JQ (Tel: Cambridge 42010). Encourages and promotes cross-country running and organizes regional and national championships each year. Honorary membership is open to individuals as well as clubs. Publishes the annual *handbook*, which includes a report of the year's activities and rules of competition.

Fell Runners' Association, Hon. Secretary: David Moulding, 127 Bury Road, Rawtenstall, Rossendale, Lancashire. The FRA aims to encourage hill and fell running. The *Fell Runner* (see 'Periodicals') is circulated to all members.

Fun Run, 7 Berkeley Lane, Canvey Island, Essex (Tel: 03743 64956). Offshoot of *RACE* magazine; will give free publicity in the magazine to organizers of fun runs.

Jogging Information Service, Stonehart Publications Ltd, 13 Golden Square, London W1R 4AG. The JIS acts as a co-ordinator of jogging groups and events and deals with enquiries from joggers and would-be joggers nationwide. Publications list available; publishes *Survival Kit*, a monthly newsletter, *Easy Jog Guide* (the latter is free) and *Jogging*.

Road Runners Club, Membership Secretary: Mrs Judith Goodsell, 10 Honywood Road, Colchester, Essex. The RRC encourages and oversees road running races in the UK.

Scottish Amateur Athletic Association, 16 Royal Crescent, Glasgow G3 7SL (Tel: 041 332 5144). The governing body for amateur athletics in Scotland. Promotes Scottish National Championships and issues an annual handbook containing rules of competition.

READING ABOUT RUNNING

Periodicals

Athletics Weekly, 344 High Street, Rochester, Kent. Weekly. Oldest of the running magazines. Full coverage of all major events, news of coming events, articles on training.

Fell Runner, 66 Edwinstowe Road, Lytham St Annes, Lancashire. Issued twice yearly to all members of the Fell Running Association.

Jogging Magazine, Stonehart Publications Ltd, 13 Golden Square, London WIR 4AG. New monthly magazine from the Jogging Information Service people.

Orienteer, British Orienteering Federation, Lea Green Sports Centre, Matlock, Derbyshire DE4 5GJ. Bi-monthly. National magazine for orienteering in Britain.

Marathon, Editor: Padraig Griffin, High Street, Ballinamore, County Leitrim, Ireland. Monthly. Irish athletics magazine.

Road and Country Enthusiast (RACE), 7 Berkeley Lane, Canvey Island, Essex. Monthly. Covers road running, cross-country, race walking, and has a section devoted to joggers' interests.

RRC Newsletter, Editor: John Jewell, 296 Barkham Road, Wokingham, Berks RG11 4DA. Issued three times a year to members of the Road Runners Club.

Runner's World, PO Box 247, Croydon, Surrey CR9 8AQ. A leading American running magazine is available on subscription in the UK.

Survival Kit, Stonehart Publications Ltd, 13 Golden Square, London WIR 4AG. Monthly. Monthly newsletter of the Jogging Information Service.

Veteris, 7 Berkeley Lane, Canvey Island, Essex. Monthly. The only magazine dealing solely with the interests of the veteran runner.

A bibliography

This list is not exhaustive, but all of the important books on running and runners currently available are included. The following have lists of books on running available on request (please send stamped addressed envelope):

Amateur Athletic Association, 70 Brompton Road, London sw3 1EE. Wide range of training and coaching manuals on every aspect of the sport, including track and field, marathon running, race walking, and event organization.
RACE Bookshop, 7 Berkeley Lane, Canvey Island, Essex. Stocks most of the UK books and also many American titles.
The Sports Market, PO Box 247, Croydon, Surrey CR9 8AQ. UK distributors of *Runner's World* magazine and the books issued by that magazine.

Athletics books

Cerutty, Percy, *Training with Cerutty* (RACE).
Foster, Brendan, and Temple, Cliff. *Brendan Foster* (Heinemann).
Heaton, John. *Better Athletics—Track* (Kaye & Ward).
Heaton, John. *Better Athletics—Field* (Kaye & Ward).

Hill, Ron. *The Long Hard Road* (RACE).
Lydiard, Arthur. *Run the Lydiard Way* (from RACE).
Mitchell, Brian. *Running to Win* (David & Charles).
Sykes, Robin. *Complete Track and Field Athletics* (Kaye & Ward).
Temple, Cliff. *Jogging for Fitness and Pleasure* (World's Work/Sunday Times).
Ward, Tony, and Watts, Denis. *Athletics for the 70s* (Weidenfeld & Nicolson).
Watman, Mel. *Encyclopaedia of Athletics*.
Woodeson, Peggy, and Watts, Denis. *Schoolgirl Athletics* (Stanley Paul).

Books on fitness

Bartlett, E. G. *Basic Fitness* (David & Charles).
Carruthers, Malcolm, and Murray, Alistair. *Fitness on 40 Minutes a Week* (Futura).
Cooper, Kenneth. *The New Aerobics* (Bantam).
Gillie, Oliver, and Mercer, Derrick (eds.). *Sunday Times Book of Body Maintenance* (Michael Joseph).
Healy, Colin. *Methods of Fitness* (Kaye & Ward).
Moorhouse, Laurence, and Gross, Leonard. *Maximum Performance* (Granada).
Moorhouse, Laurence, and Gross, Leonard. *Total Fitness* (Granada).
Murray, Alistair. *Modern Weight Training* (Kaye & Ward).
Thomas, Dr Vaughan. *Better Physical Fitness* (Kaye &.Ward).
Tulloh, Bruce. *Naturally Fit* (Weidenfeld & Nicolson).

Special interest books

Disley, John. *Orienteering* (Faber & Faber).
Muckle, David. *Sports Injuries* (Routledge & Kegan Paul).

APPENDIX B
The Harvard Step Test

The Harvard Step Test is one of the simplest ways to evaluate cardiovascular fitness. It requires you to step up and down on a bench for a few minutes, then see how quickly your heart recovers from the effort.

1. Get a sturdy bench 20 inches high. Step from the floor on to the bench and down again thirty times a minute for four minutes, using a metronome or having someone time you with the second hand of a watch. You must, incidentally, straighten your knee fully each time. (If you get too tired to go on, you can stop earlier, but it will lower your score.)

2. As soon as you finish, sit quietly and take your pulse, or have someone else take it, for 30 seconds one minute after you finish, another 30 seconds two minutes after you finish, and another 30 seconds three minutes after you finish.

3. Compute your Recovery Index (RI) by using this formula:

$$RI = \frac{\text{Duration of exercise in seconds} \times 100}{\text{Sum of pulse counts} = 2}$$

If your RI is 60 or less, your rating is poor; between 61 and 70, fair; between 71 and 80, good; between 81 and 90, very good; 91 or more, excellent. The test itself is quite strenuous if you're badly out of shape, so use caution and *stop if you have any adverse symptoms such as chest pain or extreme difficulty in breathing.*

References

Chapter 1
Bassler, Thomas J. 'Quality of life.' *Western Journal of Medicine*, April 1976.
Foss, Merle L. *et al.* 'Physical training program for rehabilitating extremely obese patients.' Unpublished paper; undated.
Jones, Robert. 'Exercise training and risk factors.' In Zohman, Lenore R., and Phillips, Raymond E., eds. *Progress in Cardiac Rehabilitation: Medical Aspects of Exercise Testing and Training.* New York: Stratton Intercontinental Medical Book Corporation, 1973.
Kasch, Fred W. 'The effects of exercise on the ageing process.' *The Physician and Sportsmedicine*, June 1976.
Kasch, Fred W. 'Stopping the clock with exercise.' *The Physician and Sportsmedicine*, July 1975.
Myers, Clayton R. *The Official YMCA Physical Fitness Handbook.* New York: Popular Library, 1975.
Weiss, Paul. *Sport: A Philosophic Inquiry.* Carbondale, Illinois: Southern Illinois University Press, 1969.

Chapter 2
Anderson, Bob, and Henderson, Joe, eds. *Guide to Distance Running.* Mountain View, California: *Runner's World*, 1971.
Bahr, Robert. 'Channeling our meanness.' *Runner's World*, June 1976.
Beisser, Arnold R. *The Madness in Sports.* New York: Appleton-Century-Crofts, 1967.
Clark, Alan. Letter to the author, December 11, 1976.
deVries, Herbert A., and Adams, Gene M. 'Electromyographic comparison of single doses of exercise and meprobamate as to effects on muscular relaxation.' *American Journal of Physical Medicine*, Vol. 51, No. 3, 1972.
Glasser, William. *Positive Addiction.* New York: Harper & Row, 1976.
Harper, Frederick D. 'Jogging research at Howard University.' *The Jogger*, June 1976.
Hoffer, Eric. *The True Believer.* New York: Harper & Row, 1951.
Huizinga, Johan. *Homo Ludens: A Study of the Play Element in Culture,* London: Routledge & Kegan Paul, 1949.
Ismail, A. H., and Trachtman, L. E. 'Jogging the imagination.' *Psychology Today*, March 1973.
Kane, J. E., ed. *Psychological Aspects of Physical Education and Sport.* London: Routledge & Kegan Paul, 1972.

Kavanagh, Terence. *Heart Attack? Counterattack!* Toronto: Van Nostrand Reinhold, 1976.

Kostrubala, Thaddeus. *The Joy of Running.* New York: J. B. Lippincott, 1976.

Mock, Michael B. Letter to the author, August, 1976.

Pieper, Josef. *Leisure: The Basis of Culture.* London: Faber & Faber, 1952.

Selye, Hans. *Stress without Distress.* London: Hodder & Stoughton, 1975.

Spino, Mike. *Beyond Jogging.* Millbrae, California: Celestial Arts, 1976.

Stiller, Richard: *Pain: Why It Hurts, Where It Hurts, When It Hurts.* Nashville, Tennessee: Thomas Nelson, 1975.

Talamini, John T., and Page, Charles H., eds. *Sports and Society.* Boston: Little-Brown, 1973.

Thomas, Vaughan. *Science and Sport: The Measurement and Improvement of Performance.* London: Faber & Faber, 1970.

Veblen, Thorstein. *The Theory of the Leisure Class.* London: Allen & Unwin, 1953.

Chapter 3

Fardy, Paul S., *et al.* 'A comparison of myocardial function in former athletes and non-athletes.' *Medicine and Science in Sports,* Vol. 8, No. 1, 1976

Medical Times, May 1976.

Michener, James A. *Sports in America.* New York: Random House, 1976.

Chapter 4

Kasch, Fred W. 'The Effects of Exercise on the Ageing Process.' *The Physician and Sportsmedicine,* June 1976.

Rose, Charles L., and Cohen, Michel L. 'Relative importance of physical activity for longevity.' Unpublished report of a study conducted at the Veterans Administration Outpatient Clinic, Boston, Massachusetts.

Chapter 5

Barnard, R. James. 'The heart needs warm-up time.' *The Physician and Sportsmedicine,* January 1976.

Fardy, Paul S. 'Guidelines for Preventive Conditioning Programs.' Unpublished report; undated.

Chapter 6

Belloc, Nedra B., and Breslow, Lester. 'Relationship of physical health status and health practices.' *Preventive Medicine 1,* 1972.

Gwinup, Grant. 'Effect of exercise alone on the weight of obese women.' *Archives of Internal Medicine,* May, 1975.

Zuti, W. B., and Golding, L. A. 'Comparing Diet and Exercise as

Weight Reducing Tools.' *The Physician and Sportsmedicine*, January 1976.

Chapter 7
Doherty, J. Kenneth. *Modern Track and Field*. Bailey & Swinfen, London, 1963.
Nideffer, Robert M. *The Inner Athlete: Mind Plus Muscle for Winning*. New York: T. Y. Crowell, 1976.
Suin, Richard M. 'Psychology for Olympic champs.' *Psychology Today*, July 1976.
Watt, Edward W., Plotnicki, B. A., and Buskirk, E. R. 'The physiology of single and multiple daily training programs.' *Track Technique 49*, 1972.

Chapter 8
Albohm, Marge. 'Does menstruation affect performance in sports?' *The Physician and Sporstmedicine*, March 1976.
Browne, Natalie. 'Jogging, the mockingbird and more.' *The Jogger*, March–April 1976.
Brownmiller, Susan: *Against Our Will*. London: Secker & Warburg, 1975.
Cooper, Kenneth H. *Aerobics*. London: Bantam Books, 1968.
Dilfer, Carol. 'Jogging through pregnancy.' *The Jogger*, March–April 1976.
Erdelyi, G. J. 'Effects of exercise on the menstrual cycle.' *The Physician and Sportsmedicine*, March 1976.
Gendel, Evalyn S. 'Psychological factors and menstrual extraction.' *The Physician and Sportsmedicine*, March 1976.
Haycock, Christine E., and Gillette, Joan V. 'Susceptibility of woman athletes to injury.' *Journal of the American Medical Association*, July 12, 1976.
Lance, Kathryn. *Running for Health and Beauty: A Complete Guide for Women*. New York: Bobbs-Merrill, 1977.
Talamini, John T., and Page, Charles H., eds. *Sport and Society*. Boston: Little-Brown, 1973.
Ullyot, Joan. *Women's Running*. Mountain View, California: World Publications, 1976.
National Athletic Health Institute. 'Women and weights.' *The Jogger*, March–April 1976.

Chapter 9
Getchell, Leroy H. *Physical Fitness: A Way to Life*. New York: Wiley, 1976.
Steincrohn, P. J. *How to Stop Killing Yourself*. New York: Funk & Wagnalls, 1962.

Chapter 10
Åstrand, Per-Olaf. Proceedings of International Symposium on

Physical Activity and Cardiovascular Health, *Canadian Medical Association Journal 96*, 1967.

Bar-Or, Oded. 'Predicting athletic performance.' *The Physician and Sportsmedicine*, August 1976.

Buskirk, Elsworth R. Letters to the author, October 5, 1976.

Craig, Robert L. 'The athlete's pre-game meal.' Letter to *The Physician and Sportsmedicine*, August 1976.

McCafferty, William B., *et al.* 'Does a "Threshold Age" cancel longevity hopes of exercisers?' *The Physician and Sportsmedicine*, June 1975.

Morella, Joseph J., and Turehetti, Richard J. *Nutrition and the Athlete*. New York: Mason/Charter, 1976.

Talamini, John T., and Page, Charles H., eds. *Sports and Society*. Boston: Little-Brown, 1973.

Williams, J. G. P., and Sperryn, P. N., eds. *Sports Medicine*, London: Edward Arnold, 1976.

Chapter 13
Cooter, G., Rankin, *et al.* 'Do long hair and football uniforms impair heat loss?' *The Physician and Sportsmedicine*, February 1975.

Chapter 14
Bogert, L. Jean, *et al. Nutrition and Physical Fitness*. Philadelphia: W. B. Saunders, 1973.

Frederick, E. C. *The Running Body*. Mountain View, California: World Publications, 1973.

Goulart, Frances Sheridan. *Bum steers*. Old Greenwich, Connecticut: Chatham Press, 1975.

Goulart, Frances Sheridan. *The Ecological Eclair*. New York: Macmillan, 1975.

Goulart, Frances Sheridan. *Bone Appétit!* Seattle, Washington: Paufiz Search, 1976.

Ryan, Allan J. 'What menu before games?' *The Physician and Sportsmedicine*, January 1976.

Smith, Nathan J. *Food for Sport*. Palo Alto: Bull Publishing Company, 1976.

Chapter 16
Williams, J. G. P. and Sperryn, P. N., eds. *Sports Medicine*, London: Edward Arnold, 1976.

Chapter 17
Beisser, Arnold R. *The Madness in Sports*. New York: Appleton-Century-Crofts, 1967.

Morgan, William P. 'The Mind of the Marathoner.' *Psychology Today*, April 1978.

Chapter 18
Knott, Peter. 'The ladies' scene.' *The Fell Runner*, Autumn 1977.
McGill, Mick. 'Orienteering: A Challenge to the Athlete.' *Road and Country Enthusiast*, January 1978.
The Orienteer, January 1978.
Rand, Jim, and Walker, Tony. *This Is Orienteering*. London: Pelham Books, 1976.

Chapter 20
Hellerstein, Herman K. 'Limitations of marathon running in the rehabilitation of coronary patients: anatomic and physiologic determinants.' *The Marathon: Physiological, Medical, Epidemiological, and Psychological Studies*. New York: The New York Academy of Sciences, 1977.
Kavanagh, Terence. *Heart Attack? Counterattack!* Toronto: Van Nostrand Reinhold, 1976.
Rowell, Loring B. Contribution to the New York Academy of Sciences conference, 'The marathon: physiological, medical, epidemiological, and psychological studies.' October 1976.

Chapter 22
Costill, David L. *A Scientific Approach to Distance Running*. Unpublished manuscript.

Afterword
Miller, David L. *Gods and Games: Toward a Theology of Play*. New York: World, 1970.

Index